Term	Definition
Disk cache	A program that stores copies of frequently used disk sectors in RAM to increase performance.
Disk interface	The system for controlling the movement of read/write heads from sector to sector, and the transfer of data to and from the disk surface.
Display adapter	A circuit card that provides the signals necessary to display images on your monitor.
DOS shell	A program that provides quick and easy access to DOS functions and files.
EGA	Enhanced Graphics Adapter—IBM's first higher resolution graphics standard.
EMS	Expanded memory specification—the system upon which expanded memory is based.
ESDI	Enhanced Small Device Interface—a hard-disk interface.
Expansion slot	A socket in which you plug a circuit card to add system resources.
FAT	File allocation table—an area on the disk that maintains a record of which sectors are being used, which are empty, and which are damaged.
File chain	A list of the clusters storing each file.
Foreground application	The application you are working with in a multitasking environment.
GUI	Graphic user interface—an alternative method for working with DOS that offers mouse-compatible point-and-shoot capabilities for all functions, using graphic symbols, or icons, to represent DOS concepts.
Hard disk	A disk drive using a rigid, compact-disk-like platter for data storage, compared to flexible material used by floppy-disk drives.
Hard-disk card	A circuit card that contains a controller and hard disk.
Hercules	A high-resolution graphics monochrome system developed by Hercules Computer Technology.
HGC	Hercules Graphic Card.
Interleaving	The spacing of sectors about a track.
MCGA	Memory Controller Gate Array—a high-resolution display that only partially implements the VGA standard.
MDA	The Monochrome Display Adapter used only with TTL monitors.
Memory	Electronic storage areas holding computer data.
MFM	Modified Frequency Modulation—a frequently used system for data coding.

▶ *continued on inside back cover*

The
Hand-Me-Down PC
Handbook

The Hand-Me-Down PC Handbook

Alan R. Neibauer

San Francisco • Paris • Düsseldorf • Soest

Acquisitions Editor: Dianne King
Developmental Editors: Cheryl Holzaepfel, Deborah Craig
Copy Editor: Kathleen D. Lattinville
Technical Editor: David Clark
Word Processors: Scott Campbell, Winnie Kelly, Lisa Mitchell
Book Designer: Helen Bruno
Technical Art: Delia Brown
Screen Graphics: Cuong Le
Typesetter: Len Gilbert
Proofreader: M.D. Barrera
Indexer: Nancy Guenther
Cover Designer: Thomas Ingalls + Associates
Cover Photographer: Mark Johann
Screen reproductions produced by XenoFont.

Library of Congress Card Number: 90-70872

ISBN: 0-89588-702-9

Manufactured in the United States of America

10 9 8 7 6 5 4 3 2 1

► *To Esther*
and the memory of
Joseph Neibauer,
my parents

▶ *Acknowledgments*

*I*t takes more than an author to produce a book such as this, and I owe thanks to many others who helped complete this project. Foremost are developmental editors Cheryl Holzaepfel and Deborah Craig, who organized the overall effort, and copy editor Kathleen Lattinville, whose excellent attention to detail is greatly appreciated. Thanks again to Dianne King, for thinking of me.

Special recognition goes to technical editor David Clark. The wide variety of hardware and software discussed in this book made his job difficult but well within his impressive expertise.

Credit for the excellent figures goes to Delia Brown for technical art and to Cuong Le for screen graphics. Thanks also to word processors Scott Campbell, Winnie Kelly, and Lisa Mitchell; book designer Helen Bruno; typesetter Len Gilbert; proofreader M.D. Barrera; and indexer Nancy Guenther.

My most sincere appreciation to Barbara Neibauer, for everything she's given me and shared with me these past twenty-five years. Finally, thanks to the following companies for their support and assistance: ALL Computers, Inc.; ALR, Inc.; Bourbaki, Inc.; Cajun Edge; CalComp, Inc.; Chronologic Corporation; Departmental Technologies, Inc.; EasySoft, Inc.; Fifth Generation Software; Gazelle Systems; Gibson Research Corporation; IBM Corporation; Logitech, Inc.; Microsoft, Corporation; Peter Norton Computing; Primetime Software, Inc.; Second Ring Publishers; SitBack Technologies, Inc.; Sterling Software, Inc.; Westlake Data, Inc.; and XTree Company.

► Contents
at a Glance

9 *Understanding Monitors*   *153*

▶ *Part Three*   *Improving and Customizing Your System*

12 *Enhancing DOS*   *215*

*W*hether you've received your hand-me-down as a corporate leftover or purchased it from a friend or acquaintance, you have some challenging yet rewarding experiences ahead.

Users of new computer systems have the luxury of a warranty and the support of a salesperson. In contrast, you have to survive in the realm of *caveat emptor*—let the buyer beware. You have to survive by your knowledge, skill, and luck, forging your path through the traps and pitfalls created by your system's previous owner.

After the sale or trade is made, after all of the promises and reassurances, the hand-me-down is on your desk, silently challenging you to step forward to explore new territory.

Luckily, you are not alone. This book is the user's guide that should—but doesn't—come packaged with every used computer or first computer system. It is your personal advisor when you can't find answers in your system manual, or didn't get the documentation with your hand-me-down. It is the perfect substitute for the salesperson and the customer support staff that new computer owners can lean on.

You'll find this book helpful even if you're already familiar with PC's. Your hand-me-down may include hardware or software that is new to you. While the book is geared for novices, even more advanced users will confront some unique challenges when facing a hand-me-down computer.

What This Book Contains

The first part of the book, Chapters 1 to 4, covers the essentials: finding out what you've inherited or bought, and getting the system in working order for yourself. In

Chapter 1, you'll explore the outside of your hand-me-down to learn about your keyboard, disk drives, and monitor. You'll learn how to identify interface ports, cables, and connectors, making sure your system is properly connected.

You'll test drive your system in Chapter 2, starting with a power-up check list, setting the time and date, and checking the keyboard status. You'll also determine the capacity of your disk drives and the amount of base memory. Since hardware is useless by itself, you'll identify the software you have available, learn how to print disk directories, and determine if your software and hardware are compatible.

Chapter 3 shows you how to use DOS, the disk operating system, to communicate with your computer and software. We'll cover internal and external commands, the differences between versions of DOS, and how to deal with disks, directories, and subdirectories. This chapter also discusses file names, wildcards, and the DOS commands DIR, COPY, TREE, and TYPE.

Now that you're familiar with your hardware and software, in Chapter 4 you'll customize your system, learning how to delete files and directories, deal with copy-protected software, and prepare, or install, software so it is ready to use. You'll learn how to examine and change two important files—AUTOEXEC.BAT and CONFIG.SYS—to work with your software and hardware such as a mouse or built-in clock circuit.

Chapter 5 covers your hand-me-down's hard disk. You'll learn how to reorganize the directories and subdirectories created by your hand-me-down's previous owner. You'll also learn about advanced hard-disk management techniques, including using paths and custom batch files, converting complex paths into easy-to-use drive letters. After reading this chapter, you'll know several ways to back up the files on your hard disk for safekeeping using DOS commands, and you'll also know how to protect your disk from accidental damage.

Chapter 6 concentrates on using and organizing your floppy disks. It explains how to format and copy disks, make DOS system disks, and handle disks of different sizes and capacities. This is an important chapter if your hand-me-down uses a different type of disk than the kind your existing software is formatted on.

Chapter 7 discusses how to diagnose and solve problems with your system. Since hand-me-downs rarely include a warranty, this chapter presents an easy-to-follow troubleshooting guide to help you quickly identify and solve problems. You'll also learn how to safeguard the configuration data in AT systems and above, and how to replace the system battery.

In Chapter 8, you'll learn how to connect and use your printer, and how to trouble-shoot printer problems. This chapter includes details on setting up a serial printer, using printer drivers, and printing graphic screen images from the DOS prompt. If you're using a printer that did not come with your hand-me-down, you'll find this chapter invaluable in determining compatibility and the correct configuration and setup.

Chapter 9 takes the mystery out of monitors, explaining confusing terms, such as TTL, Composite, MDA, HGC, CGA, EGA, VGA, MCGA, and multiscan. You'll learn about your hand-me-down's video system, and how to upgrade to a color or a higher resolution—including how to work with circuit cards and expansion slots.

In Chapters 10 and 11, you'll master some additional hardware that might have come with your hand-me-down, or that you might find useful to purchase. Chapter 10 discusses alternative ways to communicate with your system, including mice, trackballs, lightpens, touch screens, and scanners. Chapter 11 discusses communicating with the world through modems, cables, and networks.

Part III of this book shows you how to upgrade your hand-me-down and use its full resources through software and hardware. In Chapter 12, you'll find out about DOS shells, dedicated backup software, and desktop environments such as Microsoft Windows. You'll learn about programs that can recover deleted files, improve the performance of your disk, and diagnose and repair hard-disk problems.

Chapter 13 shows you how to use your hand-me-down's memory, and how to add more if it is required by your application programs. You'll learn the differences between conventional, extended, and expanded memory, and ways to utilize each type for maximum efficiency.

Chapter 14 explains how to install and configure disk drives. After reading this chapter, you'll be able to upgrade your hand-me-down with additional storage and you'll know how to correct many hard-disk problems without the cost of replacement or repair.

In Chapter 15 you'll learn the benefits of multitasking software, and about hardware designed to raise your system to new levels of performance, including numeric coprocessors, accelerator cards, motherboards, and memory caches. Chapter 16 will help you determine when it is time to upgrade your hand-me-down or graduate to a new system.

Finally, the appendix is a convenient reference to several popular software programs that you might have received or purchased with your hand-me-down.

How to Use This Book

Use Part I of this book to get up and running as quickly as possible. If you're already familiar with DOS and your system has been set up and explained to you, quickly scan Chapters 1 to 3, and then focus on customizing your system in Chapter 4. Otherwise, read these chapters carefully to become familiar with your hand-me-down.

Chapters 5 through 11 are individual references to system components and peripherals (except for Chapter 7, on diagnosing and solving problems). Use these chapters to set up your hardware, and refer to them when you have specific questions or need upgrade information.

Use the last part of the book when you're ready to expand or replace your system, to get the most use of your memory, or to add and configure disk drives. Adding internal hardware such as cards and disk drives requires some mechanical skill and careful attention to detail. If you're not comfortable working inside your computer, read these chapters to help make your upgrade decisions. Then consult a computer or repair shop for the actual installation of components.

Using a hand-me-down should not limit your computing enjoyment and accomplishments. While your system might not be the most recent model, it probably offers the same capabilities as many new computers. With this book as a guide, you'll be able to use your hand-me-down to its fullest, and if needed, upgrade it to a level of performance higher than the new system that turned your computer into a hand-me-down.

Even if you don't upgrade your system, the future of hand-me-down computing is bright. With every new advance in computer technology, the level of hand-me-downs increases as well. When a company moves to AT models, the PC's and XT's filter down; when it moves on to 386 and 486 systems, the more powerful AT's are passed down. It won't be too long before the typical hand-me-down system is the most powerful computer being used today. So when you see that 386 or 486 on someone else's desk, consider it simply being tested and broken-in before being passed on to you.

Part One

Getting
Acquainted with
Your System

Chapter One

What Have You Inherited?

*O*wning a hand-me-down computer is much like owning a used car. It involves a long-term commitment—getting to know it, growing comfortable with it, and customizing it to your own tastes and needs. So before investing time and effort in any important project with your hand-me-down, make sure you understand exactly what you have to work with.

In this chapter, you'll take a tour around the outside of your new acquisition and, when necessary, plug in its power and connecting cables. There is a lot you can learn about your computer system without even turning it on. This external exam of your system is especially important if you don't have any of the original manuals, handbooks, and other literature that were packaged with the system or its components. Let's start our tour with the keyboard.

An Introduction to the PC Keyboard

The keyboards shown in Figure 1.1 and Figure 1.2, called 84-key keyboards, are those used in the original IBM PC and PC/XT computers and the IBM PC/AT computers; the keyboard shown in Figure 1.3 is the enhanced 101-key keyboard used in newer AT-class computers.

Your keyboard might vary slightly from those in the figures. The keyboards illustrated in Figures 1.1 and 1.2, for example, show the Num Lock and Scroll Lock keys above the keypad, and the Caps Lock key to the left of the keypad, near the 0 (zero) key. In Figure 1.3, the keys are positioned differently and each of these keys has a light to indicate its on or off status.

Your keyboard must match your computer: an XT keyboard will not work with an AT computer; an enhanced keyboard will not work with an XT computer. While the two

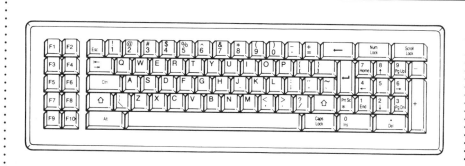

Figure 1.1: *Original IBM PC and PC/XT keyboard*

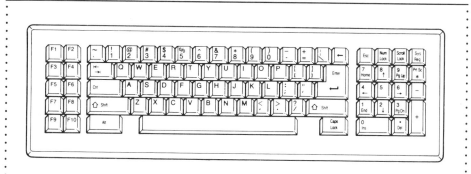

Figure 1.2: *Original IBM PC/AT keyboard*

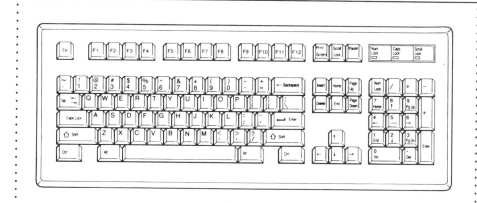

Figure 1.3: *Enhanced keyboard*

84-key keyboards look similar, they are not interchangeable. If you have an 84-key keyboard, look in the upper-right corner for a key marked SYS REQ. You'll find this key only on keyboards designed for AT-class machines.

There are, however, some keyboards that can be used with either AT or XT computers. They have a switch, usually hidden under a nameplate or cover somewhere on the keyboard, that lets you select between the two settings (Figure 1.4).

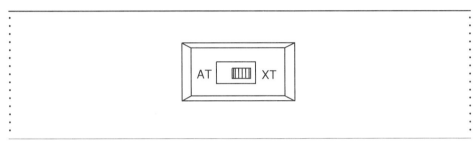

Figure 1.4: *Keyboard switch for selecting XT or AT operation*

If you know the type of computer you have, and have a switchable keyboard, make sure the switch is properly set now.

The Function Keys

Your keyboard has either 10 or 12 *function keys* labeled from F1 to F10, or F12. Some of the function keys have been programmed to perform special tasks at the *DOS* (disk operating system) level, such as pressing the F3 key to repeat the last DOS command. In addition, *application programs* such as word processors and spreadsheets use these keys for their own purposes. Most application programs that use the function keys use only F1 to F10 in order to remain compatible with all keyboard models.

You'll learn how DOS uses the function keys in Chapter 3, "Getting to Know DOS." To see how applications use function keys, consult your program's manual or one of the many excellent SYBEX books.

The Typing Keys

The largest area of the keyboard, either underneath or to the right of the function keys, contains the keys for letters, numbers, and punctuation marks needed to enter your DOS commands and to work with your programs. If you've ever used a typewriter, then you already know how to use these keys.

This area of the keyboard, however, also includes some special keys not found on a typewriter. Look for the keys marked *Ctrl, Alt, Del, Break,* and *PrtSc* or *Print Screen.* These are important keys that you will be using often with your computer, and they are not in the same position on every keyboard. Get to know their location now so you'll be ready when you use your computer.

The Cursor Movement Keys

All three keyboard designs have a combination numeric and cursor movement keypad on the right. This keypad is controlled by the key marked *Num Lock.* The *cursor* is the placemarker that shows the current editing position on the screen.

With the Num Lock key turned off, the cursor movement keys, labeled with the directional arrows and commands on the lower half of the keys, are active. In this mode, you must use the top row of the keyboard to type numbers. When you are working at the *DOS prompt*—giving commands to the disk operating system—only the left and right arrow keys (which share spaces with the numbers 4 and 6) will have any effect. When you press the left arrow key, you'll erase the character to the left of the cursor on the DOS command line. The right arrow key displays the last DOS command one character at a time. The other cursor movement keys work only in application programs that use them.

With the Num Lock key turned on, pressing a keypad key displays on the screen the number printed on the upper half of the key. In addition, this mode displays the decimal point, which shares space on the Del key, and Ø (slashed zero), which is on the Ins key.

Press Num Lock to toggle the keypad on and off, switching between the cursor movement and numeric functions. You can experiment later to see the default mode used by your system—whether the keypad is on or off when you first start your computer.

The enhanced keyboard also includes a second set of cursor movement keys between the keypad and the typing keys. You can use the keypad for typing numbers and the cursor keys for moving around the screen, without needing to switch between keypad modes.

Connecting the Keyboard to the Computer

Before going on, make sure that your keyboard is connected to your computer. In most cases, the keyboard cable plugs into a socket at the rear of the computer. Some computers have the keyboard connection on the side; others have it in the front. In a few cases, especially with portable computers, the cable is permanently connected and cannot be unplugged, and sometimes the keyboard itself is permanently attached to the computer.

If your keyboard cable is not connected, look for a cable with a round plug similar to the one shown in Figure 1.5. Notice that the plug has a series of small pins at one end and a small notch on the other. There is a matching notch on the keyboard connector so the cable can only go in one way. Rotate the plug so its pins line up with the holes in the keyboard socket and gently push it all the way in. Don't force it. If the plug won't go in, you don't have it lined up correctly. Rotate the plug a little and keep applying light pressure. The plug will fit in easily when the pins align.

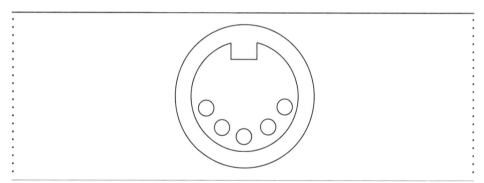

Figure 1.5: *Keyboard plug*

Setting the Keyboard Lock

Newer computer systems, especially those in the AT-class and newer, have a keyboard lock located on the front of the computer. These locks are difficult to pick and usually use a cylindrical type of key that is very hard to duplicate.

Locking the system blocks the connection between the keyboard and the computer itself, so no one can communicate with your system, even if they turn it on. This is useful if you have to leave your desk while running an application.

If your system has such a lock, look around for the key. To be honest, few people really use the lock, so don't worry for now if you can't find the key—unless the switch is in the locked position! If you can't find the key, contact the previous owner or order a new one from a computer store.

Familiarizing Yourself with Your Computer

Strictly speaking, the *computer* is a series of circuits inside the main housing. You're actually working with a *computer system* that includes the keyboard for input, the monitor and printer for output, and the disk drives for storage. It is the combination of these components that makes the system so powerful and useful.

Let's take a look at each major component.

First, look around the computer for *air vents*—cutouts in the metal or plastic that allow air to flow and cool off the hot circuits. Never place papers or other materials so they cut off the flow of air through the vents; your system could overheat. Some computers have air vents on the front. Propping pages between the keyboard and computer may block off the air vents and overheat the system. Most important, never block off the air vents outside any cooling or exhaust fan. If you have a portable computer, such as an early model Compaq, always run the machine with both side access doors fully open.

Looking at the Floppy-Disk Drives

If you have two *floppy-disk drives,* they may be mounted side-by-side vertically or horizontally, either next to each other or stacked on top of each other. The drive on the left-hand side, or on top, is normally called *drive A;* the other drive is called *drive B.* Each drive has an indicator light that turns on when the drive is in motion.

Floppy-disk drives hold either 5¼-inch or 3½-inch floppy disks, so it is obvious by the size of the drives which type you have. You may even have one of each size.

The way the drive door opens and closes with 5¼-inch disk drives varies. Many drives have a small lever that swings to the right to open and down to close after you've inserted the disk. Other drives have a tab that you lift up to open and press down to close. And some drives have a tab that you press to release the drive door.

Carefully try the latch on your drive. If it doesn't move easily in one direction, try another. Never force the latch in any direction. If it breaks you'll have to replace the entire drive.

Almost all 3½-inch drives work the same way. Push the disk all the way into the drive until it clicks into place. Release the disk by pressing a button beneath the opening.

Disk drives come in two *capacities,* or densities—normal and high. The only accurate way to tell the capacity of your floppy-disk drives is by running some tests with the machine on.

Since high-capacity disks only work in high-capacity drives, you might get a hint by examining any disks that came with your system. If you have high-capacity disks then you probably have high-capacity drives. But since low-capacity disks can be used in high-capacity drives, don't assume your drives are low-capacity based on your disks.

If you have 3½-inch floppy disks, count the number of small square openings along the sides (Figure 1.6). If there are two openings, the disk is high capacity and can store up to 1.44 million characters, or 1.44Mb (megabytes). If there is only one opening, the disk is low capacity and can store about 720,000 characters, or 720K (kilobytes). The opening with the tab that can be moved back and forth is called the write-protect notch. Its purpose is discussed fully in Chapter 4.

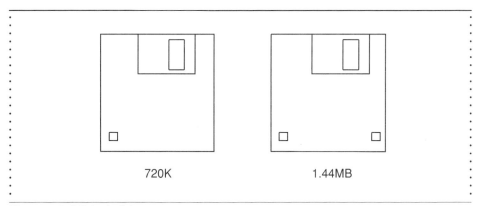

Figure 1.6: *3½-inch disks*

With 5¼-inch disks, look for a label that lists the disk's capacity. If the label reads "high density" or "96 tpi" (tracks per inch), then the disk can store about 1.2Mb. Otherwise it is a low-capacity disk that stores about 360K.

You could have a high-capacity drive and use 360K disks in it. However high-capacity disks can only be read in high-capacity disk drives. Low-capacity disks can be read in any drive. Your disks should be compatible with your disk drives.

Looking at the Hard-Disk Drive

Your computer may also have a *hard-disk drive,* a permanently installed disk-drive system that can store 10Mb or more. Hard-disk drives usually occupy one of the disk-drive *bays,* the areas in the computer where floppy disk drives can also be installed. Look for an indicator light on one of the blank panels covering a disk-drive bay. If you see a light, then you have a hard-disk drive mounted behind it. In some cases, you may have a hard disk even if there is no light on the blank bay cover. Some hard drives, for instance, are mounted on circuit cards that fit in one of the computer's expansion slots. So, you might not be able to tell if you have a hard disk without turning on the computer.

Other Storage Possibilities

Finally, it is possible your system has some form of removable mass storage device, such as a tape backup system or disk cartridge. The device will occupy one of the floppy-drive bays and will have a larger, rectangular opening.

By and large, these are add-on products that the previous owner had installed. There are quite a few different types, so look through your documentation for a manual or handbook.

Selecting the Voltage

Some systems have a switch on the back that lets you select either 115 or 220 volt operation. If you have a switch, make sure it is set for your voltage. Push the switch so the amount of your voltage is displayed. In the United States, select 115 volts.

The Power Switch and Power Devices

The computer's power switch may be on the back, side, or front of the computer, or even hidden under a little door as with some Epson computers.

Some switches are labeled ON and OFF, others as 1 (on) and 0 (off). Many just have a white dot indicating the on position. The machine is on when the white dot is pushed down. Some laptop computers have a separate switch for powering internal hard-disk drives. The switch gives you the capability of conserving battery power if you're using a floppy disk or internal memory.

You might have received a power switching device along with your system. This is either a long flat device that sits under your monitor or a multiple outlet box that lays on the floor under your desk. *Switching boxes* have a series of electrical sockets where you plug in your computer, monitor, and printer, and one master cord that you plug into the wall outlet. If you have such a device, you can leave your system switches turned on all of the time and power everything using the master switch on the device.

These power switching mechanisms usually include electrical filtering and surge suppression that protect your computer against *voltage spikes.* After a power outage or due to unusually high fluctuations of power usage, very quick pulses, or spikes, of high voltage may flow through the power lines. These high voltages may be strong enough to damage your power supply or other internal components of the computer system. Surge suppressors regulate the voltage going into your system, reducing the spikes to normal voltage levels.

You might also have a *UPS,* an uninterrupted power supply, between your computer and wall outlet that has the ability to power your system independently for a short time if your power goes out.

Other Connectors

Now that we've covered the basic equipment that makes up a computer system, let's examine the back of your computer where you'll find ports that enable it to connect with the other components of your system and with the outside world (Figure 1.7). *Ports* are the connectors where you attach cables from other components such as printers, mice, and modems. (If you have a portable computer, the ports may be located behind an access door underneath or on either side.) You should have already connected a cable to the keyboard socket.

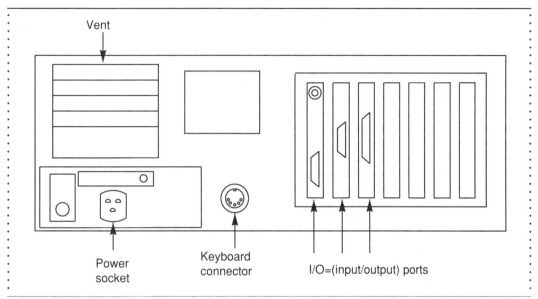

Vent

Power
socket

Keyboard
connector

I/O=(input/output) ports

Figure 1.7: *Interface ports on back panel*

You have serial or parallel ports, or both, on your computer. *Serial* and *parallel* refer to the way data is passed back and forth from your computer to devices like printers, plotters, and pointing devices.

Every character transmitted to and from your computer can be composed of eight separate electronic signals, called *bits,* which are represented by the numbers 1 and 0. The specific combination of ones and zeros is established by the *ASCII* (American Standard Code for Information Interchange) code. For example, when you want to print the capital letter A, your computer sends 01000001—the ASCII code for A—to the printer.

In a *serial transmission,* your computer sends out the bits one at a time over one wire, like a line of people waiting to get into the movie theater. The speed at which the bits travel is measured in *BPS,* bits per second. Your computer and printer must be set at the same BPS rate so the data can be transferred correctly—the printer must be ready to accept bits at the same speed the computer is sending them. (There are some other considerations in addition to BPS rate that you'll learn in Chapter 8, "Working with Your Printer.")

Serial ports have either 25 or 9 pins, and are usually male in gender, as shown in Figure 1.8. The ports may be labeled *serial, modem,* or *COM1.*

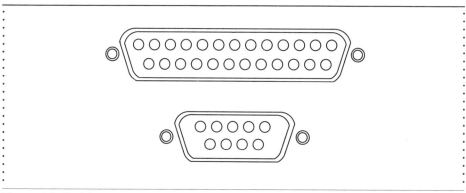

Figure 1.8: *Serial ports*

In a *parallel transmission,* the 8 bits that make up each character are all sent out at one time over 8 separate wires, like runners lined up at their starting positions for a race. Because 8 bits leave the computer at one time, parallel transmission is 2 to 3 times faster than the fastest serial transmission.

The parallel port on your computer is probably a 25-pin female connector. Parallel ports may be labeled *parallel, printer,* or *LPT.*

Inspecting Your Monitor

Make sure there is a cable connecting the monitor to your computer. In most cases, the cable connects to a socket at the back of the computer.

Figure 1.9 illustrates some typical monitor connectors. The round RCA-type connector is used for composite monitors—displays that are black and one other color, but simulate colors by shades. MDA and HGC monochrome monitors and CGA and EGA color monitors connect to 9-pin connectors. Higher resolution VGA displays use the 15-pin connector. Never try to fit a cable into the incorrect connector.

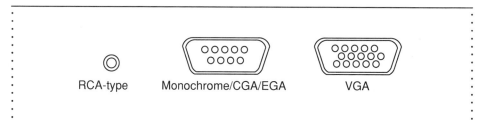

Figure 1.9: *Monitor connectors*

Next, locate the monitor's power switch and power cable. A few systems, such as early-model Epson computers, are designed so the monitor's power cord connects to a socket on the computer itself. In this case, you leave the monitor's power switch on and turn it on and off by the computer's power switch.

If you have a portable computer, the monitor is built into the system. Turning on the computer turns on the monitor at the same time.

Finally, locate your monitor's air vents and remember to keep them clear to prevent overheating.

Of Mice and Modem

Your system might include two other optional components, a mouse and a modem.

A *mouse* is a small hand-held pointing device that you roll along the desktop next to your computer. It is used to move the cursor on the screen and select options from menus. Several types of mice and mice connections are discussed in detail in Chapter 10, "Communicating with Your PC."

A *modem* is used for telecommunications—linking your computer to other computers over the telephone line. You might have a modem built into your computer, or one of several types of modems that attach to it with a serial cable. Installing and using modems are discussed in Chapter 11, "Communicating with the World."

Your system will work just as well for now if you do not connect these peripheral devices.

Connecting your Printer

Let's make a quick check to see if your printer—if you have one—is properly connected to the computer. (Details on selecting and using printers are presented in Chapter 8.)

First determine if your printer is a serial or parallel device. Most newer PC printers are parallel, which is fortunate because they are easier to attach and use than serial printers. If the printer is parallel, it will have a female Centronics-type connector, as shown in Figure 1.10. To connect it to your computer, you need a standard cable that has a 25-pin male connector at the end that attaches to the computer, and a male Centronics-type connector at the end that inserts into the printer (Figure 1.11). You can't plug the cable in the wrong way.

Serial ports may be a little more complicated. If your computer has a 25-pin male connector and your printer has a 25-pin female connector, then you need a cable with one of each type. However, the cable must be a *null-modem cable* especially designed for use with a printer.

Don't try to use a serial cable that comes with a modem, even if it looks like it would work. Null-modem cables and serial cables can look alike. If you cannot tell which

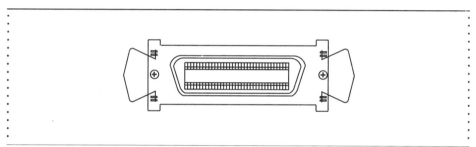

Figure 1.10: *Female Centronics port*

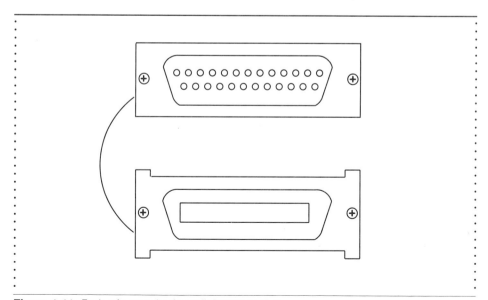

Figure 1.11: *Ends of a standard parallel printer cable*

is which, try both. If you try the wrong one, it won't function properly, but you will not damage anything.

If you use a modem cable with your printer, it's like holding two telephone handsets together. The ear pieces are connected together, as are the mouth pieces, so no communication can take place. A null-modem cable reverses some of the communication lines, which is like turning one of the phone handsets around so the voice of one goes into the earpiece of the other.

If your computer's serial port has a 9-pin connector or a 25-pin female connector, you'll need a special attachment to use most serial cables. Your computer store can sell you an adapter to connect a 25-pin cable to a 9-pin serial port. It's a short cable or plug with 9 pins on one end and 25 pins on the other. You might also need a *gender changer*—a device with two male ends that allows a female cable to connect to a female serial port .

Check the gender and size of the connectors to make sure your cable is appropriate, then plug in the printer cable. Never force the connectors together. If it doesn't fit, make sure you are holding it in the proper direction.

Your Hand–Me–Down's ID

Sooner or later you will need supplies, parts, repairs, or technical information about your hand-me-down. When this happens, you'll need to have some specific information handy about your system, such as its make and model number. You might also need its serial number to identify the exact machine you have, since some manufacturers make slight internal modifications between production runs. You should be able to find this information on a label or tag on the back of your computer.

Now that you've learned what you can from the outside of your system, let's turn it on and look inside.

Chapter Two

Test Driving Your Hand–Me-Down PC

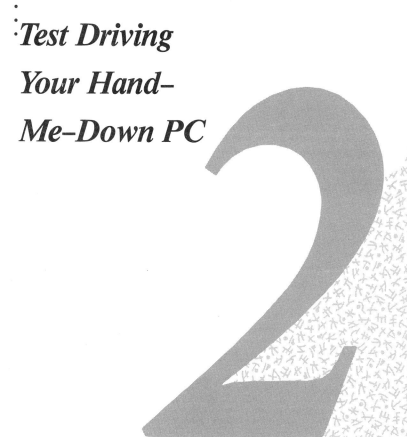

*T*here are some things about your computer that you can determine only by turning it on. In this chapter you'll learn the capacity of your floppy- and hard-disk drives, how much base memory your system has, and if it has a built-in clock/calendar. You'll also learn what software is installed on your hard disk or is supplied on floppy disks.

In an ideal world, where your system was installed and checked out for you, everything would work perfectly. But since you're dealing with a hand-me-down, and hundreds of possible system configurations, you have to consider all of the real-world possibilities. Some of the error messages and discussions in this chapter, therefore, may not apply to your system—you may have that perfect low-mileage hand-me-down that was used by a caring and considerate individual. On the other hand, your system's previous owner may have been far more typical.

Getting Started

Before turning on your system, check to see that

▶ The computer and monitor power cords are plugged into an electrical outlet.

▶ The keyboard is connected to the computer.

▶ The monitor is connected to the computer.

If you have a mouse or printer, make sure they are connected, although your system will work just as well without them attached at this time.

Powering Up Your PC

Now let's turn on, or boot, your hand-me-down. *Boot,* which means "start your computer," comes from the term *bootstrap loader,* a small program built into the computer that reads the disk operating system from your disk and starts it working.

1. If you know that you do not have a hard-disk drive, insert a *DOS system disk* in drive A. The disk will be labeled *DOS,* or *Disk Operating System.*
2. Turn on your computer and monitor and look carefully at the screen.

What you see on the screen depends on how your system was set up by its previous owner, and whether or not you've connected it properly. If everything is in order, you first may see a few messages displaying information.

These messages usually include the version and date of your DOS, and a copyright statement from the manufacturer. Other messages that appear may be generated by the CONFIG.SYS and AUTOEXEC.BAT files that give DOS some instructions during the boot process. Some AUTOEXEC.BAT files will prevent the time and date messages from appearing even when there is no built-in clock/calendar. You'll learn more about these files shortly.

Next, you'll see either a DOS prompt or a prompt to enter the date. A *prompt* appears when the system is ready for or needs some input on your part. DOS records the date and time along with the name of every file you save on your disk. A clock/calendar circuit provides DOS with the current date and time to help you organize and identify your work. This circuit is powered by a small battery. If you have a built-in clock/calendar, you'll see the DOS prompt after the system boots up properly, either

    A>

for a floppy-drive system, or

    C>

if you have a hard disk. (Depending on how the previous owner set up the system, the DOS prompt may include some other characters. You'll learn how to modify the DOS prompt yourself in Chapter 5, "Taming the Hard Disk.") When you see the DOS prompt, you've successfully started your system. Skip steps 3 and 4 and go on to step 5.

However, if you see a message such as

Current date is Tue 1-01-80
Enter new date:

your system does not contain a clock/calendar or the system is not set up properly to use one that is built in.

3. Press ◄─┘ to accept the 01-01-80 default date or type the current date in the *month-day-year* format, such as

11-25-91

then press ◄─┘.

You'll then see a message such as

Current time is 0:00:10.15
Enter new time:

4. Press ◄─┘ to accept that time as the default time or type the current time in the *hours:minutes* format, such as

9:16

then press ◄─┘. Use military time (a 24-hour clock) to indicate PM.

The DOS prompt should now appear on the screen, which means you've successfully started your system. Go on to step 5. If it doesn't, you'll need to do some investigation into the problem. Go to the section "If You Don't See the DOS Prompt," then return to this section and go to step 5.

Before you continue, you should check to see if the number keypad is active.

5. Find the Num Lock key. If the Num Lock key has a light, the keypad is in numeric mode when the light is on, and in cursor movement mode when the light is off. To use the keypad to type numbers, press the Num Lock key to turn on the light. If your Num Lock key doesn't have a light, press one of the keypad keys. No number will appear on the screen if the keypad is off. If a number appears, press the Backspace key to erase it.

Now you're ready to find out more about your system. Go to the section "Determining Disk Capacity and Base Memory."

If You Don't See the DOS Prompt

There are several things that could be wrong if a DOS prompt is not displayed—some are simple, others could require a repair. Let's look at the possibilities:

▶ If you see a prompt telling you to insert a disk, then you don't have a hard disk in your computer or, for floppy-drive systems, the disk you installed in drive A does not contain a disk operating system. Turn off your computer, insert a DOS disk, then start over.

▶ It is possible that you have a hard disk that has not been set up to start your computer or has been damaged. If you know that you have a hard disk, refer to the instructions in Chapter 5 for preparing hard-disk drives.

▶ Your computer may have detected a problem in the system. A number of computers have a self-diagnostic program that runs every time you turn on your computer. The program checks the computer's memory, connections, and other internal operations. In some cases, the program reports its results on the screen, showing, for example, the area in memory being checked or the operation being tested. Don't panic if nothing appears on the screen—your computer's self-test could be programmed to report only errors. However, if you see an error message referring to memory, CPU, ROM, parity, or some other hardware error, write down the message that appears on the screen, then turn off your computer. These are errors that involve the internal components of the computer system. The *CPU* is the central processing unit that controls the entire system, *ROM* is permanent read-only memory that contains bootup and diagnostic information, and *parity* is a system for checking your user memory. Wait a few minutes, then turn on the computer again. If the same message appears, turn off the computer and consult the manual, if you have one. You may need a repairperson.

▶ If you see a low battery message, you have to replace a small battery that is inside your computer. The battery supplies power to a special memory called *CMOS* that stores details of your system's configuration. In some systems, you'll be able to run your computer even with a low battery. If your system still boots, keep it on for as short a time as possible and replace the battery as soon as you can. If your system will not start with the low battery, replace it now following the instructions in Chapter 7, "Diagnosing and Solving Problems."

▶ If you see a keyboard error message, turn off your computer, make sure the keyboard is unlocked and properly connected, then start over. If the keyboard error still appears, you might have the incorrect type of keyboard for your system, such as an AT keyboard with an XT computer. Look for a switch on the keyboard—remember it might be hidden under a nameplate or panel that you have to pry off. Set the switch to the correct position and start over. If you do not have a switch, go back to whoever gave you the system and complain loudly.

▶ The ultimate error occurs when nothing at all happens when you turn on your system. You should at least hear a cooling fan or see a light appear somewhere on your monitor or computer. If your system is as quiet and still as a night in the Sahara, then it's not getting any power. Turn off the power switches, and check each of these items for the problem:

   ▶ Make sure the power cables are connected at both ends. Power cables are designed so they can be plugged in only one way.

   ▶ If your system includes a power switching box, either under the monitor or on the floor, make sure the master switch and any other switches are turned on. Most switching boxes have a pilot light to indicate if they are operating.

   ▶ If there is a voltage selector switch, make sure it is properly set for your power source. In the United States it should be set at 115 volts.

   ▶ Check that the wall socket you've connected the system to is live. Try a lamp or radio in the outlet. Make sure the socket is not controlled by a wall switch.

   ▶ If everything looks fine, then you might have a bad electrical cable or power supply. Try replacing the power cable. If that doesn't work you'll have to take your system in for service.

Determining Disk Capacity and Base Memory

You can determine how much *base memory* your system has and the storage capacity of disks using the program CHKDSK.COM that comes with the disk operating system. This information will help you determine what programs you can use on your system later on.

Throughout the remainder of this chapter you'll be using DOS commands to examine your system. If you are unfamiliar with DOS, just follow the step-by-step instructions. You'll learn more about DOS and DOS commands in the chapters to come.

Although you can purchase *utility programs* (programs that streamline basic operations and perform useful functions) that tell you more about your system, DOS is the one program I know you have right now. So instead of spending money on another program, we'll work with a basic set of tools that are already available. In later chapters you'll learn about hardware and software that supercharge DOS and your system to gain maximum productivity.

Locating CHKDSK on Your Disk

In order for you to run CHKDSK.COM, it must be on your floppy disk or the current directory of your hard disk. You'll use the DOS command DIR to see if the program is on your disk. Follow these steps to make sure the program is available:

1. At the DOS prompt, type **DIR CHKDSK** and press ←—⅃. If you see a listing such as

   CHKDSK COM   9832 12-30-85   12:00p

then the CHKDSK program is available for you to run and you can skip to the section "Running CHKDSK."

If the message "File not found" appears, then the program may be on another floppy disk or on a directory of your hard disk. *Directories* are sections of your hard disk that contain other programs and files. If you have a floppy-disk system, insert another DOS disk in drive A and repeat step 1 until the file is listed.

Navigating through subdirectories is a complicated process that we'll discuss in detail in Chapter 3, "Getting to Know DOS". For now, continue with the next step.

2. Type

   DIR *.

then press ←—⅃ to display a list of files with no *extensions,* one- to three-character identifiers added to the ends of the file names

(Figure 2.1). The names followed by <DIR> are directories that contain their own files and programs.

3. Copy down the list of directories for use later on, then look for a directory called BIN, DOS, PCDOS, MSDOS, or another name with the characters DOS. This probably contains the CHKDSK program.

4. Type **CD** (for *change directory*), followed by the name of the directory and press ↵. Make sure the program is there by entering

   DIR CHKDSK

   If you can't find the program on your hard disk, then locate a floppy disk containing the disk operating system.

5. Log on to drive A by typing **A:**, and then run the program as explained in the next section, "Running CHKDSK."

Running CHKDSK

Now that you've located the CHKDSK program, let's run it to get a report on your system.

```
C>dir *.

  Volume in drive C has no label
  Directory of  C:\

DBASE        <DIR>      7-06-88    9:57p
BIN          <DIR>      7-06-88    8:01a
WP50         <DIR>      7-06-88    8:43p
WP51         <DIR>     12-07-89   10:06a
FIGS         <DIR>      7-12-88    1:59p
TFIG         <DIR>      4-16-90    6:08p
TOOLS        <DIR>     10-30-88    7:24p
PUB          <DIR>     10-23-89    9:37a
FSP          <DIR>      3-17-89    2:03p
WORD5        <DIR>     10-04-88    9:57a
WIZ          <DIR>      3-15-90    1:52p
PZP          <DIR>     11-17-89   10:54a
PAINT        <DIR>      5-10-90    5:48p
       13 File(s)   17405952 bytes  free

C>
```

Figure 2.1: *Listing of directories*

1. Type **CHKDSK** and press ⏎. (Do not type the extension .COM or .EXE when executing a program.) If you're using a floppy disk with a hard-disk system, type

   A:CHKDSK C:

   After a moment you'll see a report similar to

   ```
   362496 bytes total disk space
   45056 bytes in 2 hidden files
   313344 bytes in 42 user files
   4096 bytes available on disk

   655360 bytes total memory
   580240 bytes free
   ```

CHKDSK first reports the total capacity of the disk. In this example, the disk can store up to 362496 characters. The message actually shows the capacity of your *disk,* not the maximum capacity of the disk drive. It's possible that you have a 360K disk in a high-capacity drive. So even though your drive can handle 1.2Mb disks, CHKDSK reports only 360K. The only way to know the maximum capacity of 5¼-inch drives is to try a high-capacity disk or to check your system's configuration using a utility program such as those discussed in Chapter 12, "Enhancing DOS." Table 2.1 shows the capacities of common disk formats.

Table 2.1: *Capacity of Common Disk Formats*

Type	Disk Space
360K normal capacity 5¼″	362,496
1.2Mb high capacity 5¼″	1,213,952
720K normal capacity 3½″	730,112
1.44Mb high capacity 3½″	1,457,664

CHKDSK also reports how much of the disk is being used by "hidden" system files and by your own programs and files, and how much space is still available. *Hidden files* are parts of DOS that are not shown in a directory listing.

Depending on your disk, CHKDSK might also report a number of directories and any *bad sectors,* damaged locations on the disk where DOS cannot store files. Figure 2.2, for example, is the CHKDSK report from a hard disk-drive that can store over 33Mb of data. The disk contains 19 directories and 20,480 bytes of bad sectors.

```
C>chkdsk

  33419264 bytes total disk space
    616448 bytes in 3 hidden files
     83968 bytes in 19 directories
  15304704 bytes in 792 user files
     20480 bytes in bad sectors
  17414144 bytes available on disk

    655360 bytes total memory
    559856 bytes free

C>
```

Figure 2.2: *CHKDSK report for a hard-disk drive*

The last two lines report the total amount of base memory and how much memory is available now that parts of DOS have been loaded. Base memory is not the same as total system memory. You could have expansion memory installed in your system and not be aware of it at this point. DOS recognizes only the first 640K of memory. Adding and using expansion memory is discussed in Chapter 14.

What Software Do You Have?

It is now time to see what software you received with your hand-me-down. But before cataloging your programs, you should consider a sticky legal and ethical dilemma.

Look at the labels on the floppy disks that you received with your system. If the labels are handwritten or typed on plain labels, or you have a hard disk but no floppy disks, then you have *copies* of the software, not the *distribution disks* (that is, the original disks) supplied by the software manufacturer. If you have copies, your software may be illegal.

If your software is illegal, then the person who supplied it is to blame. But by using the software, you are sharing in the responsibility. Unfortunately, your hand-me-down is of no use without any software, and you might have accepted or purchased the system based largely on the software that was supplied.

Now you certainly don't want to get fired over this issue, but if your system is a company hand-me-down, you could quietly inquire whether or not there is a policy about copying software and purchasing license agreements. Your company might have a special agreement to copy the software, either onto other floppy disks or directly onto your hard disk. Only you can decide what size waves you want to make in the corporate pond.

If you purchased your hand-me-down "on the street," you may be stuck in this quagmire. To use the software legally, contact the previous owner and request the original distribution disks and documentation. Most software license agreements allow the purchasers to transfer their rights to the program as long as they transfer the disks and documentation, and retain no copies for themselves. You could also contact the software manufacturer to see if it has a policy for upgrading an illegal copy for an authorized version. Some manufacturers will provide a copy at a reduced cost.

If you have properly labeled floppy disks, you should have no trouble identifying your software. But if you have a hard disk, floppy disks that are poorly labeled, or no documentation, you'll have to guess what a program is by its name in the directory listing.

While many applications include more than one file, Table 2.2 shows the major file names of some popular programs. As you go through the steps in the following sections, refer to the table to help identify your software.

Table 2.2: *Program File Names of Popular Application Programs*

Program File Name	Application Program
CADD	Generic CADD
DBASE	dBASE
Editor	XYWrite

Table 2.2: *Program File Names of Popular Application Programs (continued)*

Program File Name	Application Program
FP	FirstPublisher
HG	Harvard Graphics
LOTUS or 123	Lotus 1-2-3
MM	Multimate
PM	Aldus Pagemaker
PW	Professional Write
QF	Quattro
SK	Sidekick
SP	Sprint
VP	Ventura Publisher
WIN, WIN86, or WIN386	Microsoft Windows
WORD	Microsoft Word
WP	WordPerfect
WS	WordStar

Now let's see what software you have. As you go through these instructions, make a list of your programs using these suggested categories:

Word processors	Spreadsheets
Databases	Graphics
Utilities	Other

Hard-Disk Systems

If you have a hard-disk system, follow these steps:

1. Type **CD** and press ⏎ to make sure you are in the main directory.

2. Type **DIR/P** and press ⏎. The screen fills with the first listing of files and directories on your disk, and the message

Strike a key when ready...

appears at the bottom of the screen.

3. Scan the directory listing, writing down the files it contains.

4. Press any key to continue the display, and then repeat this procedure until all the files have been listed. At the end of the list you'll
see something like

   52 File(s)   25165123 bytes free

5. Scan through each of the *directories* (the file names that are followed by <DIR>). Using the list you just made (type **DIR** *. to list
directories again if necessary), examine each directory by entering
DIR/P \ followed by the name of the directory, such as

   DIR/P \WP51

6. With your list of the programs in each directory, try to identify them
using any documentation you have or the file names in Table 2.2.

Floppy-Disk Systems

Gather together the floppy disks that came with your system. You should have at
least one or two DOS disks, labeled *DOS* and *Supplemental Programs,* or *Disk 1*
and *Disk 2.*

Make a list of the other programs, noting whether or not the disks are copies or
distribution disks. If you have distribution disks, copy down any serial number or
version information along with the program name. If the disk has no label, or a label
that doesn't clearly identify its contents, follow these steps to determine the program on the disk:

1. Insert the disk in drive A.

2. Type **DIR/P** and press ◄━━┛. The screen fills with the first listing of files
and directories on your disk, and the message

   Strike a key when ready...

appears at the bottom of the screen.

3. Start a list of the files and press any key to continue the display.
Repeat this procedure until all the files have been listed. At the end
of the list you'll see something like

   19 File(s)   102316 bytes free

Printing Disk Directories

If you have many floppy-disk or hard-disk files, and a printer, you may want to print a copy of the directory listings. Some people slip a printed listing in the *disk sleeve* (the disk's paper envelope) along with the disk, or they keep a book of printed listings handy for reference.

To print your listings, follow these steps:

1. Make sure your printer is plugged in, properly connected to your computer, turned on, and supplied with paper.

2. Enter the **DIR/P** command as explained previously, but do not press key when you see the message

Strike a key when ready...

3. Press Shift-PrtSc—the Shift and PrtSc keys at the same time—then release them both. (On some keyboards, the PrtSc key is labeled Print Screen.) A copy of your screen will be printed.

If nothing happens, your printer may not be properly connected or set up. In some cases, your keyboard may lock up and not respond to your typing—you'll have to press Ctrl-Alt-Del (simultaneously) to reboot and start over. Unfortunately, this will destroy anything you were working on in an application.

Learning More about Your System

There are details about your system that you may still not know, such as the processor type and speed, total system memory, and the color and maximum resolution of your monitor. Most color monitors will appear to be black and white at the DOS level, so you could have a high-resolution color monitor and not know it.

One way to determine the type of monitor is to run, or to install and then run, an application program that adjusts for display type automatically—using color and high resolution when it is available.

You can also find out your monitor display type by installing and running any number of application programs. (*Installing* a program means getting it ready to work on your system. Instructions for installing software are presented in Chapter 4, "Personalizing Your Hand-Me-Down.") Many programs ask you to designate the type of monitor display you have. If you select the wrong one, the program won't run properly.

As an example, let's see how you can use an application program like WordPerfect to find out more about your computer. Version 5.1 of WordPerfect is shipped on low-capacity 5¼-inch disks, but requires either a hard disk or high-capacity floppy disks to run. If you can't install the program on high-capacity disks on your system, then you have only 360K drives.

After you install WordPerfect 5.1, run the program WPINFO.EXE, which you installed as part of WordPerfect either on your hard disk or on a working copy of floppy disks. You'll see a report about your hardware, as shown in Figure 2.3. Of course, your own system specifications will differ. The report shows the processor and display type, amount of base memory, and other hardware specifications. When you press a key, you'll see a listing of the AUTOEXEC.BAT and CONFIG.SYS files. These files may give you additional clues about your hardware, as you'll learn in Chapter 4.

You can find out a lot more about your system by using other utility programs that are designed to report system information. We'll discuss these in Chapter 12.

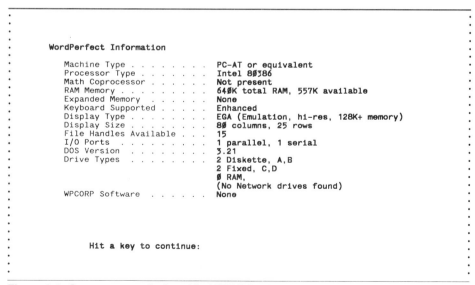

Figure 2.3: *System report displayed by WPINFO.EXE, a WordPerfect utility program*

Software Compatibility

If you have a hard-disk system or received software with your hand-me-down, you can assume that your system is adequate for the software. But if you have software from another computer or source, you cannot assume that it will run properly on your new system. All programs have certain minimum requirements, in terms of the type and number of disk drives, the amount of base or expansion memory, and the type of monitor and display adapter. The *display adapter* is a circuit card inside your computer that provides the electrical signals necessary to display images on the screen.

Check your software manuals for the list of minimum requirements. If you're not sure, make a backup of the program disks as explained in Chapter 6, "Managing Floppy Disks," then try installing and running the program. You'll quickly learn whether it will run on your hand-me-down.

If the program will not run, look for error messages on the screen, or again compare the minimum requirements with your list of specifications. You'll learn how to increase your system's resources in later chapters.

Now that you're familiar with your hand-me-down, you'll learn how to work with DOS in Chapter 3.

Chapter Three

Getting to Know DOS

*A*ll communication with your computer is through DOS. DOS serves as the link between the computer, keyboard, monitor, disk drives, and printer. It interprets your commands and wishes, letting you put data into the computer so you can get information out of it.

At one level, DOS is just the acronym for *disk operating system.* But DOS has also become the nickname for PC-DOS and MS-DOS, two versions of a disk operating system used with IBM and compatible microcomputers, so we refer simply to DOS rather than *the DOS* or *a DOS*. It may not be grammatically correct, but it serves its purpose.

You'll also often hear DOS used generically to represent that specific class of computers, as in DOS versus Apple Macintosh. In this light, DOS computers are distinguished from other microcomputers that do not use a PC-DOS type of operating system. Apple computers are not DOS machines.

The term *PC* has suffered the same fate. Years ago, PC referred generically to any "personal computer." But ever since the IBM PC—that company's specific model name for its first personal computer—the term means an IBM or compatible microcomputer, as in PC versus Macintosh. PC is also used to mean the original IBM microcomputer, compared to its later XT and AT models.

In Chapter 2, you used DOS to learn something about your computer. In this chapter you'll learn an important set of DOS commands and principles that you'll need to personalize and use your system.

DOS Anatomy

DOS is a program that is automatically loaded into your computer when you boot the system. Two hidden files, IBMBIO.COM and IBMDOS.COM, get everything going by setting up the lines of communication between your *hardware* (computer system) and *software* (application programs). (Depending on your version of DOS, the files might be called IO.SYS and MSDOS.SYS, or something similar.) Control then passes to the *command interpreter,* the program COMMAND.COM on your DOS disk or hard disk.

The DOS prompt, such as A > or C >, is DOS's way of telling you that the command interpreter is waiting for some instructions and that you are logged on to the disk drive. Being *logged on* to a drive means you can access any of the programs or other files on the disk in that drive. Everything that you type at the DOS prompt is interpreted by the command interpreter. Just type the command next to the DOS prompt and press ◄─┘.

First, the command interpreter checks to see if your command is an *internal DOS instruction*. Internal commands are built into COMMAND.COM and will not be listed individually in a disk directory. They are the most commonly used commands for manipulating the files on your disk and working with DOS. For example, they let you copy, rename, and delete files, clear the screen, and set the date and time. If your instruction is an internal command, and your *syntax*—the way you've worded the command—is correct, DOS executes it immediately. The internal commands are

BREAK	CD *or* CHDIR	CHCP	CLS
COPY	CTTY	DATE	DEL
DIR	ERASE	MD *or* MKDIR	PATH
REN	RM *or* RMDIR	SET	TIME
TYPE	VER	VERIFY	VOL

If your instruction is not an internal command, DOS looks for an external command or an executable program file with that name. *External commands* are programs supplied with DOS that perform more complex or advanced functions than the internal commands. They are not part of COMMAND.COM, but are programs that you'll be able to see listed in a directory. In order to use an external command, you must be logged on to the disk in which it is located or use the PATH command that you'll learn about in Chapter 5. The DOS external commands you'll learn in this and later chapters include

BACKUP	CHKDSK	COMP	DISKCOMP
DISKCOPY	FDISK	FIND	FORMAT
GRAPHICS	MODE	PRINT	RECOVER
RESTORE	SORT	SYS	TREE
XCOPY			

The external commands are examples of *executable programs*, programs with the .EXE or .COM extension that you can *run,* or activate, from the DOS prompt. Word processing, spreadsheet, database, graphics, and other applications that you use are also executable programs. Like the external commands, you will see these listed in the directory.

To run an executable program, just enter its name at the DOS prompt, but do not include the extension. For example, to run the program WP.EXE, type **WP,** and then press ←⏎.

If your instruction at the DOS prompt is not an internal or external command, or another executable program, DOS looks for a file with that name and the .BAT extension. These are *batch* files that contain instructions to DOS.

Finally, if DOS doesn't find a batch file with the name you entered, it displays the message

Bad command or file name

followed by the DOS prompt. You'll also see this message if you incorrectly enter a DOS internal command.

DOS Versions

Over the relatively short history of the PC, DOS has gone through a number of revisions. Each new version of DOS has included new and updated features, and additional internal and external commands. Version 1.0, for example, supported

320K disks, Version 2.0 introduced 360K disks, and Version 3.0 was the first to support high-capacity 5¼-inch disks.

Let's see what version of DOS you have by using the VER (short for *version*) internal command. Follow these steps:

1. Start your computer, and respond to the date and time prompts if they appear.

2. Type **VER**, and then press ⏎. A message will appear similar to

   BIOS Version 3.34
   MS-DOS Version 3.21

The *BIOS*—the Basic Input Output System—is a program built into your computer. The BIOS boots your disk and performs some tests of the computer's functions. In fact, it is the BIOS that determines how compatible your computer is with the IBM models.

Some computer manufacturers provide modified versions of DOS that include additional external commands that relate specifically to their hardware. For example, some versions of DOS include a SPEED command to control multispeed processors, programs to transfer files to and from laptop computers, or utilities to restore deleted files.

Still, DOS has remained remarkably consistent. The basic commands that were used five years ago are still used today.

Logging On to a Drive

The letter displayed at the DOS prompt represents the name of the disk drive you are logged on to: A> means you are on drive A, B> on drive B, C> on hard-disk drive C.

DOS needs to know the drive of all programs you want it to execute. If you enter a batch file or program name (including a DOS external command) at the DOS prompt line without specifying a drive, DOS expects to find it on the currently logged drive indicated by the DOS prompt.

For example, suppose you enter the command **CHKDSK** at the DOS prompt A>. DOS will expect the program CHKDSK.COM to be on the disk in drive A, and will display "Bad command or file name" if it is not there. (You can run an internal command from any drive or directory, however.)

To log on to a drive, just type its letter, followed by a colon, and then press ←. Let's try it now; your computer should already be on.

1. If you have a hard-disk drive, insert a floppy disk in drive A. If you have two floppy-disk drives, insert a disk in drive B.

2. Type **A:** or **B:** (depending on the drive you are using), and then press ← to log on to the disk you just inserted.

3. Type **DIR**, and then press ←. The files listed are contained on the disk you just logged on to.

4. Type **C:** or **A:** to return to the boot disk.

There are two ways to run a program that is not on your logged drive. One way is to first log on to the drive, and then enter the program name. Or, you could just precede the name of the program with its drive designator, such as B:CHKDSK to run the CHKDSK program that's in drive B.

Understanding DOS Directories and Paths

Disks can be divided into more than one directory. Each directory holds its own files and programs, so you can group together files that have a common theme. Smaller directories are more manageable than larger ones, making it easier to manipulate files using DOS commands.

The directory structure of a disk is often compared to the structure of a tree. The main directory, called the *root* directory, is like the tree trunk. Other directories are like branches coming from the root directory.

Figure 3.1 shows a graphic representation of a hard-disk drive with several directories. The disk has a root directory, and the directories WP, LOTUS, and DOS. Each of these four directories contains its own subdirectories and files, as you see.

A *subdirectory* is a further division of a directory, a branch stemming from another branch. Figure 3.2 shows subdirectories added to our sample disk.

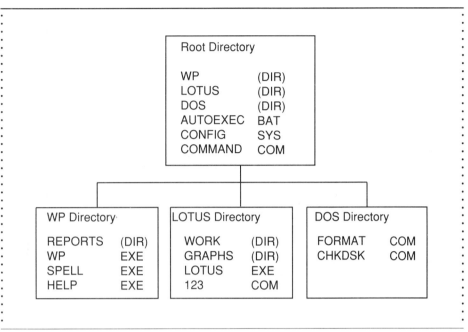

Figure 3.1: *A disk divided into sections, or directories*

In reality, all directories except the root are subdirectories since they branch from the root directory. But for simplicity, we'll refer to branches directly off of the root as directories, with subdirectories branching from these directories.

Specifying Paths

In order to take action on a file or program, DOS must locate that file or program on the disk. Since all files stem from the root directory, we can locate any file by following its path from the root through any of the directories and subdirectories.

A file's path follows this general pattern:

<disk drive:>\<directory>\<subdirectory>\<file name>

The notation *<disk drive:>* represents the drive you want to start from; *<directory>* and *<subdirectory>* are the specific branches you want to take; *<file name>* is the file you want to find. Throughout this book, we'll use italicized words

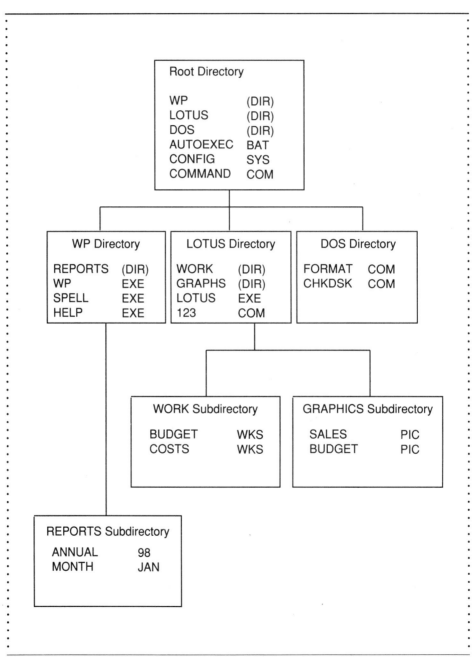

Figure 3.2: *Subdirectories are divisions of directories*

within the < and > symbols to represent the variable user input that you have to type in. Don't type in the < and > symbols themselves. So if an instruction says, type

PRINT *<file name>*

it means to type the word **PRINT** followed by the name of one of your files.

Let's look at an example of how to specify a path using the disk organization shown in Figure 3.2. Suppose you'd like to use the spreadsheet called BUDGET.WKS, which is located in the WORK subdirectory. Starting at the root directory (drive C), the file's path is

C:\LOTUS\WORK\BUDGET.WKS

Notice that each branch of the path is separated by a backslash, the \ character. The root directory is referred to as C:\, so we can locate the file through this path:

C:\	Start at the root directory (drive C)
LOTUS\	Go to the LOTUS directory off of the root
WORK\	Go to the WORK subdirectory branching from LOTUS
BUDGET.WKS	Go to the file BUDGET.WKS in WORK

If you enter a batch file or program name at the DOS prompt line without specifying a directory, DOS expects to find it on the current directory on the logged drive.

You can run a program on another directory in two ways. One way is to precede the name of program with its full path. The path includes the disk-drive letter as well as all of the directory names leading to the specific file. You can leave out the drive letter if the file is on the logged drive.

Changing Directories

Another way to run a program is first to change to its directory, and then enter the program name. To change to another directory on the logged drive, type **CD** or **CHDIR** followed by the directory's path.

For example, you would type **CD\LOTUS** to change to the LOTUS directory, or **CD** to change to the root directory. The backslash after CD tells DOS to begin the path from the root directory. So to change to the WORK subdirectory of LOTUS from anywhere on the disk, type

CD\LOTUS\WORK

This command tells DOS to go back to the root directory, and then follow the path through LOTUS to WORK.

You can quickly change to a subdirectory of the current directory by telling DOS to start at the current directory, not return to the root. If you are already logged on to C:\LOTUS, for instance, change to WORK with the command

CD WORK

Without the backslash, DOS expects WORK to be a subdirectory of the currently logged directory.

Since directories (not subdirectories) stem from the root, you can leave out the backslash when changing from the root directory to a directory, such as entering

CD LOTUS

from the root directory. However, CD WORK is invalid if you are in the root directory because WORK stems from LOTUS.

If this shorthand fails when you are trying to change directories, add the backslash and the full path.

You must be on a drive to change to a directory on that drive. You cannot log on to drives and change directories in one command. Typing **CD\D:\FONTS** is "illegal" if you are on drive C. You must first log on to the drive D by entering **D:**, and then change directories using **CD\FONTS**.

Using Wildcards

Many internal DOS commands can also accept the wildcards * and ? as part of the file name. Use * when you want to refer to any number of unknown characters in either the name or extension; use ? in place of one character.

For example, *.BAK refers to all files with the .BAK extension, while LETTER.* refers to all files named LETTER, no matter what the extension is. The shorthand *.* refers to every file on the logged disk and directory.

The ? character, on the other hand, represents a single character. The notation ?.BAK refers to all one-character file names with the .BAK extension. W?.* refers to all two-character file names starting with W, while ???.DOC refers to all three-character file names with the .DOC extension.

File-Naming Conventions

A DOS file name can have up to eight characters plus an optional one- to three-character extension. The name and extension are separated by a period. Names must consist only of letters, numbers, and the characters $, %, ', −, @, {, }, ~, !, and #.

When naming your own file, select a name that clearly indicates its contents, even though you only have a maximum of 11 characters to work with. For example, LETTR.MOM is more explanatory than just LETTER; BUDGET.93 is better than MONEY. File names like LETTER.1, LETTER.2, LETTER.3 won't have any meaning when your disk becomes full.

You should not give an .EXE, .COM, or .BAT file the same name as a DOS internal command. If you named a file COPY.BAT or REN.EXE, DOS would never execute it. When you entered **COPY** or **REN**, DOS would automatically run the internal command. You can, however, use the internal command names with no extension or an extension other than .BAT, .EXE, or .COM for files. For example, COPY and DEL.TXT are valid file names.

In addition, there are other reserved words used by DOS that you cannot use as file names. These are

aux	nul	lpt1
lpt2	lpt3	com1
com2	clock$	prn

While you can use these words as parts of file names, such as LPT105 or NULTY, you cannot use them as the full name, even with an extension.

DOS Function Keys

You can use the F1, F2, and F3 keys to quickly repeat all or part of the last DOS command you typed at the DOS prompt.

Key	Function
F1	Displays the next character from your last DOS command each time you press F1
F2 <character>	Displays the command up to the next occurrence of the specified character
F3	Repeats the remaining characters on the prompt line

For example, suppose your last DOS command was

DIR C:\WP\LETTERS\ * .DOC

Press the F1 key after the DOS prompt to display the character D. Press F1 again to display I, and once more to display R. Continue pressing F1 to display any amount of the prompt a character at a time.

If you press F2 and then **L** from the DOS prompt, all characters up to the first L in the last command would appear—**DIR C:\WP**. Press F3 from that point to display the remaining characters of the command.

By combining the Backspace and function keys, you can speed up your work with DOS. For instance, after entering the command **DIR C:\WP\LETTERS\ * .DOC**, you want to display all files with the .BAK extension on the same directory. Instead of entering the entire command line, you could perform these steps:

1. Press F3 to display **DIR C:\WP\LETTERS\ * .DOC**.
2. Press Backspace three times to delete DOC.
3. Type **BAK**, and then press ⏎.

Pausing the Display

If you want to display a long directory listing or file without printing it, use DOS key combinations to pause the display. This gives you time to read the screen before text scrolls off the top.

To pause the display, press Ctrl-Num Lock or Ctrl-S. This temporarily suspends the operation being performed. To continue the display, press any noncontrol or non-function key, such as the spacebar, a letter, or a number.

Your keyboard may also have a Pause key. Simply press Pause to suspend an operation.

Getting Out of Tight Spots

There may be times when your computer starts to misbehave—you can't pause an operation, your screen fills with gibberish, the system doesn't respond to your key-board, or your printer starts spewing pages.

These instances may call for some drastic action. Press Ctrl-Break or Ctrl-C to stop, not just suspend, an operation. If that doesn't work, you may have to reset your computer by pressing Ctrl-Alt-Del, all three keys at the same time. This performs a "warm boot" by reloading DOS again but skipping any self-diagnostic program. While a warm boot does get the computer back under control, you will lose any-thing you were working on in an application.

Finally, if your system doesn't respond to Ctrl-Alt-Del, turn off the computer, wait a minute, then turn it back on. (Some computers have a *hardware reset button* that works similarly to pressing Ctrl-Alt-Del. If Ctrl-Alt-Del doesn't work, try pressing this button before turning off and on the computer.)

Nonstandard Key Combinations

The combinations of keys discussed so far are provided by all versions of DOS. Some manufacturers have added their own unique key sequences to control spe-cial hardware or software featured in their machines.

The Compaq portable computer, for example, uses Ctrl-Alt-Plus and Ctrl-Alt-Minus to control the key clicking sound.

Zenith computers use Ctrl-Alt-Ins to run a ROM monitor program. This is a diagnos-tic and control program stored in the computer's permanent memory. If you don't have a Zenith computer, pressing this key combination may have no effect. But if you do have a Zenith, your computer will appear to reboot, losing any work you have in memory.

So don't be surprised if you get strange results from certain key combinations.

Some Useful DOS Commands

In the chapters that follow, you'll be using DOS to tailor your system to your own needs and manage your hard and floppy disks. In preparation, let's review a basic set of DOS commands that you'll be using often. This section illustrates the use of internal and external commands, as well as the principles of directories and paths. Read the discussion thoroughly, then try out the commands on your own system. Repeat them several times, using different files or options, until you're comfortable with how they work.

Listing Directories

Use the internal DOS command DIR when you want to see what files are on a disk or in a directory.

Type **DIR** and press ↵ to see a list of the files in the current directory of the logged drive. The command lists each file's name, extension, size in bytes, and the date and time it was created or last changed.

If you have a large number of files on the directory, the listing will scroll off the screen faster than you can read it. You can use the **DIR/P** command to list files one screen at a time, or the **DIR/W** command to display a wide listing, as shown in Figure 3.3. (The P or W part of the command is called an *option*.) Notice that only the names and extensions are shown with the DIR/W command, not the file size, date, and time of creation.

Use the forward slash—the / character—before an option; use the backslash (\) to separate each branch of a directory path.

Use this command:	To list the files in:
DIR	The current directory of the logged drive
DIR B:	Drive B

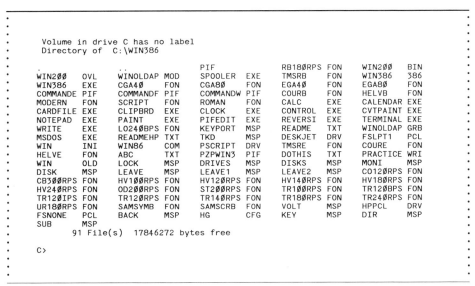

```
        Volume in drive C has no label
        Directory of  C:\WIN386

        .                    ..           PIF              RB180RPS FON   WIN200   BIN
        WIN200   OVL   WINOLDAP MOD   SPOOLER  EXE   TMSRB    FON   WIN386   386
        WIN386   EXE   CGA40    FON   CGA80    FON   EGA40    FON   EGA80    FON
        COMMANDE PIF   COMMANDF PIF   COMMANDW PIF   COURB    FON   HELVB    FON
        MODERN   FON   SCRIPT   FON   ROMAN    FON   CALC     EXE   CALENDAR EXE
        CARDFILE EXE   CLIPBRD  EXE   CLOCK    EXE   CONTROL  EXE   CVTPAINT EXE
        NOTEPAD  EXE   PAINT    EXE   PIFEDIT  EXE   REVERSI  EXE   TERMINAL EXE
        WRITE    EXE   LO240BPS FON   KEYPORT  MSP   README   TXT   WINOLDAP GRB
        MSDOS    EXE   READMEHP TXT   TKD      MSP   DESKJET  DRV   FSLPT1   PCL
        WIN      INI   WIN86    COM   PSCRIPT  DRV   TMSRE    FON   COURE    FON
        HELVE    FON   ABC      TXT   PZPWIN3  PIF   DOTHIS   TXT   PRACTICE WRI
        WIN      OLD   LOCK     MSP   DRIVES   MSP   DISKS    MSP   MONI     MSP
        DISK     MSP   LEAVE    MSP   LEAVE1   MSP   LEAVE2   MSP   CO120RPS FON
        CB300RPS FON   HV100RPS FON   HV120RPS FON   HV140RPS FON   HV180RPS FON
        HV240RPS FON   OD200RPS FON   ST200RPS FON   TR100RPS FON   TR120BPS FON
        TR120IPS FON   TR120RPS FON   TR140RPS FON   TR180RPS FON   TR240RPS FON
        UR180RPS FON   SAMSYMB  FON   SAMSCRB  FON   VOLT     MSP   HPPCL    DRV
        FSNONE   PCL   BACK     MSP   HG       CFG   KEY      MSP   DIR      MSP
        SUB      MSP
                91 File(s)   17846272 bytes free

        C>
```

Figure 3.3: *A wide directory listing*

Use this command:	To list the files in:
DIR\	The root directory of the logged drive
DIR\LOTUS	The LOTUS directory of the logged drive
DIR\LOTUS\WORK	The WORK subdirectory of the logged drive
DIR/W\WP	The WP directory of the logged drive in a wide listing
DIR B:\DOC	The DOC directory of drive B
DIR/P\WP51\DOC	The DOC subdirectory of WP51, pausing as each screen becomes full

You can use the wildcards to display selected groups of files. For example:

Use this command:	To list these files:
DIR L*.*	All files starting with the letter L
DIR L?.*	All files with two-character names starting with the letter L
DIR *.*	All files—the same as DIR by itself
DIR *.	Files without any extension, including directories

If you have trouble logging on to a directory, you're probably entering the path incorrectly, such as misspelling a directory name or leaving out one of the branches.

Listing Paths with TREE.COM

Subdirectories are not frequently used on floppy disks, but they are important for hard-disk users. It would be quite difficult to handle the hundreds of files that you can store on a hard disk if they were all on one directory.

TREE.COM is a DOS external command that displays the name of all directories and subdirectories on your disk. If you enter TREE.COM, you will see a list similar to the one shown in Figure 3.4. Each directory and subdirectory is shown with its complete path except for the drive letter. Remember, you can pause the display by pressing Ctrl-Num Lock or Ctrl-S.

```
C>TREE

Path: \WP
Sub-directories:  REPORTS

Path: \WP\REPORTS
Sub-directories:  None

Path: \LOTUS
Sub-directories:  WORK
                  BUDGET

Path: \LOTUS\WORK
Sub-directories:  None

Path: \LOTUS\GRAPHS
Sub-directories:  None

Path: \DOS
Sub-directories:  None

C>
```

Figure 3.4: *Output of the TREE command*

Copying Files with COPY

The COPY command makes a duplicate of a file, or group of files. The general syntax is

COPY <*original file name*> <*destination file name*>

Use the command to make a copy of the file on the same drive and directory, but with a different name, or to copy the file to another disk. Let's look at several examples of the COPY command.

The command

COPY LETTER.DOC LETTER.BAK

would make a copy of the LETTER.DOC file and name it LETTER.BAK. You now have two identical files on the same drive and directory but with different names.

If you issued this command:

COPY LETTER.DOC B:

DOS would copy the file from the logged drive to the disk in drive B, giving the file the same name. You now have two identical files named LETTER.DOC—one on the logged drive and one on drive B.

The command

COPY LETTER.DOC B:LETTER.BAK

would copy the file to drive B, changing the name of the copy to LETTER.BAK. The original file is not changed.

To make a copy of a file that's on another drive or directory, or to put the copy on another directory, use the full path, such as

COPY B:LETTER.DOC C:\WP\RESPONSE.DOC

This example copies and renames a file from drive B to the WP directory on drive C.

You can use the wildcards to copy selected groups of files. For example,

COPY A:*.DOC C:\WP

copies all DOC files in drive A to the WP directory of drive C.

The command

COPY *.* D:

copies every file on the logged disk and directory to the currently logged directory in drive D.

If the destination drive does not have enough room to store the file, you'll see the message

Insufficient disk space

In Chapter 5 you'll learn how to use COPY and other commands to back up your hard disk. Chapter 6 explains how to make copies of your floppy disks.

Displaying Files on the Screen with TYPE

The TYPE command displays a file's contents on the screen. The syntax is

TYPE *<file name>*

TYPE displays the ASCII files on the screen, so the command is most useful for files that contain nothing but letters and numbers, such as AUTOEXEC.BAT and CONFIG.SYS.

Files that contain binary information, such as executable programs, will appear as nonsense on the screen because the binary codes are not represented by ASCII characters (Figure 3.5). Document and data files created with application programs may appear as gibberish when displayed with TYPE.

Printing Files with DOS

PRINT is an external command that sends the contents of a file to your printer. It does so through a *print queue,* a waiting line in which a file waits until the printer is

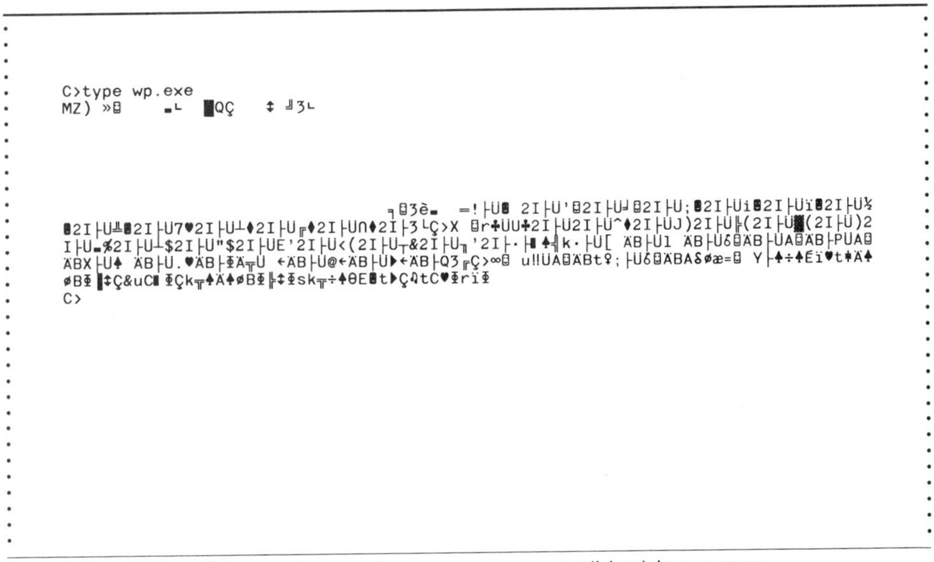

```
C>type wp.exe
MZ) »8      _ˡ  ▓QÇ    ‡ ⅃3ˡ


                           ¬83ê▪  =!├U▐ 2I├U'82I├U⅃82I├U;82I├Ui82I├Uï82I├U½
▐2I├U⅃▐2I├U7♥2I├U⊥♦2I├U▐♦2I├Un♦2I├3ˡÇ>X ▯r♣UU♣2I├U2I├U^♦2I├UJ)2I├U▍(2I├U▓(2I├U)2
I├U▪%2I├U⊥$2I├U"$2I├UE'2I├U<(2I├U⊤&2I├U⌐'2I├·├▌ ♣▌k·├U[ ÄB├U1 ÄB├U6▯ÄB├UA▯ÄB├PUA▯
ÄBX├U♦ ÄB├U.♥ÄB├‡Ä⊤Ü ←ÄB├U@←ÄB├U▶←ÄB├Q3▮Ç>∞▯ u!!UA▯ÄBt?;├U6▯ÄBAŠøæ=▯ Y├♣÷♣Éï♥t♦Ä♦
øB‡▐‡Ç&uC▌ ‡Çk⊤♦Ä♦øB‡▐‡Ïsk⊤÷♦θE▌t▶ÇⱮtC♥‡rï‡
C>
```

Figure 3.5: *Files with binary information may appear as gibberish on screen*

ready to accept it. Since it is an external command, you must be logged on to the disk or directory where the file PRINT.COM is located.

The PRINT command is similar to TYPE, in that it is best used with ASCII or text files. If you try printing a program file, you'll likely waste a great deal of paper and time since the binary information in those files cannot be translated into printable characters.

The syntax is

PRINT <*drive:*>\<*path*>\<*file name*>

as in

PRINT C:\WORD\LETTER.TXT

When you first use the PRINT command, DOS displays the message

Name of list device [PRN]:

Press ⏎ to accept the standard parallel printer. You'll then see

Resident part of PRINT installed

and a message that the file you specified is currently being printed.

You can add other files to the print queue even before the first one is printed. Just enter the PRINT command again followed by another file name. Stop printing with the command **PRINT/T**.

Although PRINT appears to be a simple command, there are many hardware considerations. Unless you tell DOS otherwise, the output of the PRINT command will go to your computer's parallel port. This is fine as long as you have a printer attached to that port.

If you have a serial printer, or more than one parallel port, then you have to give DOS some special instructions before printing the file. You'll learn these details in Chapter 8, "Working with Your Printer."

The PRINT command also has a number of options, or switches, that can be entered after it on the DOS command line. Unfortunately, the options vary between versions of DOS, especially with different manufacturers. Some versions offer greater flexibility and control over the print queue.

You can also print files, sections of files, and screen displays using the Ctrl, Shift, and PrtSc keys. In Chapter 2 you learned how to print directory listings by pressing Shift-PrtSc. Shift-PrtSc produces a *screen dump,* a quick copy of whatever is on your screen.

To print whatever will appear next on your screen, press Ctrl-PrtSc or Ctrl-P. This turns on the *continuous print function,* or *printer echo,* sending a copy of every character that next appears on your screen to your printer as well.

While Shift-PrtSc prints one screen and then stops, Ctrl-PrtSc continues printing until you press Ctrl-PrtSc (or Ctrl-P) a second time.

To print a long directory listing, follow these steps:

1. From the DOS prompt, press Ctrl-PrtSc.

2. Type **DIR**, or the directory command you want, and press ←⏎.

3. Press Ctrl-PrtSc after the listing is printed.

To print the contents of a file, follow these steps:

1. From the DOS prompt, press Ctrl-PrtSc.
2. Type **TYPE** and the file name, and then press ←⎯.
3. Press Ctrl-PrtSc after the file is printed.

Just keep in mind that every character will be sent to the printer, even error and warning messages.

Like the TYPE and PRINT commands, Shift-PrtSc and Ctrl-PrtSc work best with files that contain only ASCII characters. To produce printouts of graphic screens, you need to use some special techniques discussed in Chapter 8.

With some versions of DOS, Ctrl-PrtSc might not work correctly if there are already characters on the prompt line. In this case, make sure only the DOS prompt appears when pressing the key combination.

Now that you're familiar with DOS, let's work on personalizing your system and organizing your hard and floppy disks.

Chapter Four

Personalizing Your Hand–Me–Down

*S*ince your hand-me-down used to belong to someone else, it was set up to complement their way of working. But now that the system is yours, it should support your work and your personality.

In this chapter, you'll learn how to make some fundamental and important changes to your hand-me-down. You'll learn how to delete unwanted files, install your own programs, and modify configuration and batch files—all using resources available in DOS itself.

Deleting Unwanted Files

Although your disks may contain a great deal of useful software, they might also be burdened with personal files left over by the last owner. There may be word processing documents, spreadsheets, databases, or other files that were no doubt important to someone else, but which just take up space as far as you are concerned.

You can delete or erase files that you don't need from your disks. Deleting files is easy; making sure you don't need them is another matter. A file that looks useless to you could be a key to some important and expensive application. Even some very small files, just a few bytes in size, could be critical to an application program. Table 4.1, for instance, shows just a few of the files used by WordPerfect 5.1. Deleting any of these files could cause the program to fail or not operate fully within your configuration. So keep this golden rule in mind: Unless you're absolutely sure that you don't need the file, don't delete it.

There are retail programs that will help you undelete a file you erased by accident. But none of these programs can guarantee to restore every deleted file.

Table 4.1: *Some Files Required by WordPerfect 5.1*

ALTRNAT WPK	CONVERT EXE	CURSOR COM
EGA512 FRS	EGAITAL FRS	EGASMC FRS
EGAUND FRS	EHANDLER PS	ENHANCED WPK
EQUATION WPK	FINST COM	FIXBIOS COM
GRAB COM	HPLASERJ PRS	HRF12 FRS
HRF6 FRS	INSTALL EXE	KEYS MRS
MACROS WPK	NWPSETUP EXE	PRINTER TST
PTR EXE	PTR HLP	REBUILD BAT
SHORTCUT WPK	SPELL EXE	STANDARD CRS
STANDARD IRS	STANDARD PRS	STANDARD VRS
STY STY	TYPETHRU EXE	VGA512 FRS
VGAITAL FRS	VGASMC FRS	VGAUND FRS
WP DRS	WP EXE	WP FIL
WP LRS	WP MRS	WP QRS
WP-PIF DVP	WP{WP} SET	WP{WP} SPW
WP{WP}US HYC	WP{WP}US LCN	WP{WP}US LEX
WP{WP}US SUP	WP{WP}US THS	WP51 INS
WP51-286 PIF	WP51-386 PIF	WPHELP FIL
WPHP1 ALL	WPINFO EXE	WPPS1 ALL
WPSMALL DRS		

Since floppy disks are relatively inexpensive, use them to save the files that you're not sure about. A box of disks is less expensive than replacing an application program such as Lotus 1-2-3 or Ventura Publisher.

Guidelines for Deleting Files

There are some general rules you can follow for making those important "should I or shouldn't I" decisions:

▶ Never delete files from distribution disks, or from your only copy of a DOS or application disk.

▶ Never delete COMMAND.COM from your hard disk or DOS floppy disk.

▶ Avoid deleting an executable program from your hard disk unless you have a copy of it on a floppy disk.

▶ In some cases, but not all, you can safely erase hard-disk files that are not on the original distribution floppies.

▶ Don't delete an application from your hard disk if there is a program named UNINSTAL in the same directory. See "Copy-Protected Software" later in this chapter.

Learning from Extensions

A file's extension is often the best clue to whether you should delete it. For instance, the extensions .DOC, .TXT, and .BAK are normally those added to documents, publications, and other files created by the user. They are typically not part of an application program, except for sample and informational files. If you know the application, then you should know the file extensions it adds to user files. Table 4.2 lists extensions used for your data files by popular applications. You can usually erase these without damaging the program itself.

When files have other extensions, they are probably parts of an application—files that store program code, configuration information, or auxiliary data, for example. Be careful about deleting a file with the extensions shown in Table 4.3. There are many other extensions that are used by specific applications, such as .PIF and .FON used by Windows, and .PRD and .DAT used by Microsoft Word. Do not delete these files; they are critical to the applications.

The extensions .BAS, .PAS, .COB, and .C are used for files containing program *source code,* the instructions used to generate executable .COM or .EXE programs in BASIC, Pascal, COBOL, and C.

If you see a lot of files with these extensions, then the previous owner probably dabbled in programming. Since all but .BAS files contain all ASCII characters, you can use the DOS commands TYPE or PRINT to see their contents.

You might want to save the source code files as examples if you want to write your own programs. Some of these programs may also be useful utilities that you can

Table 4.2: *Some Common Extensions Added to User Files*

Extension	User File
.CHP	Ventura Publisher publications
.CHT	Harvard Graphics chart files
.DBF	DBASE database files
.DOC	Word and XYWRITE documents
.PIC	Lotus 1-2-3 graphs
.PM3	Pagemaker publications
.PRG	DBASE program files
.PRN	XYWRITE printer information files
.PT3	Pagemaker templates
.PUB	First Publisher publications
.SPR	Sprint documents
.STY	Word and Ventura Publisher stylesheets
.WKQ	Quattro spreadsheets
.WKS, .WK1, .WK3	Lotus 1-2-3 spreadsheets

Table 4.3: *Extensions of Files that Should Not Be Deleted*

Extension	Type of File
.AFM, .SFP, .USP	Printer fonts.
.BAT	Batch files that include commands. The file AUTOEXEC.BAT will be executed when you start your computer. Other batch files could be part of your application programs.
.COM and .EXE	Executable programs that can be run from the DOS prompt or from within Windows.
.DRV	Device driver information.
.FON	Screen fonts.
.HLP	Help files containing instructions for using your application.
.OVL	Overlay files containing additional instructions for executable programs.
.SYS	Files that contain device drivers and configuration information, such as CONFIG.SYS and MOUSE.SYS.

run yourself if you have the proper interpreter or compiler that converts the source code to executable form.

An *interpreter,* such as the program BASICA, converts and executes each line of source code one at a time. *Compilers,* on the other hand, convert the entire program to executable form so you can run it from the DOS prompt.

Renaming a File

One way to tell if a file is necessary is to rename it and then try running the application. If the application doesn't run properly, then the file is necessary, so change the file back to its original name. If the program does run properly, delete it. To change the name of a file, use the internal DOS command REN (for *rename*). The general syntax is

REN *<original file name> <new file name>*

For example, suppose you're thinking of deleting the file DBASE.SER from the DBASE directory. Use this command to rename the file:

REN DBASE.SER DBASE.BAK

Make a note of the original program extension, and then try running the DBASE program. In this case, you'd get an error message since DBASE looks for the file DBASE.SER to find your registration number and setup information.

Change the name back to its original with the command

REN DBASE.BAK DBASE.SER

To rename a file on another drive or directory, include the full path in the original file name, such as

REN C:\WP51\LETTER.DOC RESIGN.DOC

You cannot rename a file and move it to a new disk or directory at the same time, so do not include a drive or directory name in the new file name.

You can also use wildcards to rename files. For example,

REN *.DOC *.BAK

renames all files with the .DOC extension so they have the .BAK extension.

Duplicate Files

Some hard-disk users install the same program more than once, making some minor changes in configurations. They might have a copy of a program set up for a PostScript printer in one directory, and another copy of the program set up for an IBM Graphics printer in a different directory.

Other users keep several versions of the same program on their hard disk, such as WordPerfect 5.0 and WordPerfect 5.1, or Windows 3 and Windows 386.

If you only need one version or configuration, you might want to delete the other. However, don't rush to throw out earlier versions of an application just because you have a newer release. You never know when you might need the older version to read a file or perform some other function unique to that release of the software.

Copy-Protected Software

There was a time when many programs were *copy-protected,* that is, modified in some way that made it impossible, or at least difficult, to make a copy of the program or of the floppy disk. While copy-protection limited illegal duplication of software, it made it inconvenient for the legitimate user. You'd be stuck if your only copy became damaged or your hard disk crashed. You could usually exchange the faulty floppy for a new one, but you'd have to wait for the round-trip by mail.

Fortunately, consumer pressure convinced most software companies to drop copy-protection from their products. Today very few manufacturers copy-protect their programs, relying instead on our sense of honesty and fair play.

If you have a copy-protected program on your hard disk, don't delete it until you consider all of the consequences. Simply copying the program files to a floppy disk will not work—you probably won't be able to use the floppy version.

Even having the original program on floppy disks does not guarantee that you can always reinstall it on the hard disk. Some copy-protection schemes make the floppy disk unusable once it installs the program to a hard drive. If you want to know if you can reinstall a program, look on your hard disk for a program or batch file with a name like UNINSTAL. This program is designed to remove the program from the hard disk in a way that makes your floppy version usable again. If you want to delete the program from the hard disk, run UNINSTAL first.

How to Delete Files

If you decide to delete a file, use the internal DOS command DEL. The general syntax is

DEL <*file name*>

To delete a file on another drive or directory, use the full path, as in

DEL B:\LETTERS\HOME.DOC

or log on to the drive or directory first and just use the DEL command without specifying the drive or directory.

You can delete individual files or groups of files using wildcards. For example, to delete all files with .BAK extensions in the current directory on the current drive, enter the command

DEL *.BAK

To delete all files from the currently logged directory, enter

DEL *.*

Use the complete path to delete files on another directory, such as

DEL \WP50\LETTERS

When you include the directory's path, DOS defaults to *.*. DOS will prompt you with

Are you sure (Y/N)?

Press **Y** to delete the files or **N** if you change your mind. DEL *.* removes files only from the current directory. If you are on the root directory, subdirectories will not be affected.

Be extremely cautious when using the DEL command, especially with wildcards, since you could accidentally erase important files or programs. In fact, use the DIR command first to make sure only the proper files will be erased.

For example, to take a look at all files with the .DOC extension, enter the command

    DIR *.DOC

Scan through the listing to make sure you want to delete all of the files displayed. When you are sure, enter

    DEL *.DOC

The F3 key is useful when using DIR with the DEL command. After confirming the list of files with DIR command, type **DEL** and then press F3 to display the same path and file specification used in the DIR command. Press ◄— to delete the files.

Suppose you entered this command line to check on files you'd like to delete:

    DIR C:\LOTUS\BUDGET*.92

Rather than retyping the entire path, possibly making a mistake and deleting the wrong files, type **DEL** and then press F3. You can use the command ERASE as a substitute for DEL.

Deleting Directories

To delete a directory from your disk, use the command

    **RD **<*directory path*>

(RD stands for *remove directory.*)

However, you can't delete a directory if you're logged on to it or if it contains any files or subdirectories. As an example, to delete a directory called WP42 that has one subdirectory, LETTERS, follow this sequence (press ⏎ after each step):

Type:	To:
CD\WP42\LETTERS	Log on to the LETTERS subdirectory
DIR *.*	Confirm you want to delete all files
DEL *.* ⏎ Y	Delete the files
CD\WP42	Move to another directory, in this case, WP42
RD\WP42\LETTERS	Delete the subdirectory
DEL *.* ⏎ Y	Delete the files in the WP42 directory
CD\	Move to the root directory
RD\WP42	Delete the directory

Installing Software

Installing a program means getting it ready to work on your system—how you do it depends on the software itself.

Programs on your hard disk are probably already installed and ready to use. Refer to "Reinstallation" (later in this chapter) if you have problems running them. Software supplied on floppy disks might also be installed, especially if your disks are not original distribution disks. You might have a working copy of software (legal or not) that the previous owner set up.

If you have software that you just purchased, that is left over from your old system, or that doesn't seem to work properly, then you'll probably have to go through some sort of installation procedure. Programs that require installation will usually display a warning message if you run them before proper installation. If they are configured incorrectly for your system, the screen display or printed output will be unsuitable.

In Chapter 5, "Taming the Hard Disk," you'll learn how to organize your hard disk for maximum efficiency. If you have a large application to install, or one that requires you to create directories yourself, read that chapter first.

Always make a backup copy of your disks before installing any program. Instructions for making backups are given in Chapter 6, "Managing Floppy Disks."

Self-Installing Software

Many programs require no special installation procedure. You either run the program from the floppy disk or copy all of the files to the hard disk before running the program. These programs may "sense" the type of monitor you have and automatically configure themselves to your display. Others may ask you a few questions about your system the first time you run the program, and then store your responses in a special configuration file. In each case, you do not have to take any special action before using the application.

Installation Programs

Larger or more complex applications come with their own utility programs that handle installation for you. These programs are usually called INSTALL, CREATE, or something similar, and are either batch files or executable programs. Just enter the name at the DOS prompt and follow the prompts on the screen.

Some installation programs simply copy the files to your hard disk or lead you step by step through creating a working set of floppy disks. Harvard Graphics, for example, includes a program called INSTALL that copies all of the program files to a hard-disk directory called HG, creating it if necessary. The first time you use the program, however, you have to configure it for your system using a setup menu (Figure 4.1) to select your output device and set the screen colors.

Other installation programs copy the files and configure the program at one time. The installation procedure of Lotus 1-2-3 Release 3, for instance, copies all of the files to the hard disk, and then asks you to specify your hardware in a series of menus. In one menu (Figure 4.2) you designate your display type; in another, you designate your printer (Figure 4.3).

A growing number of applications are shipped as *compressed files* that have to be expanded during setup. Compression allows the manufacturer to ship fewer disks and to include files too large to fit on a floppy disk normally. WordPerfect 5.1, for instance, has several files over 450K, but ships them as compressed files on 360K disks. Its installation program has a menu that allows you to perform a first-time installation, change the configuration, or install updated disks as they are made available (Figure 4.4).

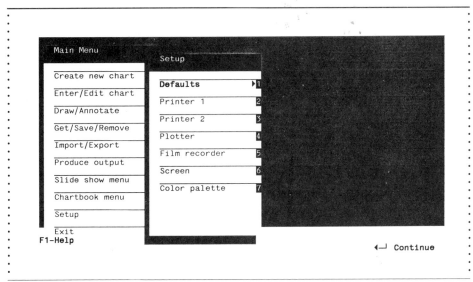

Figure 4.1: *Harvard Graphics setup menu*

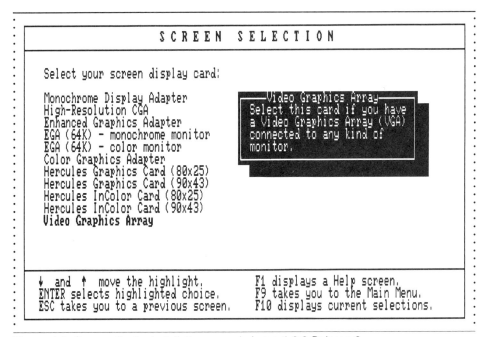

Figure 4.2: *Screen display installation menu in Lotus 1-2-3 Release 3*

```
                    P R I N T E R    S E L E C T I O N

  Select your printer manufacturer:

  Apple                              ┌──────────Apple──────────┐
  Epson                              │ Select one printer manufacturer. │
  HP                                 │ You will be able to select       │
  IBM                                │ additional printers later.       │
  NEC                                └──────────────────────────┘
  Okidata
  Toshiba
  Generic




  ↓ and ↑ move the highlight.        F1 displays a Help screen.
  ENTER selects highlighted choice.  F9 takes you to the Main Menu.
  ESC takes you to a previous screen. F10 displays current selections.
```

Figure 4.3: *Printer installation menu in Lotus 1-2-3 Release 3*

```
  Installation

     1 - Basic       Perform a standard installation to C:\WP51.

     2 - Custom      Perform a customized installation.  (User selected
                     directories.)

     3 - Network     Perform a customized installation onto a network.
                     (To be performed by the network supervisor.)

     4 - Printer     Install updated Printer (.ALL) File.

     5 - Update      Install updated program file(s).

     6 - Copy Disks  Install every file from an installation diskette to a
                     specified location.  (Useful for installing all the
                     Printer (.ALL) Files.)




  Selection: 4
```

Figure 4.4: *WordPerfect 5.1 installation menu*

Don't try to bypass or rush through an application's installation routine. Make sure you respond properly to all prompts and displays.

If you are installing a program onto a floppy disk, write-protect the distribution disks. *Write-protection* insures against accidental file erasure. With 5¼-inch disks, *write-protect tabs* are the small rectangular stickers that are packaged with blank diskettes. Fold one of the tabs over the square notch on the side of the disk. If you have 3½-inch disks, protect the disk by pushing the small tab toward the edge of the disk. If the small square is blocked, then the disk is unlocked and the files can be erased. Lock the disk by pushing the tab so the hole is uncovered. This prevents you from deleting important files if you accidentally insert the disk at the wrong time. Follow the screen prompts carefully and insert the distribution disk only when it is requested.

Never insert a distribution disk when the prompt requests a destination disk. The *destination disk* is the disk you are installing the program onto. Most prompts tell you to insert a disk and then press a key to continue, so double check that you have the proper disk inserted before pressing a key.

Reinstallation

If you're using a different display type or printer than your hand-me-down's former owner did, you might have to reinstall the program for your own configuration. A program set up for a color monitor and laser printer will not work for a monochrome monitor and dot-matrix printer.

Run the program to see how it works with your monitor and printer. If the image is clear on the screen and output prints on your printer, and then you do not have to reinstall the program. But if your screen display or printed output is blank or garbled, then you will have to reinstall it.

Look for a program or batch file on your hard or floppy disk called something similar to INSTALL, SETUP, or CREATE—the most common installation program names. Execute it from the DOS prompt, and then follow the instructions on the screen. If there is no separate installation program, run the application again and look for menu options or another function for changing the configuration.

To reinstall a program on your hard disk, you might need the original or backup copies of your distribution disk. Some installation programs only copy the system-specific files to the hard disk. These are the files needed to run the program on the hardware configuration that you designated. The information for using other monitors, printers, or mice is stored on floppy disks. When you try to reinstall the application, even when the installation program is on the hard disk, you will be prompted to insert a floppy disk in drive A. If you don't have the floppy disk you will not be able to change the configuration, so check with your system's previous owner or contact the software manufacturer.

Working with Configuration Files

If you delete, install, or reinstall any programs, you might have to make changes to the AUTOEXEC.BAT and CONFIG.SYS files, files that may be on your hard disk or DOS system floppy disk. DOS looks for these two files whenever you start your computer. If it finds them, it executes their instructions.

CONFIG.SYS gives DOS certain instructions that describe the hardware's operating environment. There may be other files with the .SYS extension, but only CONFIG.SYS and the hidden system files are used by DOS automatically.

AUTOEXEC.BAT repeats one or more DOS commands that you would normally have to enter yourself every time you start your computer. You can also run this file by entering **AUTOEXEC** at the DOS prompt. You do not have to type the .BAT extension—just the name of the file. There may be other batch files on your disk, but only AUTOEXEC.BAT is run automatically.

Examining Configuration Files

Before learning how to change these files, let's take a look at them to see if they'll tell you more about your system.

Follow these steps:

1. Type **CD** and press ◄── to log on to the root directory. If you have a floppy-disk system, make sure the boot disk is in the drive.

2. Type **TYPE CONFIG.SYS** and press ◄──.

If the message "File not found" appears on the screen, then there is no configuration file on your disk. Otherwise, you might see a listing something like this:

```
FILES = 15
BUFFERS = 15
DEVICE = EMMS.SYS
```

The FILES command designates the maximum number of open files that DOS can access. BUFFERS sets aside a number of blocks of computer memory for temporarily storing data on its way to or from the disk. The number of files and buffers in CONFIG.SYS depends upon the application programs you're using.

The DEVICE command loads a device driver into the computer's memory. A *device driver* contains information that DOS needs to communicate with components such as mice and monitors, and to use special software for managing disks and memory. In the preceding list of files, a driver is installed that accesses additional expansion memory beyond the base memory reported by CHKDSK. (You'll learn how to use expansion memory in Chapter 13.)

3. Type **TYPE AUTOEXEC.BAT** and press ←┘.

If the message "File not found" appears on the screen, then there is no automatic batch file on your disk. Otherwise, you might see a file something like this:

```
PATH C:\DOS
ASTCLOCK
```

The PATH command tells DOS to look for programs in the DOS directory if they are not in the logged drive or directory. You'll learn more about the PATH command in Chapter 5.

Computers that were designed with a built-in clock/calendar circuit will read the date and time automatically. If your machine has a clock/calendar that was added by the previous owner, however, a command must be included in AUTOEXEC.BAT that transfers the current date and time to DOS.

ASTCLOCK is a command that reads the date and time from a clock/calendar circuit made by AST Research, Inc. You'll see this command or a similar one (usually containing the word "clock" if it is from another manufacturer) if the previous owner installed an optional clock/calendar.

Modifying Configuration Files

If you add or change hardware or software to your system, you might have to make changes to AUTOEXEC.BAT and CONFIG.SYS. Both AUTOEXEC.BAT and CONFIG.SYS are ASCII text files that can contain only DOS commands and configuration information. You could use a word processing program to modify them, but you'd have to save them as ASCII files. Otherwise, the word processor might save its own formatting and control information along with the DOS commands and your system will reject the file entirely.

Another way to edit the files is by using the DOS command COPY. This isn't as convenient as using a word processor, but it insures that only ASCII characters are included in the files. You can use COPY to rewrite the entire file or to simply add additional lines to it.

In this section, we'll use both techniques to add support for using a mouse. (You'll learn about other changes to these files in later chapters.) Perhaps you had a mouse left over from your old system, or you just purchased one. To use a mouse with DOS, you must have its driver program on the disk that you use to boot your computer. If your driver program is an executable file, such as MOUSE.COM, then you have to add the MOUSE command to AUTOEXEC.BAT. If the driver is a system file, such as MOUSE.SYS, then you'll need a device command in CONFIG.SYS. If you do not see a MOUSE command in either file, you have to add it yourself.

Preparing the Driver

The first step is to determine the type of driver you have and to place it on the root directory. Search the root directory, the application directory, the application's floppy disk, or the floppy disk that came with the mouse, for a program called MOUSE.COM or MOUSE.SYS. Your application might use a different name for its mouse driver, so check the documentation if you have it. If not, look for a program with the word MOUSE in it, or contact the company that manufactured the mouse.

When you find the driver, copy it to the root directory or place it on the disk that you use to start your system. Type in

    COPY A: <*mouse driver program name*> C:\

Continue to the next section, "Rewriting or Creating Files," to add the command to the root directory or the startup disk.

Rewriting or Creating Files

Let's go through the procedure for rewriting CONFIG.SYS to include support for MOUSE.SYS.

1. Type **CD** and press ⏎ to log on to the root directory. If you have a floppy-disk system, make sure the boot disk is in drive A. If the file CONFIG.SYS is not on your disk, skip ahead to step 4.

2. Type **COPY CONFIG.SYS CONFIG.BAK** and press ⏎ to make a backup copy of the original file. If you make any mistakes when creating the new file, the original is still there for your reference.

3. Type **TYPE CONFIG.SYS** and press ⏎ to display the file on your screen so you can copy the lines to the new version. Copy down the entire file on a piece of paper, or prepare your printer and press Shift-PrtSc to print a copy of the file.

If there is a MOUSE command already in the file, just read through the remaining steps so you'll know how to rewrite the file if you later want to change it. Otherwise, continue with the next step to create the file.

4. Type **COPY CON: CONFIG.SYS** and press ⏎. The cursor will go to the next line but nothing else will happen—don't worry, that's normal. This command tells DOS to copy what you type to the file CONFIG.SYS, erasing the original contents of the file.

5. Type **DEVICE = MOUSE.SYS** and press ⏎. The cursor moves to the next line.

6. Now type any other lines that were in the original CONFIG.SYS file. Copy them exactly as they appeared in the original file, pressing ⏎ after each line.

7. Press Ctrl-Z or the F6 key, indicating the end of your input.

8. Press ⏎. The commands you entered are written to the file CONFIG.SYS.

If you want to use your mouse now, press Ctrl-Alt-Del to reboot your computer. DOS will read CONFIG.SYS and execute its commands. Otherwise, DOS will read the file the next time you start your computer.

Adding Lines to Files

You don't have to retype the entire file if you only want to add a line to it. As an example, these steps add support for the program MOUSE.COM, an executable version of the mouse driver, to AUTOEXEC.BAT.

1. Type **COPY AUTOEXEC.BAT + CON: AUTOEXEC.BAT** and press ←┘. You'll see

    AUTOEXEC.BAT
    CON

If you see the message "File Not Found," then the batch file doesn't yet exist on your disk. Type **COPY CON: AUTOEXEC.BAT** and press ←┘.

2. Type **MOUSE** and press ←┘.

3. Press F6 or Ctrl-Z to display **^Z**.

4. Press ←┘.

Adding the command does not execute it until the next time you start your computer. To use the mouse immediately, type **MOUSE** to run the driver, or **AUTOEXEC** to execute all of the batch file instructions.

Resolving Problems in Your Configuration Files

Carefully review AUTOEXEC.BAT and CONFIG.SYS for conflicts or commands that are not necessary for your hardware configuration.

If the previous owner used a serial printer, for example, you might find the lines

    MODE COM1:9600,N,8,1,P
    MODE LPT1: = COM1:

in AUTOEXEC.BAT. You must delete these lines and reboot your computer if you use a parallel printer.

When you're not sure if a line is necessary, make a copy of the BAT or SYS file, rewrite the file without the line, and then restart your system. If an application doesn't work correctly, then the line was necessary.

Time and Date Commands

If you do not have a built-in clock/calendar, AUTOEXEC.BAT may prevent the time and date prompts from appearing when you boot your system. To display the prompts, AUTOEXEC.BAT must include the commands TIME and DATE. Use either of the techniques you just learned to add the commands to AUTOEXEC.BAT, as in the batch file

```
TIME
DATE
MOUSE
```

Now that you're getting familiar with your hand-me-down, go on to Chapters 5 and 6 to tackle that hard disk or pile of floppy disks.

Part Two

Taking a Closer Look at Your PC Components

Chapter Five

Taming the
Hard Disk

*O*nce you get used to having a hard disk you'll never want to rely on floppies again. You won't have to look for a DOS disk every time you want to start your computer and you won't have to shuffle floppies trying to find an application, or swap disks in and out of drives.

But hard disks require care and caution, and there is always the possibility of a disastrous *crash,* physical damage to the hard disk that may make it, and all of your programs on it, useless.

In this chapter you'll learn how to manage your hard disk using DOS commands. You'll learn how to create and work with directories, and back up your data for safekeeping.

Since you're using a hand-me-down, you can assume that your hard disk has already been *formatted,* or prepared for use by DOS. If you can boot from your hard disk, then it has been formatted as a system disk that contains the disk operating system.

If you can't boot from your hard disk, boot your system from a floppy disk, and then see if you can log on to drive C. If you can log on to it, then the hard disk has been formatted but does not contain DOS. You'll have to transfer the system files to it. But if you can't even log on to drive C, the hard disk has not yet been formatted. You'll learn how to transfer the system files and format your hard disk in Chapter 15.

The techniques discussed in this chapter use resources that are available in DOS. Utility programs that streamline these functions are discussed in Chapter 12. If you have a DOS utility, read through this chapter anyway to become more familiar with DOS.

Organizing Files and Directories

Imagine trying to find a book in a library where the books were just stacked randomly on top of each other from floor to ceiling. Using a hard disk that is not divided into directories would be just as difficult. Just think how long your directory listing would be if your hard disk had one directory holding 20,000,000 or more bytes of programs.

Creating directories and subdirectories limits the number of files displayed in a directory listing. But more importantly, creating directories gives you a chance to organize your files and programs around a common theme, making files easier to find and use. Directories also help prevent total disaster from improper deletion commands. Deleting all of the files with the DEL *.* command will delete files only in the current directory, saving files in other directories from premature extinction.

Planning Your Hard-Disk Organization

In planning the structure of your hard disk, give your directories short, easy-to-remember names that represent their contents. As with files, directory names can be from one to eight characters—letters, numbers, and the symbols $, %, ', −, @, {, }, ~, ', !, #, (,), and &—and can include an extension, although most people don't use them. The names can reflect the software, such as LOTUS, WORD, or VENTURA, or the type of programs stored there, as with GAMES or GRAPHICS.

Select a subdirectory name along the same lines, thinking of the groupings of data files that it will contain. Call a subdirectory that stores yearly budget worksheets BUDGET93, or save documents for the research department under R&D.

Using the list of programs you collected in Chapter 2, plan how you want to divide your hard disk. Work from the root, through directories, and then to the subdirectory level. You can always make or remove directories, so don't worry about the layout at this point.

The Root Directory

Keep a minimum number of files in the root directory. The files you'll need are COMMAND.COM, AUTOEXEC.BAT, and CONFIG.SYS. You'll also need the mouse driver if you added it in a device command in Chapter 4.

Aside from these few files, the DIR command will serve as a table of contents, listing the major applications or divisions of the hard disk.

Directories

Create a separate directory for each major application. You might have a directory to hold your word processor, one for a spreadsheet program, and another for a database, and another for DOS external commands. If you have more than one type of major application, such as two word processing programs, plan a separate directory for each.

Group smaller applications in a directory with a central theme. You could create one directory for small utility programs, and another for games. Draw a tree diagram of your directories as shown in Figure 5.1.

Many software installation programs will automatically create and name a directory for the application during the installation process. Don't worry about that for now, because planning for the directories will prepare you to install the program and decide on the overall layout of your disk.

Subdirectories

Keep your data files in a subdirectory of the application you used to create them. For example, store your word processing documents in a subdirectory of the word processing program. The subdirectories will make it easier to locate and back up your work later on. Write down the subdirectory names on your tree diagram (Figure 5.2).

You might want to keep data files that are used by more than one application in their own directory, not in a subdirectory. This will make it easier to access the files when you are using an application program. For example, perhaps you have PFS:First Publisher set up for a dot-matrix printer on C:\FPDOT and for a laser printer on C:\FPLASER. If you store your files on C:\FPLASER\PUBS, you'll have to enter that long path when you want to recall a publication for either version. Keeping the files in C:\PUB will reduce keystrokes.

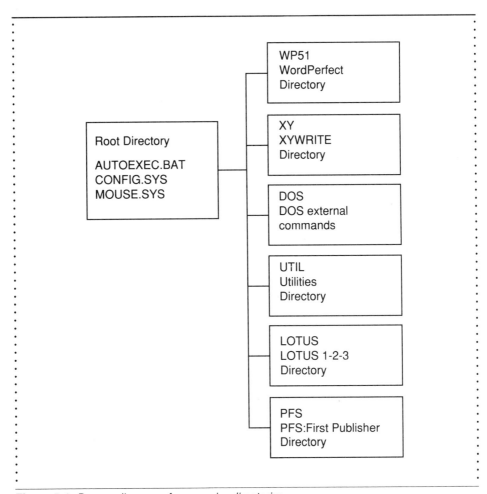

Figure 5.1: *Draw a diagram of your major directories*

Existing Files

Before installing any new programs, fit your existing files and directories into your plan. Make a note of which files should be moved into your planned directories and which directories you can leave as they are. If you plan to keep an existing directory, add its name to your chart or change a name that you've already written.

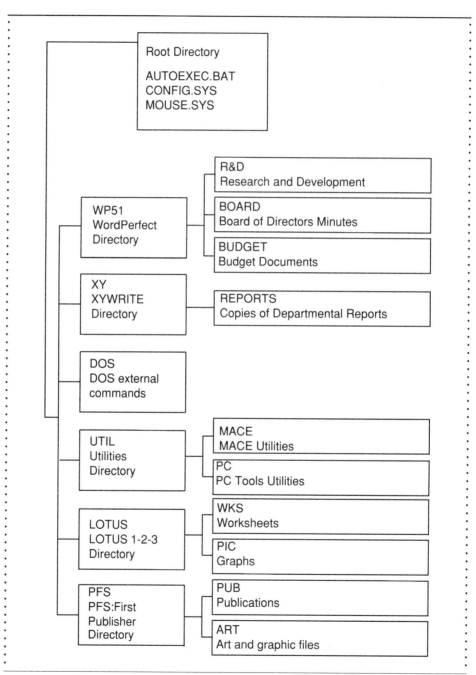

Figure 5.2: *Add subdirectories to store data files*

To create a new directory, type **MD** (for *make directory*), followed by the directory name, as in

    MD\XYWRITE

The backslash tells DOS to make a directory branching off of the root directory. If you are logged on to the root directory, the backslash is optional.

Once the directory is created, make the subdirectories. If you're on the root directory, use the entire path to create subdirectories, as in

    MD\XYWRITE\REPORTS

If you are already logged on to the XYWRITE directory, use the shorthand

    MD REPORTS

Finally, copy the files onto the new directories. Use wildcards, if you can, to make the process go faster. Then delete the files from their original location. Delete the original directory if it contains no files.

Renaming Directories

You cannot change a directory name using DOS commands. If you don't like the name of a current directory, you have to copy all of the files to a new directory, and then delete the originals. Just make sure the disk has enough space to store two versions of the same files temporarily.

For example, suppose the previous owner put all DOS external command files on a directory called BIN, short for *binary*. Here are the steps to change the directory's name to DOS (press ⏎ after each step):

Type:	To:
CD\	Log onto the root directory
MD\DOS	Create the DOS directory
CD\BIN	Log onto the BIN directory
COPY *.* \DOS	Copy the files to the DOS directory

Type:	To:
DEL *.* ↵ Y	Delete the files from the BIN directory
CD\	Log on to the root directory
RD\BIN	Delete the BIN directory

You'll have to change any PATH commands (discussed later in this chapter) that refer to the original directory.

Using Directories

As you work with your system, you'll start to add files to directories and subdirectories. Periodically scan your disk to see that your directory structure plan is still in force.

If the number of files in a subdirectory becomes too large and unmanageable, consider regrouping them into two subdirectories along some other lines. Keep a close eye on your application directories, copying data files to the appropriate subdirectory.

Displaying Directories

When you start switching between directories, it is easy to lose track of your location. Losing track of which directory you're in can cause problems, such as entering **DEL** *.* ↵ Y ↵ only to realize too late that you're logged on to the wrong directory.

You can find out where you are by displaying the current directory path—just enter **CD** from the DOS prompt line. You can also have the directory path appear as part of the DOS prompt by adding the command

PROMPT pg

to AUTOEXEC.BAT. This changes the DOS prompt to include the directory name as well as the drive letter, followed by the > sign, as in

C:\LOTUS>

PROMPT is an internal DOS command that can also add the date, time, and DOS version number to the DOS prompt. This command

PROMPT pg$_time = t_date = d_Please enter your command:

creates a four-line DOS prompt that looks like this:

```
C:\LOTUS>
time = 12:25:45.12
date = Thur 10-17-1991
Please enter your command:
```

The underline character in the PROMPT command performs the line feed/carriage return.

Managing Directories

Running an application program that is not on the root directory can be a chore. You have to remember what directory the program is on, and change to that directory using the CD command before executing the program. This is almost as cumbersome as using floppy disks.

You can avoid this problem by using any combination of these three methods—establishing a DOS path, writing batch files to change directories, and substituting a drive designator for a path.

Using Paths

A PATH command in AUTOEXEC.BAT lets you execute a program in a directory without needing to log on to that directory first. For example, the command

PATH C:\DOS;C:\WP51

establishes a *path,* or channel, to two directories—DOS and WP51—telling DOS that if a program isn't on the current drive or directory, look for it on the DOS and WP51 directories of drive C.

By placing all external DOS commands in the DOS directory and using a PATH command, you can run all external DOS commands from any drive and directory.

Adding and Deleting Paths

You might add paths to AUTOEXEC.BAT if you've installed new programs on your hard disk. You should definitely remove paths to directories that you've deleted. Add or delete paths using the COPY command that you learned in Chapter 4.

If there was no path in the original file, type **PATH** followed by the complete directory path you want to add to the file. For example, add a path to WP51 by typing **PATH C:\WP51**. Separate multiple paths with a semicolon, as in

    PATH C:\BIN;C:\WSTAR;C:\LOTUS;C:\WP51

If there was a PATH command in AUTOEXEC.BAT already, copy it exactly as it appears, but leave out any directories you may have deleted. When you've copied the command, add any new paths desired.

In some instances, a PATH command must be placed in the proper location within AUTOEXEC.BAT. For example, if your mouse driver program, MOUSE.COM, is in the DOS directory, the following batch file would not work because DOS would attempt to run the MOUSE program before knowing the path to follow:

    MOUSE
    PATH C:\DOS

Instead, enter the batch file this way:

    PATH C:\DOS
    MOUSE

Try to place the directories that you use most frequently at the beginning of the PATH command, since DOS searches through each directory in the path, from left to right, until it finds the file.

Writing Custom Batch Files

Adding paths to AUTOEXEC.BAT, unfortunately, may make it difficult for some applications to access files. In the example above, for instance, you could have added a path to WP51 in order to run WordPerfect from any drive or directory. Although WordPerfect will run properly, it will look for document files in the current directory, not necessarily WP51. If you tried to edit a document in WP51, you'd get a "File not found" message unless you entered the full path at the "Document to be retrieved" prompt.

Instead of using a path, write the commands to change to WP51 and run Word-Perfect in a separate batch file with a name other than AUTOEXEC. The file won't execute automatically when you start your system, but it will let you change to the directory and run the application in just a few keystrokes.

Let's create a small batch file on the root directory for doing just that.

1. Type **CD** to log on to the root directory. If you have a floppy-disk system, make sure the boot disk is in drive A.

2. Type **COPY CON: WP.BAT** and press ←┘.

3. Type

   ```
   CD\WP51
   WP
   CD\
   ```

4. Press Ctrl-Z or the F6 key, and ←┘.

When you want to run WordPerfect, you only have to type **WP** from the root directory. The batch file changes to the WP51 directory and then runs WordPerfect. When you exit Word-Perfect, the command CD\ returns you to the root directory. Since the file is on your root directory, you can't run it from any other directory. To access a file from any directory on the disk, copy the batch file to your other directories and subdirectories.

To run this batch file automatically, include the file's name as the last line in AUTOEXEC.BAT.

Substituting Drives for Paths

You can also streamline the task of changing directories by using the SUBST command, which substitutes a drive letter for a directory path. This command was first available in DOS Version 3.0.

The syntax is

SUBST *<drive:> <directory>*

For example, the command

SUBST D: C:\LOTUS

tells DOS to treat the LOTUS directory as drive D. When you want to change to that directory, type **D:** just as if you were logging on to an actual drive D.

You can substitute any unused drive from A to E for a directory path. Some versions, however, let you assign drive letters from A to Z by adding a command such as

LASTDRIVE = Z

to CONFIG.SYS.

If you forget what substitutions you made, type **SUBST** by itself on the command line. DOS will report the substitutions, as in

D: = > C:\LOTUS

Add the SUBST command to AUTOEXEC.BAT to have it executed when you start your computer. Otherwise, the substitution stays in effect until you turn off your computer or disengage the assignment with the command SUBST D:/D. Some versions of DOS may not disengage a substitution if you have a complex configuration of device drivers and other hardware. If this happens, reboot your computer.

Backing Up Your Hard Disk

Even though your hard disk is sealed inside the computer, it is not immune to damage. Smoke and dust particles can find their way onto the disk, and vibrations and electrical surges can wreak havoc with your data. When your hard disk crashes, some or all of your files can be destroyed, and the wonderful benefits of the hard disk are wiped out in an instant.

Making a *backup* of your hard disk—a duplicate of your files—is the only insurance you can rely on. You can make image, full, or incremental backups.

An *image backup* is a complete duplication of every bit of data on your hard disk. Rather than copy your disk file by file, the backup records each bit it encounters, including bits not being used for active files, but which still remain physically on the disk. When you restore the data to the hard disk, the bits are replaced at their original locations. DOS commands can only make an image backup of a floppy disk, not the hard disk.

A *full backup* copies every file on your disk, even files that were unchanged since the last time you performed a full backup. An *incremental backup,* on the other hand, copies only those files changed since your last backup using an *archive flag* that DOS saves along with the file name in the directory. When you create or edit a file, DOS turns on the archive flag to indicate that that file has not yet been backed up. The incremental backup saves only the files with the archive flag turned on, skipping over files that have not been changed since the last backup. The flag is turned off after the file is copied, indicating that it has been backed up.

Full and incremental backups copy your data as files, not as individual and unrelated bits. When you restore the data, the files are placed on the hard disk but not necessarily in the original locations.

You should have to make only one full backup of your hard disk, since many files will not change as you work. You should already have individual backup copies of your DOS and application distribution disks, so there's no need to back up these files on a regular basis. After performing one full backup as a safeguard, use incremental backups to save your ongoing projects.

Performing a hard-disk backup can be time consuming. (Backing up your hard disk is not the same as making a backup copy of your floppy disks.) You can purchase programs that are designed to produce backups in the shortest time possible. We'll look at these in Chapter 12. In this section, let's see what backup options we have in DOS.

Using the BACKUP and RESTORE Programs

DOS does not provide a means of performing an image backup. But starting with Version 2.0, DOS provides the BACKUP and RESTORE programs for performing a full backup of your hard disk or selected directories.

BACKUP saves your files in a format that DOS itself does not recognize. This means that you cannot use files on the backup disks until you restore the files with the RESTORE program, a fact that has caused many users some sleepless nights.

Because BACKUP and RESTORE have been modified slightly with each release of DOS, you must use the RESTORE program from the same version of DOS as the BACKUP program you used—another version's RESTORE might not work. This is one reason to always have a floppy-disk copy of the DOS version that is on your hard disk. Chances are you'll use the BACKUP program on your hard disk for making backups. If your hard disk crashes, you'll have to use the RESTORE program from your floppy disks. If you have a version of RESTORE that doesn't match the BACKUP version you used, your backup disks might be useless.

Using BACKUP

Before backing up your hard disk, make sure you have enough floppy disks on hand to store your files. You'll need roughly either three 360K disks, two 720K disks, one 1.2Mb disk, or one 1.44Mb disk for each megabyte of files.

Some versions of BACKUP will format a floppy disk for you, if necessary, as long as the DOS program FORMAT.COM is in the current directory or path. Earlier versions of BACKUP, usually before Version 3.0, require the backup disks to be formatted already.

The syntax for the command is

    BACKUP <source drive:>\<path>\<file name> <destination drive:> <path>
    <file name>/<options>

Enter the file names or paths containing the files you want to back up, and then the disk drive where you'll insert floppy disks. To back up the LOTUS directory on drive C to floppy disks in drive A, for example, enter

    BACKUP C:\LOTUS*.* A:

Options on the command line allow you to customize the backup operation. These vary with versions of DOS, but the most useful is the /S option that tells DOS to back up files from the current directory and all of its subdirectories. The command to back up your entire hard disk onto floppy disks in drive A is

    BACKUP C:*.* A:/S

BACKUP will start copying your programs, prompting you to insert a disk as each becomes full, assigning each disk a volume number starting with 1. Files larger than the capacity of your floppy disk will be divided between two or more disks, an important feature, since some applications have files larger than 360K. When you restore the file, the sections are added together.

Some versions of DOS let you save time and floppy disks by excluding groups of files from the backup procedure with the /E option. For example, exclude executable program files, which you should have on floppy disk already, from the backup using the command

>   **BACKUP C:*.* A:/S/E:*.COM + *.EXE**

BACKUP will exclude files with the .COM and .EXE extensions.

Newer versions of BACKUP let you make incremental backups. As you add or change files on your disk, use the /M option to back up only files with the archive flag set. For example, the command

>   **BACKUP C:*.* A:/S/M**

performs an incremental backup, saving files that you created or edited since the last backup. Some versions of DOS use the /W option for this purpose.

Some BACKUP options are listed in Table 5.1. Check your DOS manual to see which ones are provided by your version of DOS.

Restoring Backup Files

If you accidentally delete a directory or even a single file, you can retrieve it from your backup disks using the RESTORE command. The general syntax is

>   **RESTORE** *<backup disk:>\<path>\<file name>* *<hard disk:>/<options>*

To perform a total restoration, use the command

>   **RESTORE A:*.* C:/S**

The /S options tells DOS to restore files to all directories on drive C.

Table 5.1: *BACKUP Command Options*

Option	Function
/A	Appends files to those already on the backup disk
/B:DATE	Backs up files dated on or before the date specified
/D:DATE	Backs up files dated on or after the date specified
/E	Excludes files from the backup
/F	Formats destination disks without prompting
/M	Performs incremental backup of new or edited files
/N	Does not format destination disks
/Q	Requests confirmation before backing up each file
/R	Rings a bell to prompt for responses
/S	Backs up current directory and all subdirectories
/T	Backs up only files with today's date
/V	Verifies backup

Restore files to a single directory using a command such as

    RESTORE A:\LOTUS*.* C:

Restore a specific file using a command such as

    RESTORE A:\WP51\RESUME C:

Backup files maintain their link with their original directory. When you restore a file, the directory must exist on the disk.

Table 5.2 lists options available in some versions of RESTORE. Check your DOS manual to see which options are available in your version.

Using COPY and XCOPY

Because disks made by BACKUP cannot be read by DOS, you might find the program awkward for saving your everyday work. To save your new or important files on a daily basis, use the DOS commands COPY or XCOPY. COPY saves files in the

Table 5.2: *RESTORE Command Options*

Options	Function
/B:DATE	Restores files dated on or before the date specified
/D:DATE	Restores files dated on or after the date specified
/E:TIME	Restores files modified at or earlier than the time specified (Some versions use /E to exclude files from the RESTORE operation.)
/F	Restores all files to the current directory
/O	Restores operating system files
/P	Prompts to restore read-only files and files that have been changed since the last backup
/Q	Requests confirmation before restoring each file
/R	Rings a bell to prompt for responses
/S	Restores files to current directory and all subdirectories
/T	Restores only files with today's date
/V	Verifies restore

normal DOS format so they can be used without a formal RESTORE procedure. Newer versions of DOS also have an XCOPY command that can make full or incremental backups of a file in the normal DOS format. XCOPY and COPY, however, cannot save a file that is larger than what a floppy disk can hold.

Both programs require you to use a formatted disk. If you do not know how to format a disk, refer to the section "Formatting Data Disks" in Chapter 6.

Using COPY

In Chapter 3 you learned how to copy files using the internal COPY command. COPY is not adequate for making a full backup of your hard disk. If you wanted to perform a full backup, you'd have to keep track of your progress manually, inserting a new disk when one became full and noting what files fit on each disk.

But COPY is useful for making day-to-day backups of your current work. Save any documents or other files you create or modify each day on a floppy disk. You could create a separate hard-disk directory for your current files. Don't store more files in it than can fit on a floppy disk. When you're done for the day, log on to the directory, insert a blank floppy disk in drive A, and then enter

COPY *.* A:

COPY will only copy files from the current directory, not from any subdirectories. You must manually log on to each subdirectory to copy files. If you have files on several directories or are working with a large number of files, however, you'll find the XCOPY command more convenient.

Using XCOPY

XCOPY is an external command provided in DOS 3.2 and later. It saves files in normal DOS format, and its syntax for copying individual or groups of files is identical to the COPY command. For instance

XCOPY C: A:

saves all of the files on the current directory to drive A.

XCOPY has a number of options that let it serve as a full or incremental backup utility. These options are shown in Table 5.3.

Table 5.3: *XCOPY Command Options*

Option	Function
/A	Copies files that have their archive flag set, but does not change the archive flag
/D:DATE	Copies files dated on or after the date specified
/E	When used with /S option, recreates any empty directories from the source disk to the target disk
/M	Copies files that have their archive flag set, but changes the archive flag afterward
/P	Prompts to confirm that you want to copy each file
/S	Copies files in the current directory and all subdirectories
/V	Verifies each copy
/W	Waits and displays a message before copying files; press any key to begin the operation, or press Ctrl-Break to abort

To make an incremental backup of your hard disk, use the command

XCOPY C:\ A: /S/M

The options tell XCOPY to copy files from every directory on the drive (/S), but to copy only files that have the archive flag set (/M)—that is, files that have been created or modified since the last backup. DOS turns off the archive flag after copying the file, so it will not be copied again unless it is edited.

DOS will display the message

Disk Full

on the screen when a floppy disk becomes full. Insert another formatted disk, press F3 and ◄— to repeat the XCOPY command. Because DOS changed the archive flag of files already copied, XCOPY will continue where it left off, skipping over the already copied files.

When you use the /S option, XCOPY will duplicate the directory structure on the floppy disk. If you specify a directory, such as

XCOPY C:\GAMES A:\GAMES

but the directory is not on the floppy disk, XCOPY will display the prompt

Does GAMES specify a file name
or directory name on the target
(F = file, D = directory)?

Press **D** to create the directory.

Finally, you can use the /D option to copy files based on their date. For example, the command

XCOPY C:\WSTAR\DOCS A:/D:10-22-91

copies only files created on or after October 22, 1991. Before leaving work for the day, use XCOPY with the date option to back up that day's work.

Setting the Archive Flag

To use XCOPY to make a full backup of your hard disk, you have to make sure that all files have the archive flag turned on. Otherwise, the /A and /M options will only make an incremental backup. Turn on the archive flag using the DOS ATTRIB external command:

ATTRIB +A C:*.* /S

This command turns on the archive flag of files in every directory using the /S option. With the flags on, the command

XCOPY C:*.* A: /S/M

will now perform a full backup.

By using both the ATTRIB and XCOPY commands, you can exclude certain files or directories from your full backup. For example, perhaps you have directories that you never add files to or change, such as DOS or GAMES. Since you have the files on their original distribution disks, you don't want to waste floppies by backing them up.

After using the

ATTRIB +A C:*.* /S

command to prepare your files for a full backup, enter the commands:

ATTRIB – A C:\DOS*.*
ATTRIB – A C:\GAMES*.*

The – A command turns off the archive bits of those files so XCOPY will skip over them when it performs a full backup. Use the same technique to exclude .EXE and .COM files from the backup with the commands

ATTRIB – A C:*.COM /S
ATTRIB – A C:*.EXE /S

Protecting Your Hard Disk with PARK

Hard-disk drives are built to exacting tolerances. They have a *read/write head* that floats just above the surface of the disk. The head reads data from the disk and writes information onto it. If you move your computer or accidentally bump against it, the read/write head could crash against and damage the disk's surface. But damage can result even if you're careful. Every time you turn on your system, electrical surges through the disk drive's read/write head can weaken or destroy the data stored beneath it.

As a precaution, you should park your disk every time you turn off your computer. *Parking* moves the read/write head over an area of the disk where no data is stored. If the head does strike the disk, no data will be lost.

Most versions of DOS provide an external command called PARK or SHIP that "parks" the read/write head. Place the program on a directory included in your PATH command and execute it every time you turn off your computer.

Chapter Six

Managing
Floppy Disks

6

*P*reparing, using, and maintaining a library of floppy disks requires thorough planning and organization. There is nothing as frustrating as wasting valuable time swapping disk after disk in search of a single file, or discovering that your only copy of an important disk has been accidentally reformatted or damaged.

In this chapter you will learn how to manage your floppy disks. You'll learn how to copy and format floppy disks, how to make system disks, and how to work with disks of multiple sizes and capacities.

Making Backups

You should make copies of your application disks before attempting to use or install them. Because disks can wear out from use, an extra set of disks is simply a precaution against losing your valuable programs.

First, write-protect your application disks as a precaution against accidentally erasing your programs. With a 5¼-inch disk, place a write-protect tab over the small notch on the edge of each disk. If you have a 3½-inch disk, protect it by pushing the small tab toward the edge of the disk.

Do not lock or write-protect the blank disks that you will be copying onto. You want these disks free so that you can transfer your programs to them.

Making Backups with DISKCOPY

The DOS external command DISKCOPY makes an image backup of one floppy disk onto another. It copies everything on the disk, including hidden system files that are not shown in a directory listing. Use DISKCOPY when you want an exact duplicate of a floppy disk.

DISKCOPY will format the disk for you if you're copying onto a new blank disk. Otherwise, it will erase all of the files that are already on the disk. So if you're not using a blank disk, make sure it doesn't contain any programs or files that you want.

Systems with Two Floppy Disks

Follow these instructions to make a copy of a disk on systems with two identical floppy-disk drives, whether or not you have a hard disk as well. If your disk drives are not the same size or capacity, use the techniques under "Hard-Disk Systems with One Floppy."

1. Turn on the computer and respond to the date and time prompts if they appear.

2. Make sure the DOS program DISKCOPY.COM is on the current drive, directory, or path. If not, insert a DOS disk that contains the program or move to the appropriate subdirectory with the CD\ command.

3. Type **DISKCOPY A: B:** and press ←┘. The screen will display

    Insert SOURCE diskette in drive A:
    Insert TARGET diskette in drive B:
    Strike any key when ready...

The *source diskette* is the original disk that you will be copying from. The *target diskette* is the blank disk that you are copying to. *Never* insert the original disk in drive B—the disk will be erased if you forgot to write-protect it.

4. Place the disk you want to copy in drive A. For a 5¼-inch disk, you should have a write-protect tab on it, or for a 3½-inch disk, the tab should be moved to the locked position.

5. Place a blank disk, or a disk containing files that you no longer need, in drive B. Do not write-protect this disk.

6. Press any key to begin the copy. When the copy is completed, the message

    Copy Another (Y/N)?

appears.

7. Remove the disks and immediately label the copy accordingly. Write the name of the disk on the label before sticking it on the disk. If you write on the disk itself, the impression of a pen or pencil could damage the recording surface. If you must write on a disk, use a felt-tipped pen and write very lightly.

8. Press **Y** and repeat this process for all of your disks.

Place the original disks in a safe location and use the copies for everyday work.

Hard-Disk Systems with One Floppy

During this procedure, you must be very careful to follow the instructions displayed on the screen. Remember to write-protect your disks as a precaution against accidentally erasing them.

1. Turn on the computer and respond to the date and time prompts if they appear.

2. Make sure the DOS program DISKCOPY.COM is on the current directory. If not, move to the appropriate subdirectory with the CD\ command.

3. Type **DISKCOPY A: A:** and press ←┘. The screen will display

> **Insert SOURCE diskette in drive A:**
> **Strike any key when ready...**

You will be making a copy using only one disk drive. During the process, you will be instructed to insert either the source diskette or the target diskette into drive A. *Never* insert the original disk when you are asked to insert the target disk—the programs on the disk could be erased.

4. Place one of your original disks in drive A. You should place a write-protect tab on 5¼-inch disks, or move the tab to the locked position on 3½-inch disks.

5. Press any key. Soon the message

> **Insert TARGET diskette in drive A:**
> **Strike any key when ready...**

appears.

6. Remove the original disk and insert a blank disk in drive A. You can also use a disk that contains files you no longer need.

7. Press any key to begin the copy. You will be told several times to switch disks until all of the information on the original disk has been copied on to the blank disk. Be certain that the original disk is in the drive only when the screen requests the source diskette. When the copy is completed, the message

Copy Another (Y/N)?

appears.

8. Remove the disk and immediately label the copy accordingly. Write the name of the disk on the label before sticking it on the disk. If you write on the disk itself, the impression of a pen or pencil could damage the recording surface. If you must write on a disk, use a felt-tipped pen and write very lightly.

9. Press **Y** and repeat this process for all of your disks.

Place the original disks in a safe location and use the copies for everyday work.

Making Backups with COPY

You can also back up disks using the COPY command. Unlike DISKCOPY, COPY transfers data file by file, ignoring hidden system files. So, you cannot use COPY to duplicate a system disk.

To make a backup of a floppy disk using COPY, insert the original disk in drive A and a blank formatted disk in drive B, then type **COPY A: B:**.

If you have a hard disk and one floppy-disk drive, you can copy files from a floppy disk to another floppy disk via the hard disk. Create a directory on the hard disk where you'll temporarily store the files from the floppy disk. Copy the files from the source floppy disk to the directory, insert a blank formatted disk in the drive, and then copy the files from the hard disk to the target floppy disk. Delete the files in the temporary directory, and then repeat the process for any other disk. When you're done, delete the directory.

For example, here are the steps to copy a disk in drive A via the hard disk (press ↵ after each step):

Type:	To:
MD\TEMP	Create a directory to store the files
CD\TEMP	Log on to the directory
COPY A:*.* C:	Copy the files from the floppy disk to the directory
	Remove the disk in drive A and insert a blank formatted disk
COPY *.* A:	Copy the files from the hard disk to the new floppy disk
DEL *.* ↵ Y	Delete the files from the hard-disk directory
CD\	Log on to the root directory
RD\TEMP	Delete the directory

Just remember that COPY transfers only files from the currently logged directory, ignoring subdirectories. If you are on the root directory of a floppy drive, the command COPY A: B: will just back up the root directory, not the entire disk. You must log on to each subdirectory and copy it yourself.

DISKCOPY versus COPY

Both DISKCOPY and COPY can be used to back up the files from one disk to another. Table 6.1 shows some very important differences between these two methods.

Table 6.1: *Differences between DISKCOPY and COPY*

DISKCOPY	COPY
Formats the target disk, if necessary.	The target disk must already be formatted.
Erases all existing files on the target disk, whether formatted or not.	Adds files to a disk. Deletes only files that have the same names as files you are copying. Since existing files will not be erased, there might not be enough room for the new files.
Copies hidden files.	Copies only the current directory.
Should not be used with disks of different sizes or capacities.	Can copy files between disks of any size and capacity, but only until the disk becomes full.

Formatting Data Disks

To use a new blank diskette that will hold your data, you have to format it with the FOR-MAT command. *Formatting* prepares the disk so it can be used by DOS. These instructions are for computers with two disk drives and no hard disk. (If your system has two drives of different sizes or capacities, refer to "Working with Mixed Disk Formats.") The DOS disk will be in drive A; the blank disk will be in drive B. If you have a hard disk and one floppy-disk drive, you can use these instructions, but you should place the blank disk in drive A and use drive A instead of drive B in each of the steps below. Check with your DOS manual if you have any problems with the following procedure.

1. Start your computer.

2. Make sure the DOS program FORMAT.COM is on the current drive, directory, or path. If not, move to the appropriate subdirectory with the CD\ command or insert a DOS disk with the FORMAT program. Make sure the disk is write-protected.

3. Type **FORMAT B:** and press ◄┘. The screen will display

   Insert new diskette for drive B:
   and strike ENTER when ready...

4. Place a blank disk in drive B and press ◄┘. It will take a few minutes, but the blank disk will be formatted. On some systems, the message

   Volume Label (11 characters, ENTER for none)?

   will be displayed.

A *volume label* is a disk name that is displayed when you list the directory. It could be any name that will quickly identify the nature of the documents on that disk.

5. Type a volume label for the disk and press ◄┘, or just press ◄┘ if you don't want to give the disk a label. The screen will now display

   Format another (Y/N)?

6. Press **N** to stop the program or **Y** if you have other disks to format.

Formatting a System Disk

You should always have a floppy-disk copy of DOS available. If something happens to your only copy of DOS, your hard disk, a configuration file, or the internal battery, you may not be able to start your computer without a floppy disk.

The FORMAT command by itself does not add the disk operating system to a disk. You'd be able to save your files on the formatted disk but not start your computer with it. A disk that can start your computer is called a *system disk*.

You can create a system disk by using DISKCOPY to copy an existing system disk or by using the /S option to copy the DOS programs when you format a blank disk.

Follow these steps to create a system disk using the FORMAT command. These instructions are for computers with two disk drives. If you have a hard disk and one disk drive, place your target disk in drive A and use drive A instead of drive B in each of the steps below.

1. Start your computer.
2. Make sure the DOS program FORMAT.COM is on the current drive, directory, or path. If not, move to the appropriate subdirectory with the CD\ command or insert a DOS disk containing FORMAT.COM.
3. Type **FORMAT B:/S** and press ←.
4. Place a blank disk in drive B and press ←. DOS will format the disk and transfer the two hidden system files, IBMBIO.COM and IBMDOS.COM (or IO.SYS and MSDOS.SYS).
5. Press **N** at the prompt

    Format another (Y/N)?

With some versions of DOS, the formatted disk will now contain enough of the operating system to start your computer. However, other versions of DOS do not copy COMMAND.COM to the target disk. You should check to see if this file is on the new system disk and, if not, copy it from the DOS disk.

6. Type **DIR B:** to see if COMMAND.COM is on the newly formatted disk.
7. If it is not on the disk, type **COPY COMMAND.COM B:** and press ←. This instruction copies the program onto the disk in drive B.

If you already formatted a disk without the /S option, you might still be able to make it a system disk. The SYS external command transfers the two hidden system files— but not the command interpreter—from one disk to another.

To make a formatted disk on a floppy-drive system into a system disk, insert the DOS disk in drive A and the formatted disk in drive B. Type **SYS B:** and press ◄┘. With a hard disk system, insert the formatted disk in drive A, type **SYS A:** and press ◄┘. Check to see if COMMAND.COM is on the disk. If not, copy the program from the hard disk or a floppy system disk onto the new system disk.

SYS might not work if you already have files on the disk. Unlike most files, system, or DOS, files must be in specific locations on a disk. If SYS finds system files in those locations already, it will copy the files only if the new and old files take up exactly the same space. The system files from earlier versions of DOS might be smaller, so you cannot update the disk to the new version using SYS—you'll have to format a blank disk with the /S option and then transfer the files with COPY or XCOPY.

SYS will *abort* (stop running) if it finds any nonsystem files or programs where the system files belong.

Working with Mixed Disk Formats

It is possible that you have two disk drives that are not the same size or capacity. You might have one 5¼-inch and one 3½-inch drive, or one normal and one high-capacity drive.

While some versions of DISKCOPY may work between some combinations of drives, there are too many variables to give definitive guidelines. So use the command DISKCOPY as if you have only one drive. Copy a disk in drive A to drive A, and a disk in drive B to drive B using the general procedure outlined in "Hard-Disk Systems with One Floppy."

The SYS program will copy the system files from one disk to a disk of a different size or capacity, as long as the target disk has enough space to store the system files at the appropriate location.

When formatting disks, try to use a disk that matches the maximum capacity of the drive. If you do not have a hard disk, this means you might have to format a disk in drive A. For example, suppose you have a 1.2Mb drive A and a 360K drive B. To format a 360K disk, just follow the instructions in the section "Formatting Data Disks."

To format a 1.2Mb disk, however, you'll have to use drive A for the entire procedure. Boot your computer from a DOS disk in drive A, type **FORMAT A:**, and press

↵. When you see the prompt to insert the target disk, *remove* your DOS disk. Insert a blank disk in drive A and press ↵.

With the variety of disk capacities available, you might want to format a lower capacity disk in a high-capacity drive. Not only are these disks less expensive, but you might have to share a disk with someone who has only low-capacity drives.

To format a 360K disk in a 1.2Mb drive (5¼-inch), use the command

FORMAT A:/4

The /4 option is only available in DOS Version 3.0 and later, the only versions that support high-capacity 5¼-inch drives.

To format a 720K disk in a 1.44Mb drive (3½-inch), use the command

FORMAT A:/N:9

You can read and write 720K 3½-inch disks in high-capacity 3½-inch disk drives without ruining the disk for normal-capacity drives.

Using a 5¼-inch disk in drives that do not match its maximum capacity is more complex. You can read and write 360K disks in high-capacity drives. But once you write on the disk, you might not be able to read it in a 360K drive. There are some methods of formatting and writing to low-capacity disks in 1.2Mb drives that do not always ruin it for use in 360K drives, but don't trust the disk with important files. If you have both 360K and 1.2Mb disk drives, only write to your low-capacity disks in the 360K drive.

Selecting and Purchasing Floppy Disks

Just a few years ago, a box of ten 360K disks could cost $29 or more, a box of 1.2Mb disks were at least $40, and a box of 1.44Mb 3½-inch disks required a second mortgage. To save money, many computer users opted for generic brand bulk disks under the theory that if only 5% or 10% were unusable they'd still be ahead of the game. Luckily prices have dropped, especially for lower capacity disks. You can now buy ten standard quality 360K disks for $5, or nationally known brands starting at about $10 for a box of ten. Prices have dropped on all types of disks, although the high-capacity variety can still be costly.

There are several theories about selecting and purchasing floppy disks. One school of thought feels that you should never take chances with your data or disk drives and only buy national brands, regardless of price. To these users, the higher cost is worth the feeling of security.

Others, however, believe that there is little difference between the known brands and the generic disks advertised in the back of computer magazines. They feel that the generic brands are just as good, only cheaper because they're not paying for the advertising and fancy boxes.

There are also those users who buy a mix of brand name and generic disks. They use the more expensive disks for important programs and files, and the cheaper disks for backups and less critical data.

While your own finances will guide you, there are some advantages to this last method. Disks have an almost unlimited shelf life if stored properly, but a limited life span when used. Each read, write, or erase operation, each rotation in the drive, each puff of smoke that passes over it, takes its toll on a disk. As insurance against disaster, select high-quality disks for those programs and files that you use often and for your only backups of programs or files. Better quality disks last longer and are likely to withstand the wear and tear. Use the more questionable-quality disks for trading your own files or public domain programs with friends, or for making extra sets of backups.

High quality doesn't necessarily mean national brands. There are many generic disks that are good quality, perhaps even better than some you buy in the best computer stores. If you do opt for generic disks, select ones that come in disk sleeves, preferably packed in a box, with a lifetime guarantee.

If you have a high-capacity disk drive, you can stretch lower capacity disks beyond their limits for noncritical applications. For instance, you can format 360K disks in a 1.2Mb drive using the FORMAT command with no options. DOS will attempt to format the disk as high capacity. While you'll probably get a number of bad sectors, you might be able to store at least twice as much data as on a standard 360K disk. Because of the bad sectors, use the disk only for extra backups or for trading files with friends. Run CHKDSK often to check files that you copy onto the disk.

However, you can't use FORMAT to extend the capacity of 720K 3½-inch disks because high-capacity drives look for the square hole opposite the write-protect tab. There is a device that can transform the disk into a 1.44Mb disk. The Cajun Edge is a small hand-held steel punch similar to a one-hole paper punch except that it cuts a perfectly square hole. Version 2 of the punch has an alignment guide that places the hole in the exact position. You just slide the disk into the guide and press down to punch the hole through the disk's plastic jacket. The punched 720K disk can now be formatted to 1.44 Mb. But since there are always potential problems when physically altering a disk, use punched disks only for backup copies and noncritical data. The Cajun Edge company recommends that you use a good quality 720K disk and that you run CHKDSK after formatting the punched diskette. For information on the punch, contact:

Cajun Edge
117 S. Oak Street, Suite C
P. O. Box 2457
Hammond, LA 70404
(504) 542-0410

Diagnosing and Solving Problems

*C*hapter 2, "Test Driving Your Hand-Me-Down PC," outlined some common problems you may encounter when you start your computer. In this chapter, you'll learn how to diagnose, correct, and prevent a wider range of problems using DOS and utility programs.

In cases where the problem is due to a breakdown in hardware, you'll need to replace or repair the part in question. If you are mechanically inclined and do not mind working inside your computer, you'll be able to make many repairs yourself by substituting a new part for the old one. But if you are at all unsure about working with circuit cards, integrated circuits, and wires, take your system to a repair shop.

Most shops can repair or replace the more generic type of parts, such as disk drives and monitors. It usually doesn't matter if these parts are replaced by units not exactly like the originals. The more technical circuits, however, often require special parts or knowledge that only an authorized repair shop or one specializing in your system will have available. An authorized repair shop is one that is recommended by the manufacturer of your computer. Many manufacturers have toll-free telephone numbers that you can call for a list of repair facilities. If you have no idea what is wrong with the system, use an authorized repair shop or a retailer specializing in your model.

Selecting a repair shop for general maintenance and repair is a combination of research and luck. If possible, visit the shop and discuss the problem. Look to see if they have computers like yours already in the shop for repair, or if they are familiar with your make and model. A reputable shop will guarantee their work in writing.

Recording CMOS Information

Rather than learning how to solve problems after they occur, you can prevent a problem before it happens. Later-model computers have a special area in memory called *CMOS* that stores critical information about your system configuration. A battery powers the memory so the data is retained when your computer is turned off or unplugged. If the battery is dead, or goes below a minimum charge, the data is lost and your system might not boot or operate fully. (Depending on your hardware, this battery may also power the clock / calendar.)

CMOS memory also is erased when you remove the battery to replace it. After inserting a new battery, you'll have to reenter the configuration information. It's a good idea to record this information·*before* you need to replace the battery so you'll know what to reenter. In some cases, you'll find the data in your system documentation. But the configuration could be unique for your own combination of memory and floppy- and hard-disk drives, and you won't be able to enter the data unless you have a record of it.

Before the battery needs replacing, use your system's method for displaying the setup information on the screen. In general, the CMOS setup is accessed by pressing a key or key combination during bootup or by using a program provided on disk with the system, usually called SETUP.EXE or something similar. With Zenith computers, for example, you press Ctrl-Alt-Ins to display the CMOS prompt, and then type **SETUP**. Check your documentation for the method used by your computer, or consult the previous owner. When the data is displayed, copy it down completely or press Shift-PrtSc for a printed copy and store it in a handy place.

You access CMOS in the same way to change or reenter the data. Follow the prompts on the screen or, if a menu is displayed, use the arrow or tab keys to move to each choice, and then enter the data you copied down or want to change.

Diagnosing and Troubleshooting Techniques

The first step in solving a problem is to verify that a problem actually exists and to isolate a possible cause. In this chapter, you'll learn how to diagnose all problems except those relating to your printer. Printer problems are discussed in Chapter 8, "Working with Your Printer."

Computer Self–Test Programs and Error Messages

Some computers have a self-test program supplied either on disk or as part of the ROM. The programs test all key system components and display error messages if there is a problem with your system.

Early Compaq portable computers, for example, included a program called TEST on the DOS disk. The program first analyzes the system, reporting the amount of memory, interface ports, and disk drives (Figure 7.1). It then runs a check on your processor, memory, keyboard, video circuits, disk drives, and *display memory pages* (the areas of memory that store the image displayed on the screen).

The Zenith TEST command is an example of a ROM-based diagnostic program. It is run through what Zenith calls the Monitor, a general-purpose diagnostic utility accessed by pressing Ctrl-Alt-Ins.

Check your user's guide or other system manuals to see if a self-test program is built into ROM, or look on your DOS disk for a program called TEST. You might also have a disk labeled *Diagnostic Disk* or *System Utilities* that contains diagnostic

```
                     The COMPAQ PERSONAL COMPUTER

                              DIAGNOSTICS


        THE FOLLOWING DEVICES ARE DETECTED:

            1 - SYSTEM BOARD
            2 - 640KB MEMORY
            3 - KEYBOARD
            4 - PARALLEL PRINTER
            5 - VIDEO DISPLAY UNIT
            6 - 2 DISKETTE DRIVE(S)
           11 - ASYNC COMMUNICATIONS
           17 - 1 FIXED DISK DRIVE(S)


        Are all the installed devices listed ? (Y or N)
```

Figure 7.1: *Compaq diagnostic program*

software. If you can't find a diagnostic program or self-test procedure, contact the manufacturer or a dealer who handles your make of computer.

When you run into a problem, you will often see an error message on the screen. Although some error messages are the same for all versions of DOS, others have been added by individual system manufacturers. It would be impossible to list every error message that might appear on your screen.

Many error messages, however, are self-explanatory, presenting enough information to let you diagnose the problem. For instance, if you see the message

DISK ERROR: drive not ready

or

No system

then you probably do not have a formatted system disk in the drive, or the drive door is not closed.

When the problem is not so obvious, look for a chapter or appendix in your DOS, system, or software manuals that explains error messages. If you don't have the manuals, follow the "Troubleshooting Guide." Narrow down the problem until you can attempt a solution or identify that you need professional help.

Troubleshooting Guide

If your system doesn't include a self-test program, or the error message is not self-explanatory, you'll have to track down the cause of problems yourself. Auto mechanics, electricians, physicians, and others whose job it is to fix things use a problem-solving technique called *troubleshooting*. They start by asking questions to identify the part of the system that might be causing the problem, such as "Where does it hurt?" or "Does anything happen when you turn the key?" The responses help isolate the faulty system that most likely contains the specific breakdown or problem.

You can use similar techniques to solve problems you encounter with your hand-me-down. Figure 7.2 is a guide for isolating the causes of problems. Troubleshooting guides such as this work like branches of a tree or paths of a directory. You start

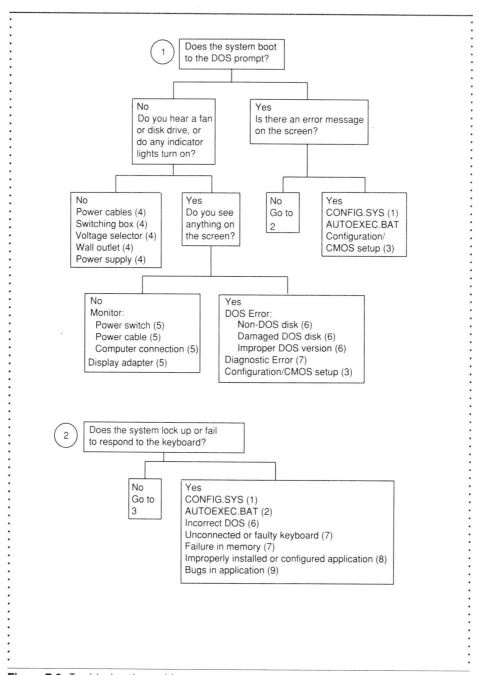

Figure 7.2: *Troubleshooting guide*

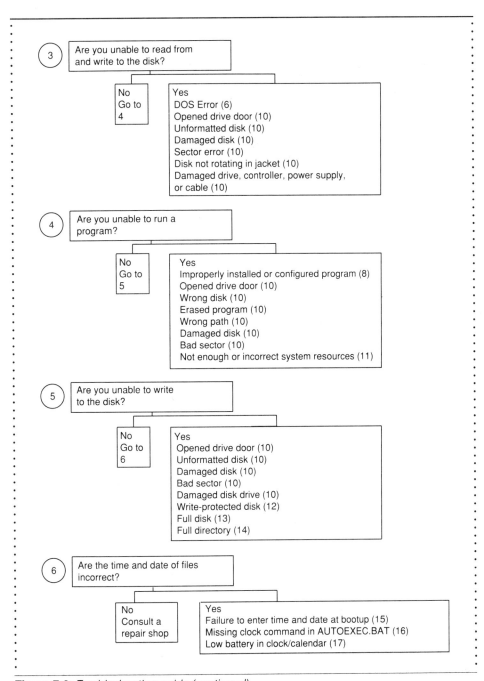

Figure 7.2: *Troubleshooting guide (continued)*

at the root—the first question—and then work your way through the series of questions based on your responses. The numbers in parentheses in the "Troubleshooting Guide" correspond to sections in the "Troubleshooting Reference" later in this chapter. Check the appropriate reference for an explanation of the problem and for possible solutions.

When you encounter a problem, start with the first question in Figure 7.2, "Does the system boot to the DOS prompt?" If you answer yes to that question, work your way through the Yes path, which asks "Is there an error message on the screen?" If you do not see the DOS prompt, work through the path starting with "Do you hear a fan or disk drive, or do any indicator lights turn on?"

If you see the DOS prompt but no error messages, go to question 2, which asks specific questions about the problem. When you reach a point where there are no more questions to answer, you've isolated a possible cause of the problem.

As an example, let's look at a hypothetical situation:

> You turn on your computer. You hear the system's fan and see the disk drive indicator light go on. Then the message "General failure error" appears on the screen.

What's the problem?

Since you don't see the DOS prompt, you choose the No path at the first question. You can hear the fan and see the light, so you follow the Yes path next. Since you see the error message on the screen, you follow the Yes path again.

The problem is either a DOS, CMOS, or configuration error, or an error displayed by the system's diagnostic self-test. Refer to the appropriate section in "Troubleshooting Reference."

Now consider this situation:

> Your system boots properly and you start to run a word processing program. Every time you try to save a document, however, an error message appears on the screen.

The DOS prompt appears, so you follow the Yes path. There is no error message (at this point), so you then follow the No path and go to question 2. The response to questions 2, 3, and 4 are no, but since you can't save, which is a function of writing to the disk, the answer to question 5 is yes. Check the possible causes listed in that question.

Troubleshooting Reference

The numbered items in this section correspond to the items indicated in parentheses in the "Troubleshooting Guide."

▶ **1. CONFIG.SYS**

There might be a command in CONFIG.SYS that cannot be executed or conflicts with your hardware. For example, DOS might be unable to locate a device driver referenced in a device command. Display the file by entering **TYPE CONFIG.SYS**. Make sure each of the commands is appropriate for your hardware and is worded correctly.

▶ **2. AUTOEXEC.BAT**

As with CONFIG.SYS, there is probably an improper or inappropriate command in the file. Check for PATH commands that reference nonexistent directories or hardware that is not installed.

▶ **3. System configuration or CMOS setup**

There could be two problems. First, the actual hardware you have installed might not match the hardware specified in your ROM setup. Check your system manual for instructions on how to set up your CMOS configuration.

Second, the system's diagnostic program might have found an error that is not serious enough to prevent the system from booting. See item 7, "Diagnostic Error," and check your system manual.

▶ **4. Power Failure**

Your system, or a part of it, is not receiving power. Refer to the section in Chapter 2 called "If You Don't See the DOS Prompt."

▶ **5. Display Failure**

There is an error in the display of characters on your screen. Make sure your monitor is plugged in, connected to the computer, and turned on. Make sure you have the correct monitor for your display adapter. If the monitor's indicator light is not on, you may have a disabled monitor.

▶ **6. DOS Error**

DOS errors result from two types of problems. First, you may be trying to boot from a nonsystem disk or a damaged system disk. Replace the disk and try again. If you have a hard disk, boot with a floppy disk and then log on to drive C. If you can read and write to the hard disk, then the DOS boot information might be lost. Try using the command SYS C: to transfer the boot data back to the hard disk. If that doesn't correct the problem, back up all of the data you can read from the disk. Either reformat the hard disk or purchase a hard-disk maintenance utility such as Spinrite II, that can format the bad sectors without erasing other files.

Second, you may be using the wrong version of DOS. Some computers require a version of DOS supplied by the manufacturer and will not boot with another version.

▶ **7. Diagnostic Error**

The system's diagnostic program has found a hardware or CMOS problem. If the system does not boot, then you might have to consult a repair shop.

Look for an indication of these five types of errors:

Disk	Faulty drive, controller, cable, or power supply. Check your documentation to see if your system has options for booting from drives other than A or the hard disk. If you don't have documentation, consult a computer store that sells your system or contact the manufacturer.
RAM or ROM memory, CPU	Write down the exact message that appears on the screen. Turn off the machine, wait a few moments and then turn it back on. If the message appears again, consult your manual or a repair shop.
CMOS	This could be a hardware error resulting from a configuration problem. If your system has a setup program, check for proper configuration. This could also be caused by a low battery.

| Low battery | The battery that powers your CMOS is running low. Replace it. |
| Keyboard | Make sure your keyboard is connected and of the proper type. You might have a bad keyboard or keyboard cable. |

▶ **8. Program Installation**

The program may not be properly installed or configured for your hardware. Install or reinstall the program.

▶ **9. Faulty Application**

There can be errors in the application that will not let it operate properly on your hardware. Check the application's manual, the software supplier, or the manufacturer.

▶ **10. Disk Problems**

A number of problems can be caused by a problem with the disk or disk drive.

Opened drive door	Make sure the disk drive door is completely closed. Try removing and reinserting the disk.
Unformatted disk	You're using an unformatted disk. Replace the disk with one that you know is formatted.
Damaged disk	Dirt, lint, smoke, or other foreign particles have damaged the disk. The disk might be bent or scratched. Backup any files you can from the disk, then throw it away.
Sector error	The area on the disk where the file is located is damaged. Try reading the file again. Even if the disk is damaged, other files may still be readable. Copy them to another disk.
	The area on the disk where DOS is trying to write a file is damaged. Save the file to another disk. Copy files from the original, then reformat.
	There is a damaged FAT or directory. Try running CHKDSK or a utility program such as those

discussed in Chapter 12, "Enhancing DOS." If you have a large number of errors with a hard disk, back up all of the data you can read from the disk. Purchase a utility program that will either reformat the bad sectors or use the DOS command DETECT to determine which sectors are bad, and then reformat the drive so DOS will ignore the bad sectors.

Disk not rotating	The walls of the *disk jacket* (the permanent plastic envelope that encases the disk) are pressing against the disk, preventing it from rotating. First try removing and reinserting the disk. If that doesn't work, hold the disk in a corner, slip two fingers inside the center hole and carefully rotate the disk. If this fails, hold the disk just below the two top corners and try to flatten the edge on a hard surface or table top.
Damaged disk drive, controller power supply, or cable	If no disk works correctly in the drive, have the drive serviced or replaced.
Wrong disk, erased program	The program you are trying to run is not on the disk. Replace the disk. If the program was accidentally erased or the disk formatted, a DOS utility program might be able to reclaim the file. (See Chapter 12.)
Wrong path	The program you are trying to run is not on the directory. Change to another directory. Check your PATH command.

▶ **11. Not enough or incorrect system resources**

The program requires more memory or other facilities than your system has available. Check the documentation for minimum requirements. Add memory or memory drivers. Try installing or reinstalling the program.

▶ **12. Write-protected disk**

The disk is protected by a write-protect tab. Remove (for 5¼-inch disks) or lower (for 3½-inch disks) the tab, and then try again.

▶ **13. Full disk**

There is no room on the disk for the file. Delete some unnecessary files or save on another disk.

▶ **14. Full directory**

Although free space might be shown with DIR or CHKDSK, the directory is full and cannot hold any more entries. Delete some unnecessary files or save the file on another disk.

▶ **15. Failure to enter time and date when booting**

You did not enter the date and time when booting, or you entered it in the incorrect format. Return to DOS and run the TIME and DATE internal commands.

▶ **16. Missing clock command in AUTOEXEC.BAT**

The clock command is incorrect or missing. Check AUTOEXEC.BAT.

▶ **17. Low battery in clock/calendar**

See the section "Finding and Replacing the System Battery" (later in this chapter) for instructions.

Using CHKDSK

The CHKDSK program not only reports on disk usage and memory status, but can isolate and repair two common disk problems: lost clusters and cross links. These are errors that relate to the disk directory and the FAT, or file allocation table. The *FAT* maintains a list of which disk sectors are being used, which are empty, and which are damaged. Information is stored in *clusters,* the smallest number of sectors that DOS can use to store a single file. The FAT maintains the *file chain,* a list of clusters storing each file.

To locate a file, DOS finds its name and the location of its first cluster in the directory, and then consults the FAT to locate additional clusters of the file. A *lost cluster* is a file chain in the FAT that doesn't have a corresponding directory entry. That is, the FAT is reserving clusters for a file that doesn't exist. A *cross link* occurs when a cluster is included in two FAT chains, even though a cluster can only be used to store one file.

Both of these problems are commonly caused by rebooting the computer when you're not at the DOS prompt. Changes being made to the directory or FAT by the application were not completed so they contain incomplete or conflicting records.

CHKDSK will report these errors and ask you if it should attempt to repair the damage. But no matter what your response is, it will not actually solve the problem unless you start the program with the /F option. Type

CHKDSK /F

to begin CHKDSK in Fix mode. The program scans the directory, attempting to fix problems it encounters.

Let's examine some typical messages that CHKDSK reports and the actions it takes to correct them if you use the /F option.

Message	Explanation
Allocation error, size adjusted	The size of the file recorded in the directory does not match the actual number of clusters allocated to the file by the FAT. CHKDSK will change the directory entry to match the FAT.
All files specified are contiguous	All the files specified in the CHKDSK command are stored in contiguous sectors. This message will only appear if you include a file specifier with the CHKDSK command, such as CHKDSK *.*. CHKDSK takes no action.
Cannot check a SUBSTed drive	You cannot use CHKDSK on a drive that you've substituted for a directory path. CHKDSK takes no action.
Contains n noncontiguous blocks	The file is fragmented, or stored in nonconsecutive clusters. CHKDSK reports the number of blocks (n), but takes no action.
n lost clusters found in n chains. Convert lost chains to files (Y/N)?	CHKDSK has found lost chains and reports the number of lost clusters and lost chains (n). If you respond **Y**, the clusters indicated in the chain are written to a series of files named FILE0000.CHK,

Message	Explanation
	FILE0001.CHK, FILE0002.CHK, and so on, in the root directory. Display the files on the screen with the TYPE command to determine if you need the data. If you respond **N**, CHKDSK removes the file chain from the FAT so the clusters can be reallocated for other files.
Errors found. F parameter not specified. Corrections will not be written to disk	You did not specify the /F option. Errors are reported but not corrected.
Insufficient room in root directory	The root directory is full and cannot store the recovered lost chain files.

Finding and Replacing the System Battery

The battery that powers your clock/calendar and CMOS can last for years. Its life depends on how much of the time your computer is turned off, the only time when battery power is required.

To replace your system's battery, you have to remove the computer's cover. This will not void any warranties, and is a task that many computer users perform themselves. As with other repairs, if you are at all unsure about working inside the computer, have a repair shop replace the battery for you.

If you decide to replace the battery yourself, make sure you unplug all of the power cords before starting. Just turning off the power switch is not adequate protection against possible disaster to both you and your computer.

Some systems use a small, flat, circular battery; others use a cylindrical battery similar to a battery you'd use in a portable radio and tape player. You must replace the battery with the exact same type. If you can't find the type of battery in your system manual, you'll have to remove the old battery before purchasing a new one.

Locating the Battery

Depending on your system, the battery may be located on a circuit card or on the computer's backplane. A *circuit card* is a thin rigid board containing electronic components. Most circuit cards are attached to your system at the rear panel that contains the interface ports. The *backplane* is the bottom part of the computer that contains the *expansion sockets* (the area where small circuit cards are connected to the main circuit board). Some systems use a *motherboard,* a large circuit card that contains the microprocessor, the major electronic circuits, and the expansion sockets. Others have the microprocessor on a CPU circuit card, and use a separate backplane to which all cards are connected.

If a clock/calendar circuit is built into your system, the battery will be on the motherboard or the backplane. If the circuit was added to your system by the previous owner, it will be on a separate circuit card attached to the rear panel.

Make sure you have a copy of the CMOS information before removing the battery. While the exact methods for accessing the battery differ, follow these general steps. First, find out where your battery is located and its type.

1. Turn off the computer and unplug the power cable. Do not try to work inside the computer with the plug connected.

2. Remove the computer's cover. Most systems have small Phillips screws holding the cover to the side or the back. Remove the screws and try pulling the cover up and away from the computer.

If the cover does not move, look for two or three screws along the top edge of the back panel. There may be other screws on the back panel that fasten internal components, such as the power switch or cooling fan, to the back of the system. Start by removing the two screws in the corners. If the cover does not move, look for one in the exact center of the top edge. If the cover and front panel appear to be one unit, slide the cover toward the front of the computer.

The early Compaq portable computer has a plastic cover you must pry off from the end where the carrying handle is located. Underneath the cover is a metal plate held on by several nuts. Remove the nuts with a nut driver, pliers, or wrench.

3. Look for a small battery on the backplane or a circuit card. Go to the next section for instructions on removing and replacing the battery.

Replacing the Battery

Follow these steps to replace a battery located on the backplane:

1. Remove the battery, noting the position of the positive and negative terminals (Figure 7.3). Pull the battery with one hand, holding the battery socket with the other. This will prevent accidental damage to the socket or backplane.

2. Replace the battery with the new one. Make sure the positive and negative terminals are positioned properly.

3. Replace the cover, and then reconfigure CMOS as explained in "Recording CMOS Information."

A circuit card battery is usually circular. When you remove the battery, pay particular attention to the markings showing which surfaces are the positive and negative terminals, and which terminal faced down toward the card.

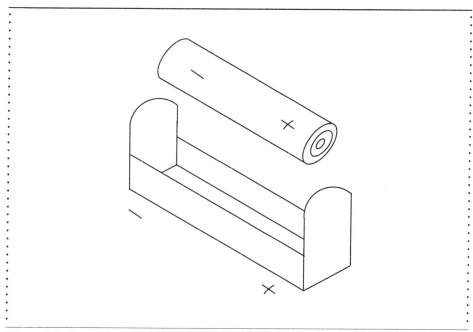

Figure 7.3: *Removing a backplane battery*

1. Remove the battery. There is usually a small retaining clip holding it. Lift the clip up *slightly* with your finger or a small screwdriver, and then pry the battery out of the holder. Be careful not to pull on the holder itself, or you could damage the circuit card. If you do not have enough clearance to access the battery, refer to the section "Working with Circuit Cards" in Chapter 9.

2. Insert the new battery in the socket, under the clip. Make sure the correct surface or terminal is facing toward the card.

3. Replace the cover, and then reconfigure CMOS as explained in "Recording CMOS Information."

Chapter Eight

Working with
Your Printer

You may have received a hand-me-down printer with your hand-me-down PC, or you might be using a printer that you already had. Each situation presents its own challenges.

If you're using your old printer, you already know how it operates. Your major task is to make sure it is connected and set up properly for your hand-me-down. Refer to "Communicating with Your Printer" and the "Printer Troubleshooting Guide" in this chapter if you have any problems.

However, if your printer is a hand-me-down, you'll have to examine it in a little more detail. In Chapter 2, you learned how to connect serial and parallel printers to your computer. In this chapter, you'll learn more about your printer—how to make it communicate with your computer, and how to diagnose and correct printing problems.

Understanding Printers

There are many types of printers. Some printers use an *impact* mechanism in which a physical element strikes a ribbon to transfer an image to the paper. With *non-impact* printers, the image is transferred without any moving part physically striking a ribbon. For example, thermal printers transfer the image by applying heat to specially coated paper. The paper turns color where the heat is applied.

There are also character, line, and page printers. *Character printers* print one character and then move to the next; *line printers* transfer text a line at a time; *page printers* print the entire page at once.

However, printers are usually classified according to how they transfer the image.

Daisy-Wheel Printers

Daisy-wheel printers are impact character printers that work much like electric type-writers. They use a flat plastic or metal disk with petal-like projections. On the end of each projection is a fully formed character. The wheel spins so the appropriate character is opposite the printhead. The *printhead* contains a small pin that is thrust out and strikes the element against the ribbon, transferring the entire character to a sheet of paper.

You can remove the wheel and exchange it for one with a different *font,* or style of type, such as italic. While you can get some slightly smaller and larger fonts, the printers are limited by the physical size of the wheel.

Daisy-wheel printers are relatively slow because the wheel has to spin for each character, but they produce output that looks exactly as if it were typed on a standard typewriter.

Dot-Matrix Printers

Dot-matrix printers are also impact character printers. Instead of using fully formed characters, however, they use pins that form characters as a series of small dots.

The number of pins determines the quality of the printed character. Printers with 24 pins form characters that more closely resemble daisy-wheel output in a mode called *near letter quality* printing, or NLQ.

Nine-pin printers may also have a near letter quality setting. In this mode, the printhead strikes the same position a second time, but slightly offset from the first. The offset fills in some of the space between the dots, creating a more polished look.

Dot-matrix printers are not only usually faster than daisy-wheel printers, but they can also print various sizes and styles of characters, and graphics as well.

Laser Printers

Laser printers are non-impact page printers that produce high-quality text and graphics. This type of printer works by using static electricity to attract and hold powdered ink, or toner, to the paper. The printer heats the toner, which adheres to the page.

The printing is page oriented—the process doesn't start until the printer has all of the information it needs for the complete page.

There are two general classes of laser printers, PostScript and Hewlett-Packard PCL. While both can print text and graphics in various sizes, most PCL printers require that you have each font in the proper size before you start printing. Post-Script printers create fonts of all sizes from *outlines,* files that generically describe each character's style and shape. (The LaserJet III, however, uses scalable fonts much like PostScript printers.)

Inkjet Printers

Inkjet printers produce an image by ejecting streams of ink through a small spraying mechanism, called the *print cartridge.* The cartridge contains dot-sized ink jets that can print with the same quality as many laser printers. In addition, DeskJet inkjet printers made by Hewlett-Packard use the same commands as PCL laser printers.

Learning About Your Printer

Of all hand-me-down peripherals, printers have the most variation in features. At one end of the spectrum are printers that produce just uppercase characters on 2-inch wide rolls of paper. At the other end are high-speed color laser printers capable of publication-quality output.

No matter where your printer falls in this range, there are some key features that you should be aware of before putting your printer to work.

Paper Feed Selection

Your printer may accept paper by tractor feed, friction feed, or both.

Tractor feed uses continuous paper with sprocket holes on the sides. This assures an even, straight flow of paper, so once you line up the paper, you can print a long document without worrying. If your printer has *only* tractor feed, you cannot use individual sheets of paper.

Friction feed uses built-in rollers that pick up and guide the paper, much like the rollers on a typewriter. You can use individual sheets of paper such as printed letterheads, memo forms, and index cards. You can also use continuous paper, although it tends to slip in some friction feed mechanisms so you have to check alignment every few sheets.

Many printers have both tractor and friction feed capabilities. You select the feed type with a lever usually located on the top right or left (Figure 8.1). Push the lever into the tractor position to disengage the friction rollers so continuous paper can be pulled easily by the sprockets. To feed individual sheets of paper, place the lever in the friction position. In some printers, you can remove the tractor mechanism for better access to the rollers.

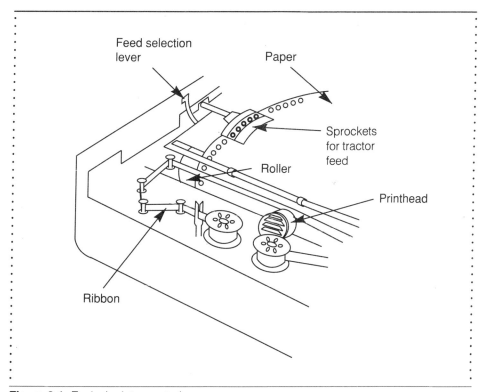

Figure 8.1: *Typical printer controls*

It is important to know the type of paper feed before setting up applications such as word processors. If the program is configured for friction feed, it may stop before printing each sheet, waiting for you insert paper. This wastes time when you are using continuous paper.

On the other hand, when you're using individual sheets, make sure the program is not set for continuous feed. It will attempt to print a page even when you don't have paper loaded.

Maximum Paper Size

Printers are either letter size or wide carriage. *Letter-size* printers handle paper up to 9 ½ inches wide—8 ½ inches plus an extra inch for the sprocket holes in continuous paper. *Wide-carriage* printers accept paper 17 inches and wider, and are useful for large spreadsheets and landscape printing on daisy-wheel and dot-matrix printers. Landscape printing allows you to print text and graphics across the length (as opposed to the width) of the page.

If your printer only handles letter-size paper, you may still be able to print wide spreadsheets by selecting a small font or by printing in landscape.

Experimenting with Fonts and Styles

A *font* is a collection of characters, numbers, and symbols in one size and style. Font sizes are measured in *points*. A point is a printer's measure of about $1/72$ of an inch, so there are 72 points in an inch. Font styles are classified by *families,* the name given by the font's designer. Times 14 point, for example, is a font of the Times family in the 14 point size. Other popular font families include Courier and Helvetica.

If you have a daisy-wheel printer, each printwheel represents a different font. Insert the appropriate wheel when you want to print in a certain font.

Most dot-matrix printers have a number of fonts built in. There may be an italic font, a small compressed font, and a larger expanded font. A number of dot-matrix printers can also accept font cartridges that plug into slots in the front, and fonts that are downloaded into the printer's own memory.

Laser printers have three sources of fonts: internal, plug-in cartridges, and soft-fonts. *Internal fonts* are built into the computer's hardware, *cartridge fonts* plug into the printer, and *softfonts* (or *downloadable* fonts) are typefaces stored on a disk that are transferred to your computer's memory when needed. The number of fonts you can use at one time is determined by your printer.

You select fonts either through your application program or by using buttons on the printer's control panel. Use a compressed font to print wide documents on 8½ by 11-inch paper; use larger fonts for headlines and signs.

Setting Printer Controls

Your printer has a control panel where you manage its operations, as shown in Figure 8.2. While some control panels have special facilities for selecting fonts or various paper sources, there are certain functions that you can perform with almost every printer.

Online

When the printer is *online,* a indicator light is lit and the printer is ready to accept characters from the computer. When the online indicator is off, the printer is *offline,* and the computer will not transmit any characters. To switch between online and offline, press and release the online button. (The online button and indicator light may also be labeled *Select.*)

You must turn the printer offline to use any of the other controls on the panel. Just remember to put the printer back online when you're ready to print.

Form Feed

Press the form feed button to eject the sheet of paper in the printer. (Remember, the printer must be offline.)

You could eject the page by just pulling it out of the printer, or turning the roller, but this can create problems with some printers and applications. You shouldn't turn the roller

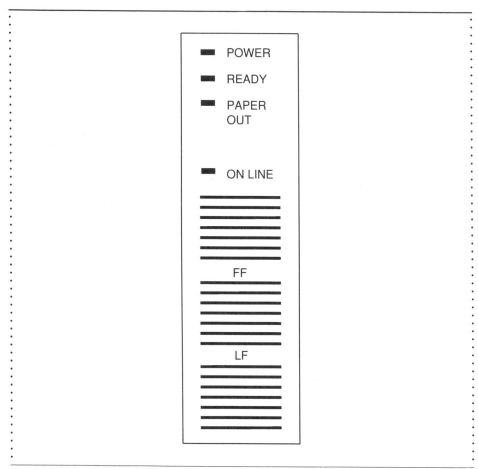

Figure 8.2: *Typical printer control panel*

manually when the printer is on. This could damage plastic gears that are engaged in the feeder mechanism. Turn the printer off first to disengage the mechanism.

Taking the paper out manually could also throw off the *top of form* setting. When you print a document, the application keeps track of the number of lines printed on the page. It assumes that you started the print job with the top of the sheet at the proper position in the printer. When the page becomes full, the application issues a form feed command that ejects the sheet.

Some printers also keep track of the lines per page, automatically feeding the paper when it comes to the end of the page. When you first turn it on, the printer assumes that the top of the form is aligned with the printhead and the printer counts each line it prints from that point.

When you pull out a sheet of paper and insert a new one while the printer is counting lines, it doesn't know to start counting again from the top of the page. It will pick up from where it left off, print some lines, and then eject the page before it becomes full.

Pressing the form feed button ejects the paper and sets the line counter back to the top of the form. In fact, some printers label this control *TOF.*

With a laser printer, the form feed button also clears the printer's *buffer*—a memory area where your document is stored after being received from the computer. Don't press the form feed button unless you're sure all of the data has been transmitted, and the page doesn't eject by itself. If you use form feed in the middle of a print function, you may lose some of your text.

Line Feed

Most dot-matrix printers use the line feed button to feed the paper one line at a time. Use this control when you want to advance the paper but not eject it from the printer. These line feeds will be added to the printer's line count for determining the top of form.

Manual Feed

Laser printers have a manual feed control to accept paper or envelopes from the manual feed tray instead of the paper cassette. The *paper cassette* is a tray that contains sheets of paper and that is inserted into the printer. When you do not insert paper into the manual tray, or press the manual feed button, the printer uses paper from the cassette.

Even without your pressing manual feed, most laser printers can detect when sheets of paper are in the manual tray and they will use those sheets instead of paper from the cassette. If you want the printer to wait until you've inserted paper manually, press manual feed so the printer ignores the cassette. (With the Apple LaserWriters and compatible printers, you can only switch to manual feed through your application programs or printer control software.)

You can use manual feed to print on two sides of a sheet of paper or to feed a sheet that does not fit in your cassette. You can also use manual feed when you want to print on legal-size paper but only have a letter-size paper tray. Follow these steps:

1. Press the online button until its light goes out.
2. Press the manual feed button.
3. Press the online button to turn its light back on.
4. Insert a sheet of paper into the manual feed tray.
5. Set up your application for legal-size paper.
6. Initiate printing.

The printer will wait until you insert a sheet of paper into the manual feed tray, even though the paper cassette is available.

Self-Test

Most printers can perform a test of their functions, printing a sample of their fonts and styles. While some laser printers have a self-test button that initiates the process, most printers use some combination of other controls. You may have to hold down one of the buttons as you turn on the machine, or press two of the controls at the same time. Check your printer's manual.

Other Indicators

In addition to the online indicator, most printers have a power light showing that the printer is turned on, and a ready light indicating that the printer is ready to accept characters.

Many printers also have a buzzer or light that warns of error conditions, such as being out of paper, ribbon, or toner.

Communicating with Your Printer

While it's best if you have a copy of the printer's operating manual, you can usually get along without one if you have a parallel printer. Parallel printers require no special setup.

Serial printers, on the other hand, require coordination between computer and printer, and the careful establishing of the serial protocol. (Serial, parallel, and interface ports are described in detail in Chapter 1.)

Setting Up a Serial Printer

Each time you start your computer, you have to tell it how you want to communicate with your serial printer. This is done with commands in AUTOEXEC.BAT similar to these:

```
MODE COM1:9600,N,8,1,P
MODE LPT1: = COM1:
```

The MODE command establishes the serial protocol by which data is transmitted by the computer and accepted by the printer. These particular commands are required with a Hewlett-Packard laser printer using default serial settings. Your own commands depend on how your printer is configured.

Most serial printers let you change their protocol through a series of small switches (Figure 8.3). Look for switches around the outside of the printer, under an access panel, or inside the printer's case. In some cases, there will be a label indicating the values of the switch settings. In most instances, however, you'll need the printer's manual.

The settings in the MODE command *must* match those of your printer. Take a look at these individual commands in detail:

MODE   Uses the program MODE.COM, an external DOS program that configures the system's serial circuit.

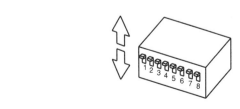

Figure 8.3: *Switches for selecting serial protocol and other settings*

COM1:	Determines the serial port attached to the printer. Use COM1: if you have only one serial port, or if your printer is attached to the first of several serial ports. If your printer is connected to the second serial port, use COM2:.
9600	Specifies the baud rate (speed of transmission) at which the printer is set to receive characters. Possible settings are 110, 150, 300, 600, 1200, 2400, 4800, and 9600. Some versions of DOS only require you to enter the first two characters of the number, such as 30 or 96.
N	Sets the parity, a communications system for checking the accuracy of transmitted data. Possible settings are N (None), E (Even), and O (Odd).
8	Specifies the number of bits that compose each character, usually 7 or 8.
1	Specifies the number of *stop bits* used to indicate the end of each character. May be 1 or 2. The stop bits are used to separate each transmitted character, and are discussed in detail in Chapter 11.
P	Indicates that the serial port is being used for serial printing, not for a modem.
LPT1: = COM1:	Tells DOS to direct all characters going to the LPT1: port (the default parallel port) to the serial port. (Use COM2: if your printer is attached to the second serial port.)

Check your AUTOEXEC.BAT file to see if these lines already exist. If not, add them using the techniques you learned in Chapter 4.

Now whenever you start your computer you'll see a message something like this, depending on the version of your operating system:

REDIRECTING LPT1: TO COM1:

Printing from DOS

If your computer and software are configured for your printer, you'll be able to print anything the application can produce. However, there may be some complications when printing from the DOS prompt, as explained in Chapter 3.

Graphics

Just as you can't display on the screen an executable file with the TYPE command, you can't print a screen of graphics using Shift-PrtSc. The screen's graphic image is not composed of printable ASCII characters. If you try to produce a screen dump of a graphic image, you'll get a page of gibberish.

Most versions of DOS, however, include a program called GRAPHICS that modifies the Shift-PrtSc function to print a graphic image on a printer compatible with the IBM Graphics dot-matrix printer. To run the program, log on to the disk or directory where it is located, or include it in the PATH command, and then type **GRAPHICS**.

The program will not work with daisy-wheel or laser printers, and many versions will only print screen dumps of 320 x 200 CGA screens, not higher resolution EGA or VGA screens.

Fortunately, there are programs that can print high-resolution screen dumps and output to laser printers. Pizazz Plus, for example, can print graphics from CGA, EGA, VGA, and MCGA displays on a wide variety of dot-matrix and laser printers.

You can also use utility programs to capture the image into a graphic file format, and then print the image with programs such as Ventura, WordPerfect, and Word. These are similar to Grab, which comes free with WordPerfect, and Capture, provided with Word.

Ejecting Paper in Laser Printers

Laser printers only eject a sheet of paper when a page becomes full or when they receive a form feed command. If you print less than a full page from the DOS prompt, you have to eject the page manually using the printer's control panel. Follow these steps:

1. Press the online button until its light goes out.

2. Press the form feed button to eject the page.

3. Press the online button to turn its light back on.

Don't forget the last step, or your next print job won't work.

Using Printer Drivers

Most printers can print directory listings and text screen dumps from DOS without any problem. (PostScript printers may require some special setup, and most will not produce listings and screen dumps generated from DOS without special software.) However, to use your printer's special features, such as various fonts and graphics, you must use a printer driver supplied with your application program.

When you install your application, look for a menu of supported printers. If you're not given a choice of printers, the program outputs plain text characters and doesn't use your printer's optional fonts. When you are given a choice, make sure you specify the make and model of your printer. For example, selecting **LaserJet** when your LaserJet II is listed as an option will prevent you from using softfonts.

You might also be asked to specify the resolution for printing graphics. Many dot-matrix printers, for instance, can produce graphics in several resolutions. While the highest resolution looks the best, large graphics can take quite some time to print. Some LaserJet printers need additional optional memory to print a full page at 300 dots-per-inch (dpi) resolution. If you select 300 dpi during the setup and are unable to print an entire page, reinstall the program and select a lower resolution.

If your printer is not listed among those supported by the application, look for a compatible printer. Check your printer's documentation if you're not sure. If you don't have documentation, can can try these settings:

If you have:	Try this setting:
Dot-matrix	Epson or IBM Graphics
Daisy-wheel	Diablo
Laser	LaserJet or PostScript

You may be able to set your printer to emulate one of these standards by using switches. In fact, some laser printers can emulate IBM Graphics and Diablo printers as well.

Troubleshooting Printer Problems

Printers are less complicated than entire computer systems, but a printer break-down can be extremely frustrating—you can see your work on the screen, but you just can't get it to print.

If you find that gibberish, or nothing, is being printed, run the printer's self-test. If the printout is acceptable, the problem is most likely in the interface between the printer and your computer or application. Refer to "Interface" in the "Troubleshooting Reference."

Use the "Printer Troubleshooting Guide" (Figure 8.4) for tracking down other problems. Locate the problem you are having, and then refer to the appropriate section in "Troubleshooting Reference."

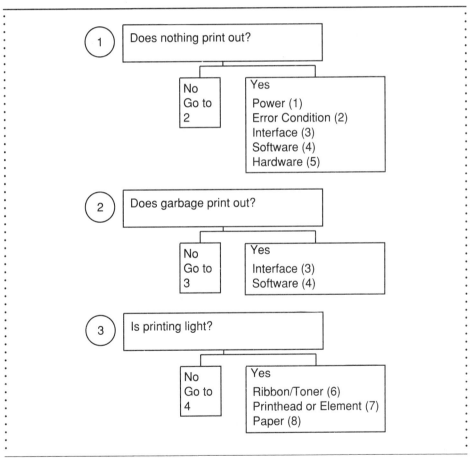

Figure 8.4: *Printer troubleshooting guide*

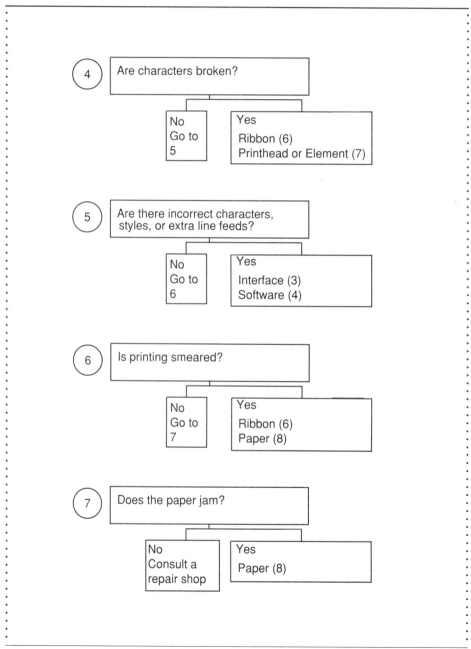

Figure 8.4: *Printer troubleshooting guide (continued)*

Troubleshooting Reference

► **1. Power**

Make sure the printer is plugged in, turned on, and online.

► **2. Error Conditions**

If you hear a buzzer or see a light, an error condition has suspended printing. Common conditions are paper jams, broken or damaged ribbons, and broken or damaged printheads. Correct the problem and then put the printer back online.

► **3. Interface**

There is a data communication problem between the computer and the printer.

Cable	Make sure you have the proper cable, firmly seated at both ends, in the proper connector. If you have a serial printer, make sure the cable is designed for a printer, not a modem.
Printer switches	Make sure the switches are set properly for your system. The switches often determine the default print style or character set. Check the settings, for example, if every character is italic, compressed, or enlarged.
	Some printers have a setting that performs a line feed each time it receives a carriage return from the software. If the printer receives a line feed and carriage return from the software, its own line feed is unnecessary. Check for switches that control the line feed and carriage return commands. Set the switch so it is not in the automatic line feed position.
	Some older printers and cables were designed to perform a line feed automatically with each carriage return. This is most common with *older* Radio Shack hardware. If changing software or changing the printer's switches does not correct the problem, you might need to have your cable modified. Snipping line 14 will usually correct the problem. This changes

	the electronic signals that activate the automatic line feed function. Take the cable to a repair shop if you don't feel comfortable making the modification yourself.
CONFIG.SYS, AUTOEXEC.BAT	Check the contents of these files for the proper commands. If you're using a serial printer, look for the MODE command. Confirm that the settings match those of the printer and your software.

▶ **4. Software**

Your application program may be configured for a different printer or serial protocol. Check your software manual for instructions on selecting or configuring printer drivers.

Determine how your software and printer treat the line feed and carriage return commands. Some older programs can be configured either to separate or combine the commands.

▶ **5. Hardware**

Your printer might have a hardware error that requires repair.

▶ **6. Ribbon/Toner**

Make sure the ribbon is still inked (rub the ribbon between your thumb and index finger as a quick test). Some ribbons can only be used once—make sure your ribbon has not reached its end.

Make sure the ribbon is properly seated between the printhead and the ribbon guide (Figure 8.5).

Check the toner usage indicator on your laser printer. You can extend the life of the cartridge by about 100 sheets of paper by rocking it back and forth to distribute the toner.

Check the printer cartridge if you have an inkjet printer; dried ink may be clogging the printhead.

▶ **7. Printhead or Element**

Check the distance between the printhead and ribbon. Most daisy-wheel and dot-matrix printers have a lever that adjusts the printhead for various thicknesses of

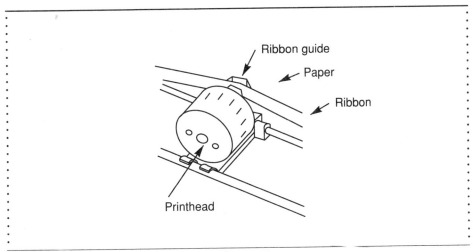

Figure 8.5: *Make sure the ribbon is properly seated*

paper (see Figure 8.1). Move the printhead closer to increase the impact and darken the image.

Look for broken pins on a dot-matrix printer. You can usually unscrew and replace damaged printheads yourself.

Look for broken or missing characters on a daisy-wheel printer. Clean the area around the printhead of any dirt or paper.

▶ 8. Paper

Confirm that you are using the proper type and thickness of paper for your printer. Keep in mind that coated papers tend to smear and light spots may appear on humid or damp paper.

The paper may not be feeding properly—check its size. Make sure it is loaded properly and is fully seated in the tractor. Be sure to set the tractor/friction feed setting appropriately.

Your printer should last a long time with the proper care. Keep the areas around the printhead and paper-feed path clean. Vacuum the areas periodically to remove pieces of paper, lint, and dust.

Chapter Nine

Understanding
Monitors

*W*hile it only has a few controls, the television-like monitor that came with your hand-me-down is one of the most complex parts of your system. In many ways, it is the least understood peripheral, probably because we take it for granted.

Most of us will just plug in the cables and turn on the computer, feeling satisfied to see the DOS prompt. Depending on what applications you use, you might not have to do anything else, or learn anything more about your monitor. But the monitor is just one part of your computer's display system. Inside of your hand-me-down is a *display adapter,* or *video card,* that controls what is displayed on the screen. The adapter and monitor must work hand in hand—they must be compatible or nothing will display. In fact, using incompatible equipment could seriously damage the monitor.

As long as your monitor and adapter are compatible, you'll be able to run DOS commands and many applications without further thought. But DOS is a very forgiving piece of software—many application programs require special software to use your monitor's more sophisticated features.

In this chapter, you'll learn about the types of monitors and display adapters, and how to upgrade your hand-me-down. *Upgrading* may include moving from a monochrome to a color monitor, or increasing the resolution of displayed text and graphics.

Measuring the Quality of Display

The heart of the monitor is the CRT (cathode-ray tube), a glass vacuum tube with the screen at one end and an *electronic gun* at the other. The electronic gun focuses a concentrated beam of light on the inside of the screen. The beam starts at the top left of the screen, and scans back and forth in lines until it reaches the bottom right corner, when it returns to the top left and starts over. The movement of the beam from the bottom of the screen to the top is called the *vertical sweep* and it occurs either 50 or 60 times each second, depending on your system.

The computer's video circuit turns the beam off and on, lighting up individual dots, or *pixels,* to form the image. The greater the number of dots in each square inch, the higher the picture resolution and the finer the image.

Resolution is measured by the number of dots horizontally and the number of rows vertically. For example, a 640 x 200 resolution screen has 640 dots in each of its 200 rows. This is not the same as the number of character rows and columns. Most monitors can display 2000 characters, 25 rows of 80 characters, with each character created by a matrix of dots, much like the dots from a dot-matrix printer.

If you divide your system's resolution into 2000 individual boxes, you get the character box in which each character fits. With a 720 x 400 resolution display, for example, each character has a 9 x 16 space in which it can fit.

Types of Monitors

Now let's look at the types of monitors that you may have. There are basically two types of monitors: monochrome and color.

Monochrome Monitors

Monochrome monitors display a black background with one other color for the image—either white, green, or amber, determined by the phosphor coating on the inside of the picture tube. At one time, white displays were shunned because of their hard contrast and tendency to create eye fatigue. Green and amber displays were found to be easier on the eyes and more readable.

The popularity of desktop publishing, however, has started to reverse the trend. Monochrome monitors that use a white background are gaining acceptance because they resemble the familiar look of printing on white paper. In fact, a class of *page-white* displays are available with a softer, warmer shade of white that more closely matches bond typing paper.

There are three types of monochrome monitors. Transistor-to-Transistor Link (TTL) monitors require a special monochrome display adapter. They were originally designed just to display text, but can now be used for graphic applications. TTL monitors are the traditional monitors used with monochrome systems.

Composite monitors display black and one other color but can be used with low-resolution color graphics display adapters. Instead of displaying only one shade of the nonblack color, composite monitors simulate color with shades, using a dark green, for example, to represent a dark color like red, and a light green to represent a light color like yellow. You can identify a composite monitor by its *connector,* which looks like the round plug used in the back of video cassette recorders and stereo equipment.

VGA, or Video Graphics Array, is a high-resolution color graphics standard originally introduced by IBM. Because VGA color monitors can be expensive, some users opt for a monochrome version that displays graphics in shades of gray, something like a high-resolution composite monitor.

Color Monitors

Color monitors can display at least 16 colors, including various shades of gray. The number of colors displayed at one time depends not necessarily on the monitor, but on the display adapter and the display mode.

We usually classify color monitors by the maximum resolution they can display. Since this depends on the display adapter installed in your computer, we'll discuss color monitors along with their compatible display cards.

Special-Purpose Monitors

There are many special monitors designed primarily for desktop publishing. These are high-resolution monitors capable of displaying one or two full pages of text and graphics at a time, rather than the one-third of a page normally displayed by CGA monitors, or the one-half of a page shown on EGA and VGA displays. These monitors allow designers to visualize and work with a full page, or two facing pages, without scrolling from one section or page to another.

There is even a monitor than can be swiveled or turned sideways to automatically display images in a landscape orientation.

These special monitors require their own adapter cards and software.

Types of Display Cards

The *display card* provides the monitor with electronic signals to create the image. In fact, this card has more to do with the variety and quality of your display than the monitor itself does.

Monochrome Cards

There are two basic monochrome standards, MDA and Hercules. MDA (Monochrome Display Adapter) cards can be used only with TTL monitors. While the card cannot display graphics, text characters appear at a high resolution of 720 x 350, making it an option for text-only applications such as basic word processing. Each character is formed within a 9 x 14 box; the average character is a 7 x 9 matrix. The MDA card includes a 9-pin D-shaped connector.

Even though TTL monitors were designed to work with MDA cards, they are physically capable of displaying high-resolution graphics. To take advantage of the monitor's capabilities, Hercules Computer Technology developed a 720 x 348 resolution monochrome graphics card.

The Hercules card became so popular with TTL users that MDA quickly faded into the background and the Hercules, or HGC, standard was born. In order to use HGC for graphics, however, your software must include a special driver that converts its output to Hercules-compatible signals. The standard is so widely accepted that this isn't much of a problem.

Color Cards

There is a wide variety of color systems, but we can relate them all to the video standards established by IBM. Some other manufacturers add additional features to their display cards while trying to maintain compatibility with the standard. Your own card, for example, might offer a resolution or graphic capability not found in the IBM version. But since most software is designed for the general class of IBM machines, it is the standard features that are initially important.

Table 9.1 summarizes the maximum resolutions of the popular video standards. Not all colors are available in each mode, however.

Table 9.1: *Maximum Resolution of Video Standards*

Monitor Type	Text	Graphics
CGA	640 x 200	640 x 200
MDA	720 x 350	none
EGA	640 x 350	640 x 350
VGA	640 x 480	720 x 400
HGC	720 x 348	720 x 348

CGA

The Color Graphics Adapter was IBM's original alternative to MDA. It provides a resolution of up to 640 x 200 and can be used with CGA-compatible color and composite monitors. The typical character is 7 x 7 in an 8 x 8 box.

The number of colors displayed on the screen depends on the *graphics resolution*. CGA can display 16 colors in 160 x 200 low resolution, four colors in 320 x 200 medium resolution, or one color in 640 x 200 high resolution mode. The available colors are shown in Table 9.2. Notice that there are five colors in two levels of intensity, plus yellow, brown, black, white, and two shades of gray.

The CGA screen can also have a border surrounding the 25 x 80 character text area. This border can be in any of the 16 available colors.

CGA monitors are often called RGB or RGBI because of the red, green, and blue phosphors that they use to create up to 16 colors.

IBM's original CGA card included three different connectors: a round composite-type plug, a 9-pin D-shaped connector, and a 4-pin adapter for use with special hardware to display images on a standard television set.

Table 9.2: *Colors Available with CGA Displays*

Foreground colors	Background Colors
Black	Black
Blue	Blue
Green	Green
Cyan	Cyan
Red	Red
Magenta	Magenta
Brown	Brown
Light Gray	White
Dark Gray	
Bright Blue	
Bright Green	
Bright Cyan	
Bright Red	
Bright Magenta	
Yellow	
White	

EGA

The low resolution of CGA graphics severely limited the PC's ability to compete in graphics-intensive applications. The EGA (Enhanced Graphics Adapter) was IBM's first higher resolution graphics standard.

EGA systems support 640 x 350 resolution of 64 colors (eight colors in four levels of intensity plus black and various shades of gray); up to 16 can be displayed at one time. Characters are typically 7 x 9 in an 8 x 14 matrix. The unused dots allow for more readable descenders and spacing. You use a 9-pin D-shaped connector to connect an EGA monitor.

VGA

IBM introduced the VGA standard with its PS/2 line of microcomputers. VGA (Video Graphics Array) is capable of 640 x 480 graphics resolution and 720 x 400 text resolution. Text characters fit in a large 9 x 16 box. VGA monitors use a 15-pin D-shaped connector.

TTL, CGA, and EGA monitors work with a digital video signal. *Digital* signals are square waves which turn the monitor's electronics either off or on. These two distinct states limit the range of colors that can be displayed to specific combinations of the red, blue, and green phosphors.

VGA monitors, on the other hand, accept *analog* signals that do not have definite on or off states but can vary in almost infinite degrees. The VGA card converts the computer's digital signals to the monitor's analog, so it can display up to 256 of 256,000 possible colors at a time—256 colors at 320 x 200, 16 at 640 x 480, and 16 in the 720 x 400 text mode.

When you power up your system, the VGA card senses which color signal paths are completed between the card and the monitor. If it finds that only the green signal path is completed, it assumes that you're using a monochrome monitor and converts color information to 64 possible shades of gray.

Monochrome VGA monitors are less expensive than their color counterparts and they can display a wide range of shades at high resolution. They are popular for desktop-publishing applications which require a high-resolution black-on-white display.

Other Standards

While MDA, HGC, CGA, EGA, and VGA are the most popular standards, a number of other video display systems are in use today. The most popular offer resolutions higher than standard VGA, or implement just part of the VGA standard for use with less expensive hardware.

Super VGA monitors, for example, are high-resolution VGA systems that require special display adapters to output 256 colors in 640 x 480, 800 x 600, or even 1024 x 768 resolution.

IBM's own 8514/A video card, for example, allows up to 16 colors on a 1024 x 768 resolution display. The board contains its own coprocessor to speed up display operations, freeing your own CPU for other tasks.

You can use the 8514/A in addition to the system's standard VGA card, driving two monitors at a time. You can have high-resolution graphics displayed on one monitor, and text on another. Because the card has its own coprocessor, one monitor can create complex drawings while you word process on the other.

The 8514/A card, however, requires the Micro Channel bus architecture available in more expensive IBM and compatible models.

At the opposite end of the high-resolution spectrum is the MCGA (Memory Controller Gate Array) display standard. Used in several less expensive IBM PS/2 computers, MCGA implements part of the VGA standard to offer high resolution for less cost. MCGA offers a text resolution of 640 x 400 in 16 colors, using an 8 x 16 character box. Graphic modes include four-color 320 x 200, two-color 640 x 200, and one-color 640 x 480.

Multiple-Mode Displays

In many ways the display standards compete with each other. Each uses its own scanning frequency and requires its own type of monitor and software configuration. If you ran an application set up for a standard different than your own, your screen would be filled with meaningless characters, if anything appeared at all.

Multiple-mode displays based on the VGA standard can run software designed for all common standards. For example, you can easily run software created for CGA or even HGC displays on multiple-mode displays.

Multiscan Monitors

The speed with which the electronic beam scans the face of your monitor from left to right is called the *horizontal frequency.* For your card and monitor to be compatible, each must be synchronized at the same rate (see Table 9.3). For example, a CGA monitor running at 15,720 cycles per second (cps) could not handle the 21,800 cycles from an EGA card.

Multiscan monitors can automatically synchronize with signals from 15,500 to 31,500 cps instead of being locked into one scanning rate. Because the monitor can adjust to the scanning rate of the signal, it can display MDA, HGC, CGA, and EGA images, and you can use software designed for any graphic standard.

Table 9.3: *Scanning Frequencies of Video Standards*

Monitor Type	Cycles per Second
CGA	15,750
MDA	18,432
EGA	21,800
VGA	31,500

Multiscan monitors are also called *multisynchronous* monitors. The trade name MultiSync belongs to NEC, which developed and manufactured the first monitor of this type.

Multiple-Mode Display Cards

The benefits of a multiscan monitor can also be achieved with a display adapter that automatically switches modes. Most VGA cards, for example, can emulate MDA, HGC, CGA, and EGA images as analog signals at 31,500 cycles. So even though the monitor isn't multiscan, it can still display the full range of video images, because the card switches automatically to match the software.

Connecting Your Monitor

Monochrome, CGA, and EGA monitors all use identical-looking 9-pin connectors. While the connector itself is physically the same, the electronic signals transmitted through the pins are not, and you can damage your monitor if you connect it to the wrong adapter card.

If you see horizontal or vertical lines or a flash of light, or hear a high-pitched noise, immediately turn off your monitor. You may have caught the problem in time to prevent any serious damage. Check your documentation to determine the type of adapter card you have installed, and compare the specifications with those of your monitor.

Since only composite monitors use RCA-type plugs, you can't make a mistake with their connection. While both VGA and 8514/A use 15-pin connectors, no damage will result if they are mismatched. Both work just as well with either card.

The 9-pin and 15-pin connectors look very much alike from the outside, but they are not interchangeable. Never try to force in a monitor cable that does not contain the same number of pins as the adapter connector.

Setting Your Computer's Switches

The original PC and XT computers have a pair of switches for setting their hardware configurations. Two of the switches on the first switch block must be set to match the display adapter. The switches are located on a circuit card inside the computer and should be set as shown in Figure 9.1.

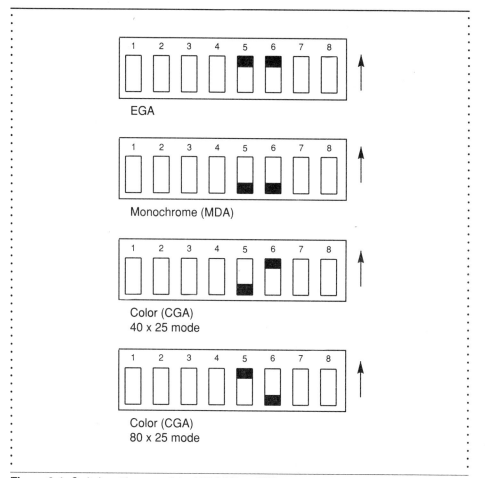

Figure 9.1: *Switch setting on original IBM PC and XT computers*

IBM's AT computers have a single switch on the display adapter that determines whether the monitor is color or monochrome. Push the switch toward the back of the computer if you have color, or toward the front for monochrome.

If you have an AT-compatible, check your documentation or contact the manufacturer for the location of the switch and how to set it for your monitor.

A number of EGA and VGA cards also have switches that can be set to emulate CGA and monochrome displays. Check your documentation for a list of the settings if you have any display problems.

Using Graphics on Your System

Since graphics are not built into DOS, you need graphic drivers to use the full capabilities of your monitor. A *graphic driver* is a special program that sends the appropriate signals to your video card. In most cases, your application program will include drivers for displaying graphics in CGA, HGC, EGA, and VGA resolutions. You have to select the driver during the installation procedure or in the program's configuration menu.

The drivers let you display graphics in the highest resolution possible on your system and select between text modes capable of displaying 43 or more lines of text on your screen, depending on the adapter.

Some display cards may not be fully compatible with the IBM standards that they emulate, so the manufacturer will include a disk of drivers for popular application programs. Many application programs even include their own graphic drivers for the more popular display cards.

Be careful when selecting drivers. Usually the worst that can occur is that your screen will be blank or garbled. But your video card may transmit signals that can damage your monitor. Don't experiment with drives that you know are incompatible with your display system.

Using the MODE Command

You can use the external DOS command MODE to take advantage of many display system features. For instance, if CGA images look bad on a monochrome composite monitor, turn off the color with the command:

MODE BW

Table 9.4 lists other options available with versions of DOS. Select the options that match your display system.

Table 9.4: *Mode Options for Controlling the Video Display*

Mode Options	Video Display
MODE 40	40 characters per line
MODE 80	80 characters per line
MODE BW40	Disable color, 40 characters per line
MODE BW80	Disable color, 80 characters per line
MODE CO40	Enable color, 40 characters per line
MODE CO80	Enable color, 80 characters per line
MODE GR40	320 x 200 resolution
MODE GR80	640 x 200 resolution
MODE MONO	Monochrome 80-character display
MODE HGC,FULL	Hercules graphics display using full video memory
MODE HGC,HALF	Hercules graphics display using half of the video memory
MODE *n*	Some laptop computers use this command to turn off the display after *n* minutes elapse without keyboard activity

Either enter the command at the DOS prompt, or include it in your AUTOEXEC.BAT, if you want to execute it when you boot your computer.

Upgrading Your System

If you're not satisfied with the display system on your hand-me-down, consider upgrading to color or to a higher resolution by purchasing another monitor and card. The cost of monitors and display cards has dropped, so even EGA color systems cost less than monochrome did just a short time ago.

Make sure you purchase a card and monitor that are compatible. If they are used, ask to see documentation that proves their compatibility or ask to see them operating in a system before they are removed. If you purchase new hardware, buy both the monitor and card from the same source—many retailers even package both components together at a special price.

You can upgrade the original PS/2 models with MCGA systems to full VGA by adding a circuit card. The board turns off the built-in MCGA adapter so you must attach your monitor to a connector on the VGA board.

To move up from one graphic standard to the next, you'll need both a video card and a new monitor. Some EGA and VGA cards can only fit in AT-class machines, not PC models, so make sure the card is compatible with your system before you purchase it.

Remove your existing card and select and install the new one using the techniques discussed in the next section. Double-check all switch settings before replacing the cover, and then reconfigure or reinstall any software that requires color or high-resolution drivers—most applications require this.

Working with Circuit Cards

When you upgrade to a new display system, you might have to insert a new video card into an unused expansion slot. Working with cards is easy as long as you work carefully and slowly.

Many cards contain switches or jumper blocks that must be set according to your specific configuration. A *jumper block* is a series of upright pins. Following the documentation that comes with the card, you set the switches or connect specific pins together using the hardware provided. When working inside your computer or with circuit cards, do not change any switch or jumper block settings unless instructed to do so in the documentation.

Removing Circuit Cards

Follow these steps to remove a circuit card from your system:

1. Turn off the computer and unplug the power cables.

2. Remove the computer's cover.

3. Disconnect any cables from the card, noting the exact way they plug in.

4. Carefully remove the Phillips screw that secures the support bracket to the computer (Figure 9.2). Be careful not to drop the screw into the computer.

5. Grasp the card with both hands and pull it straight up.

6. If you have to remove the card entirely, lay it on a nonconducting surface (such as wood or plastic) with the component side facing up.

Selecting Slots

If you are reinstalling a card, place it in the slot in which it was originally located. If you are installing a new card into your system, however, you have to insert it in one

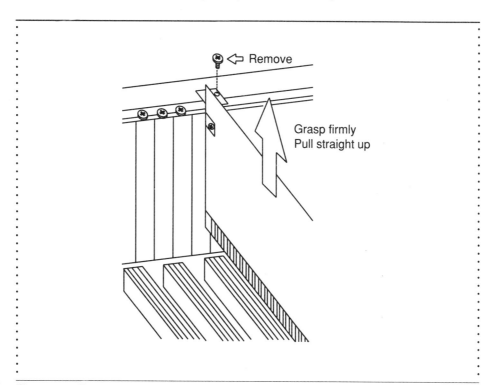

Figure 9.2: *Removing a circuit card*

of the empty card slots. It doesn't matter which slot you select, as long as it is physically compatible with the edge on the card.

Figure 9.3 shows some common card configurations. The section of the card that extends down, fitting into the card slot, is called a *descender*.

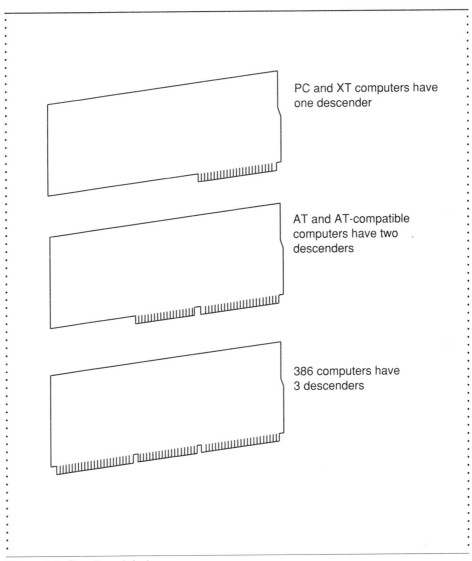

Figure 9.3: *Circuit card design*

Cards designed for PC and XT computers will have one descender. AT-compatible cards have two descenders, and some 386 cards have three. The size and number of descenders should match the card slot in the computer (Figure 9.4).

However, some cards are designed to work in a variety of computers, as shown in Figure 9.5. Some cards have two descenders but still can be used in PC and AT machines. Others with one descender can be used in all machines. If the card edges do not match the slots exactly, check the manual before inserting the card.

Installing Circuit Cards

If you are reinstalling a card you just removed, skip ahead to step 6. Otherwise, follow these steps to install a card into your system:

1. Turn off the computer and unplug the power cables.
2. Remove the computer's cover.
3. Decide in which vacant card slot you want to install the new card.
4. Remove the Phillips screw that secures the support bracket to the computer.

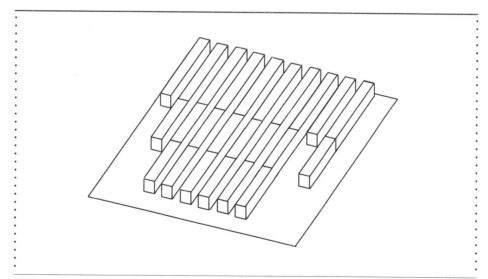

Figure 9.4: *Card slots*

5. Set any switches or jumper blocks as instructed in the documentation.

6. Hold the card level, with the edge connector facing down.

7. Position the edge connector over the card slot, with the support bracket aligned against the back panel. Some computers have plastic card guides on the opposite side for handling full length cards. Make sure the back of the card fits into the guide.

8. Lower the card into the computer so the edge card fits into the card slot. A small tip on the support bracket should line up with a corresponding groove.

9. Apply even but firm pressure to push the connector into the card slot.

10. Replace the screw that secures the support bracket to the computer. Be careful not to drop it.

11. Install any connector cables.

12. Replace the cover.

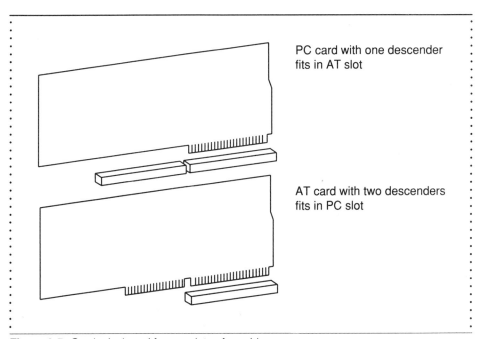

PC card with one descender fits in AT slot

AT card with two descenders fits in PC slot

Figure 9.5: *Cards designed for a variety of machines*

Chapter Ten

Communicating
with Your PC

Your hand-me-down's keyboard is a common device for getting data into your computer. While it is not the only input device that you can use, it is the only one that allows quick entry of a virtually unlimited combination of letters, numbers, control, and function keys. It is also the only one that works with every program that you can buy.

Even with these benefits, however, there are reasons to use other methods of input. In this chapter you'll explore some other input devices that you might have received with your hand-me-down, or that you would like to add to improve performance.

Overcoming Keyboard Restrictions

When you use a keyboard, the cursor movement keys provide movement only along the X and Y axes—right, left, up, and down. Reaching a point not along these four paths means moving in discrete steps, such as moving up and over to reach the upper-right corner.

Even if the 7, 9, 1, and 3 keys could be programmed for diagonal movement, you would still have to move the cursor in discrete steps to reach positions not along those paths.

This limitation not only affects drawing and painting programs, but slows down the process of selecting commands and working with your application programs.

When the keyboard is your only means of communicating with the PC, application programs give you two ways of selecting commands and performing functions. The most common method forces you to remember and enter a series of key-strokes for each task that you want the program to perform. As an example, you'd have to know that Ctrl-X moves the cursor down a line in WordStar, or that F6 makes text bold in WordPerfect.

Some applications also use the *point-and-shoot* method. The available options are listed on the screen. You just have to move the cursor to the desired option and press ◄─┘. While this method is certainly easier to learn than memorizing key-strokes, it is still limited to the paths of the cursor movement keys.

If you had unlimited flexibility in cursor movement, however, the point-and-shoot concept could be applied to almost any program. You would no longer have to press numerous keys, or move the cursor in a series of horizontal and vertical steps to reach some out-of-the-way position on the screen.

Working with Mice

A *mouse* is a small device that you move along the table top next to your PC. You might have received a mouse with your hand-me-down. Look for a device about the size of the palm of your hand with one or more buttons. The mouse will have a cable that connects to the back of your computer. If you did not receive a mouse, you should consider adding one to your system—particularly if you use a desktop-publishing, drawing, or painting program, Microsoft Windows, or another program designed for mouse input.

When you move the mouse, instructions are sent to the program to move the pointer mouse on the screen in a corresponding way. Since you can move the mouse in any direction, it gives you total flexibility to point anywhere on the screen without moving in row and column increments.

With graphic programs, use the mouse as you would a pencil or pen on a piece of paper. Draw on the screen by *dragging* (moving) the mouse on the table top.

Mouse Buttons

On top of the mouse are one or more buttons (Figure 10.1). In point-and-shoot operations, you merely have to move the mouse until the cursor is on the option you want, and then *click* (quickly press and release) one of the mouse buttons. In this way, you can initiate a command without even lifting your hand from the mouse itself. Some programs also support *double-clicking,* two clicks in a row that perform a more complex function than a single click.

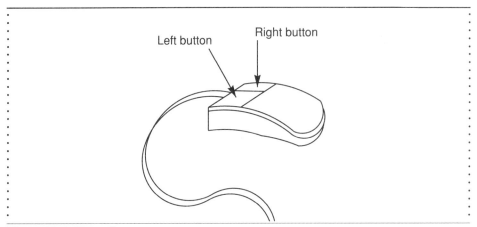

Left button

Right button

Figure 10.1: *Mouse buttons*

Since most mice have two or three buttons, programs designed to work with mice will have left and right mouse commands. Click the right button to perform one function; click the left button for another.

Mouse Drivers

In order to use your mouse, you must install a mouse driver. Instructions for loading the driver are in Chapter 4 in the section "Modifying Configuration Files."

Your mouse system disk, however, might come with additional drivers for use with specific application programs. The drivers install menus for selecting program options with the mouse, even when the program itself does not support a mouse. Figure 10.2, for example, shows a mouse menu installed in Lotus 1-2-3. Move the mouse to highlight the option you want and then click a mouse button.

Some mice even have programs that let you create your own menus, so you can use the mouse to run applications or perform DOS functions (Figure 10.3).

If the mouse has more than two buttons, you probably need special software supplied by the manufacturer to use anything other than the left and right buttons. The Powermouse from Prohance Technologies, for example, has 38 keys in addition to left and right mouse buttons, including a full numeric keypad that duplicates your

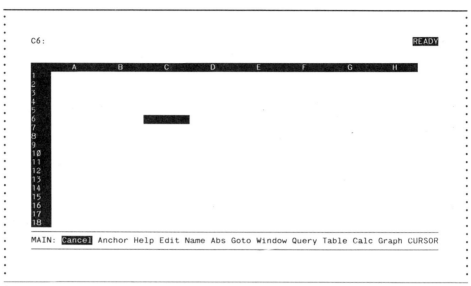

Figure 10.2: *Mouse menu in Lotus 1-2-3*

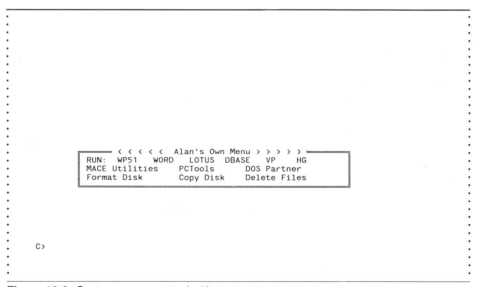

Figure 10.3: *Custom menu created with mouse support program*

computer's ten function keys. Its drivers program the remaining keys to automate certain application functions, such as copying and deleting blocks in WordPerfect and summing a range of cells in Lotus 1-2-3.

The more buttons on the mouse, the more functions you can perform, but also the more you have to rely on the manufacturer's own drivers. If you have an application not directly supported by the mouse, a generic driver may not work.

The standard of compatibility is the two-button Microsoft mouse. You can use a Microsoft mouse with every program that supports a mouse. The most compatible mice will work with a Microsoft mouse driver, no matter who the manufacturer is. Select a noncompatible mouse only if it is supported by your application or has its own drivers.

Types of Mice

Mice can operate either mechanically or optically. This depends on the method used by the mouse to convert its movement into the instructions transmitted to your program. In order to draw or accurately position the mouse pointer on the screen, even the smallest mouse movements must be detected.

Mechanical Mouse

In the bottom of a *mechanical mouse* is a small rubber ball that rolls along the table top as you move the mouse. On the inside, the ball rotates against two rollers that convert the physical movement into electronic signals that are transmitted to the computer. There is a third roller that holds the ball tightly against the other two, but does not record any movement.

There are only two rollers that detect movement, so diagonal activity is detected when both rollers rotate at the same time. The process occurs so fast, and in such small steps, that it appears to provide total flexibility and cursor control.

The problem with mechanical mice is that they require a clear, flat space next to your computer. Also, the ball often picks up dirt and lint, and must be cleaned regularly.

Optical Mouse

Rather than using a rubber ball, *optical mice* sense movement using sets of light beams and photodetectors mounted at right angles to each other. (A *photodetector* is a device that converts light into electronic signals.) You move the mouse across a specially constructed mouse pad printed with a grid pattern. The mouse detects variations of light, and converts them into electronic signals.

You need a clear surface on your desktop for the mouse pad, and you must use the pad supplied with the mouse.

Connecting Your Mouse

A mouse can be connected to your hand-me-down in three ways—through a serial port, through the mouse's own interface board, or through a dedicated mouse port. The type of connection, however, does not change how you use the mouse, just how the movement instructions enter your system.

Serial Mouse

Serial mice connect to a computer's serial port—the same type of port that you could use for a printer or modem. Many mice use a 9-pin connector, but some come with an adapter for use with a 25-pin serial port.

Bus Mouse

Since many systems have only one serial port, you might not want to use it for a mouse. An alternative is a mouse that comes with its own circuit board that you plug into an empty expansion slot in the computer. This type of mouse is called a *bus mouse* because it uses the system's *internal bus,* the electronic pathway connecting the computer's various parts. With the bus mouse, you can use your serial port for a modem, printer, or other peripheral while using your mouse to draw and point.

The circuit boards provided with bus mice are designed to work in almost any computer. Because of differences in hardware, however, the boards usually contain a *jumper block* to configure the board to your system. Following the instructions provided, you determine which of the pins should be connected together to complete the correct signal path for your system.

The Microsoft bus mouse jumper block, for example, has four sets of pins (Figure 10.4). You select the appropriate set of pins for your system by eliminating pins that you cannot use, as shown in Table 10.1. Cross out any of the items that pertain to your system, and then connect together one of the remaining sets using a *jumper* that you push onto the pins.

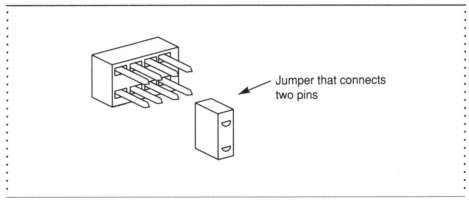

Jumper that connects two pins

Figure 10.4: *Jumper block on bus mouse board*

Table 10.1: *Eliminate Hardware to Determine the Jumper Setting for Your System*

With this hardware:	Do not use this jumper:
IBM PC with fixed disk	5
IBM 3270 PC with fixed disk	5
IBM PC/XT	5
Asynchronous Communications Adapter on first serial port (com1)	4
Binary Synchronous Communications Adapter on first serial port (com1)	4
Synchronous Data Link Control Communications Adapter	3
Asynchronous Communications Adapter on second serial port (com2)	3
Binary Synchronous Communications Adapter on second serial port (com2)	3
IBM PC AT	2
IBM 3270 PC (with or without fixed disk)	2

Dedicated Mouse Port

Many systems come with a port dedicated to mice. In most cases, these ports are 9-pin female connectors that resemble a 9-pin serial port, but are labeled *mouse*. Some mice can plug directly into the port, but others cannot. If your hand-me-down has a dedicated mouse port, check your mouse documentation. If it does not work with the mouse port, then it connects either to a serial port or to its own circuit board connector.

Mouse Features

When selecting a mouse, consider the type of interface that is best for your system and which mice support your applications. Other features to look for are resolution, tracking, and acceleration.

Resolution

The mouse rollers or photodetectors transmit movement as a series of small points, or dots, which are converted into pixels on the screen. The number of dots per square inch of desk (or mouse pad) space is called the *resolution*. The higher the resolution, the more exact your movements and the less you have to move the mouse for a corresponding movement on the screen. Most mice have a resolution from 200 to 400, although some, like the Logitech Series 9 mouse, can be adjusted to have a resolution range of 50 to 19,000.

Resolution isn't critical for text applications, such as selecting menu options or working with word processors. You'd probably see little difference in the 200 to 400 range. It is, however, more important for desktop-publishing, drawing, and drafting applications where you want precise movement in small increments.

Tracking

Tracking is the ability of the mouse to glide smoothly on a desk or mouse pad. Like driving a car that pulls to one side, using a mouse with poor tracking can be a chore. You have to push the mouse constantly to compensate for its defect.

Unfortunately, there are no predetermined standards for tracking—it is more of a personal feeling of comfort, and it depends on both the mouse and the surface being used. Test the mouse before purchasing it. If you can, run a painting or drawing program and see how easy it is to draw straight horizontal and vertical lines. Difficulty in drawing straight lines can indicate a mouse with poor tracking.

Acceleration

In menu selection and cursor positioning, you'd like a mouse that moves quickly from one screen position to the next and responds to sudden movements. A mouse with high *acceleration* can accurately translate quick movements, positioning the cursor at the proper screen location.

Again, you have to test drive a mouse to judge its acceleration. Run a program that allows mouse selection of menu items, and quickly move the mouse to select items that are some distance apart.

Alternatives to Mice

While mice are the most commonly used alternative to the keyboard for drawing and cursor positioning, there are a number of other pointing devices. It is unlikely that your hand-me-down includes one of these peripherals, but they do offer some advantages over a mouse and might be a worthwhile addition to your system.

Trackballs

If you'd like a mouse but can't clear space on your desktop, consider a *trackball*. These are basically mechanical mice turned upside down, with the roller ball facing up on the same surface as the buttons (Figure 10.5). Instead of rolling the mouse around the desk, you roll the ball with your fingertips.

While you gain some desk space with a trackball, you lose the feedback you get from seeing and feeling how far you've moved the mouse. You also lose the ability to use a straight edge for drawing lines. But since you don't have to move your wrist or arm, many users find trackballs less tiring.

Digitizers

There are other pointing devices that you can use as an alternative to a mouse. A *puck* is identical to a mouse except it has crosshairs in front to indicate its exact

Figure 10.5: *Logitech Trackman*

location. *Crosshairs* are intersecting lines; you use the point where the two lines meet to position the mouse pointer. Pucks are used for tracing and drawing, or where precise positioning is required. You can also use a *digitizer pen* that gives you the feeling of drawing on paper.

Both devices use a *digitizer tablet*, a pad-like device which has a fine grid of wires just beneath the surface. The pointing device determines its position electronically by sensing the coordinates of the grid.

The WIZ, manufactured by CalComp, is a puck input system with an optional pen. The pen has a button on the side and a tip that acts as a mouse button when pressed against a hard surface.

You can use both the puck and pen for drawing and interacting with programs that work with mice. What makes pucks and pens unique is that they work with a collection of templates and drivers designed for popular applications that are not mouse-compatible, such as WordPerfect 5.0 and Lotus 1-2-3. Each template contains a series of menus that include the program's major functions. You place the template on the digitizer tablet and then access a function by pointing to the item and clicking the puck, or depressing the tip of the pen (Figure 10.6). There is even a template for DOS, so you can display directories and manipulate files without typing DOS commands, even from within application programs.

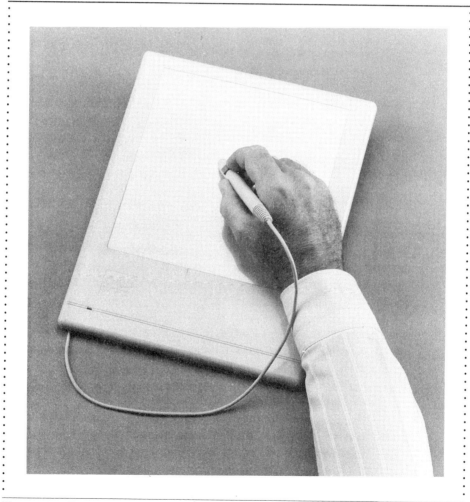

Figure 10.6: *The WIZ pen can select menu items from application templates*

The WIZ can also be configured for relative and absolute positioning. With *relative positioning,* the screen position is determined by the distance you move the puck or pen. As with a mouse, you can lift up the pointer and move it elsewhere without changing the screen position.

Absolute positioning, on the other hand, duplicates the X and Y coordinates on the pad with those of the screen. To point to a specific part of the screen, position the pointer on the corresponding position on the tablet.

The tablet, puck, and pen use electrical power. However, you don't need to connect them to a wall outlet; instead, they get their power directly from your system. The tablet plugs into the serial port and attaches to the keyboard interface using a Y-connector. The mouse or pen plug directly into the tablet. If your keyboard is permanently connected to your hand-me-down, you need to purchase a separate power supply.

Using Light Pens

Instead of simulating the face of the screen on a pad or your desktop, light pens allow you to work directly on the screen. You draw a line by drawing on the screen itself—you select a menu option simply by pointing to it.

When you point to the screen, the light pen senses the exact moment the monitor's scanning line passes under its photodetector. The vertical sweep rate is so fast (about 50 times per second) that the pen appears to react instantly, signaling the driver software to perform some action based on that coordinate position.

For example, suppose you point to a menu item that is between character positions 65 and 70 on the screen's fourteenth line. The pen transmits a signal to the computer when it senses the scanning line. The computer calculates where the scan line was at that time, and determines which menu option was at that position.

Many IBM adapters have a 6-pin light-pen interface built into the card. Other light-pen interfaces look like modular-telephone plugs.

Touch Screens

A few PC's have point-and-shoot systems built into the monitor that allow you to use your finger as the pointer. Hewlett-Packard, for example, developed a system called the Touch Screen. The monitor's screen is surrounded by a series of light beams and photodetectors that create an invisible 16 x 16 grid pattern. When you point to an option on the screen with your finger, you break the pattern, telling the computer to act on that coordinate.

The obvious advantage of the Touch Screen is that you don't have to pick up a pen or move a mouse. The added electronics, however, make Touch Screen monitors expensive. In addition, the grid pattern is far from precise. The small tip of a light pen or the crosshairs of a mouse cursor can pinpoint a single pixel. You certainly couldn't say the same for your finger.

Scanning Graphics and Text

All of the pointing devices discussed earlier are designed for selecting menu options or cursor movement, duplicating a single keystroke at one time.

Through scanning, you can quickly input larger amounts of text or graphics without having to type or draw them yourself. A *scanner* directs light onto a printed surface, and then uses a sensor to record the amount of reflected light at regular intervals— the *scanning resolution.* The data recorded by the sensor is converted into a graphic file that you can import into your application.

Scanners can either capture full pages or small sections of text. With full-page scanners, the sheet to be copied either sits flat under the scanning head or face down on glass, as on a photocopier. This makes it easy to scan pages from a book or magazine.

Lower cost "hand scanners" capture images from three to five inches wide. You slowly move the hand-held device across or down the page (Figure 10.7).

It is important to differentiate between the scanning of graphics and the scanning of text, or optical character recognition (OCR).

Scanning Graphics

When you scan a drawing or signature, the resulting file is an image of the original that you can merge into your desktop publisher or print as a figure with a word processor that handles graphics. The scanned images are printed as a series of dots, which is

Figure 10.7: *Logitech ScanMan Plus*

fine as long as the scanned image is just solid black and solid white, such as a signature, but not for photographs and other images that have shades of gray.

Photographs are called *continuous tone images* because they contain shades that range over the entire gray scale from white to black. Scanners handle the gray scale in three ways.

The least expensive scanners only capture two shades: solid black and solid white. These scanners, called *bit-map* or *line art* scanners, convert every shade of gray to either black or white dots. Obviously, this type of scanner is not suitable for capturing photographs and similar artwork.

Other scanners simulate the gray scale by a process called dithering. In *dithering,* each shade of gray is represented by a different number of dots in a square grid: the darker the shade, the more dots. The scanner reads a sample, then converts it into a dither pattern instead of a single black or white dot. When printed, the dither patterns give the illusion of gray.

More expensive scanners can capture gray scales digitally, instead of as collections of dots. Gray-scale scanners record each sample of the photograph as a series of bits representing the actual shade of gray. The more bits used, the more shades represented and the finer the reproduction.

Scanning Software

While scanners come with their own software for capturing images, you can use other programs to manipulate graphics. Publisher's Paintbrush, for instance, lets you edit and manipulate the gray-scale patterns, controlling how the gray scale data will appear when printed. You can even use drawing tools to edit, size, crop, or mirror sections of the image, and then save it in a format for importing into Aldus PageMaker or Ventura Publisher.

For maximum control over scanned images, use scanning software such as PB/Scan, a part of Publisher's Type Foundry. This program works directly from within PC Paintbrush for Windows, and scans images into the Paintbrush environment. The program includes its own drivers for popular scanners, so the program can be set up specifically for your hardware, and can be used to set the brightness and contrast of the image (Figure 10.8).

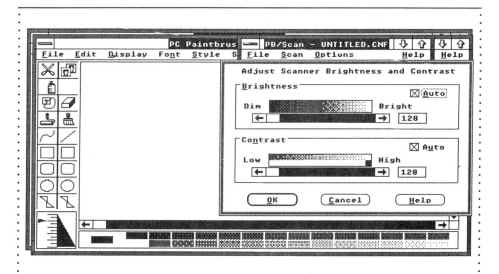

Figure 10.8: *PC Paintbrush brightness and contrast controls*

Desktop-publishing software also lets you control the quality of scanned images. For instance, Aldus PageMaker has options for controlling the line resolution and angle of the patterns that simulate the gray scale when it prints a page.

Scanning Text

If you scan a paragraph of text using any of the techniques just described, you'll get a graphic image of that paragraph. The image will be just a series of dots and lines with no meaning, not individual letters or numbers. Your word processor won't recognize the letters in the image, and you won't be able to edit the words as you can text.

For your word processor to recognize a scanned image as text, you need OCR (*optical character recognition*) software that converts the dots and lines into ASCII characters—individual, recognizable letters, numbers, and punctuation marks.

Most OCR systems, however, can only recognize a few standard typefaces and sizes. Some systems contain a number of other fonts in memory, which you select from before scanning. However, the scanner is still limited to the fonts it stores on disk.

A newer technology is ICR, *intelligent character recognition*. When the system doesn't recognize a font, that font's characteristics can be "taught" to the software. After learning more characteristics of the font, the program can recognize the characters and may even go back to previously scanned characters to assign the correct ASCII codes.

CatchWord is an ICR program designed to work with Logitech Corporation's line of hand-held scanners. The program uses the spacing between characters to divide a scanned image into individual objects. It then checks each object against its store of characters to find a matching model. You can enter the model for characters that the program cannot match up, and it then applies that model to similar objects in the file. Once it learns the model from you or its own database, it applies that model throughout the entire document. CatchWord can also save the scanned text in formats compatible with popular word processing programs.

While the process can be slow, I found it useful for scanning complicated program listings that would be difficult to type. I let CatchWord match models and objects while I do other things around the office.

Product Resource Guide

For more information about input devices and products mentioned in this chapter, contact

CH Products
1225 Stone Drive
San Marcos, CA 92069
(619) 744-8546
Trackball

Kensington Microware, Ltd.
251 Park Avenue, South
New York, NY 10010
(800) 535-4242
Trackball

Keytronic, Inc.
P. O. Box 14687
Spokane, WA 99214
(509) 927-5515
Mouse

Logitech, Inc.
6505 Kaiser Drive
Fremont, CA 94555
(415) 795-8500
Mouse, trackball, scanner

Microsoft, Inc.
16011 N. E. 36th Way
P. O. Box 97017
Redmond, WA 98073
(206) 882-8080
Mouse

Mouse Systems, Inc.
47505 Seabridge Drive
Fremont, CA 94538
(415) 656-1117
Mouse, trackball

Prohance Technologies, Inc.
1307 S. Mary Avenue
Sunnyvale, CA 94087
(408) 746-0950
Mouse

WIZ
CalComp, Inc.
2411 W. La Palma Avenue
Anaheim, CA 92801
(800) 458-5888
Trackball

Communicating
with the World

11

*U*sing the universal language of binary communications, you can link your computer instantaneously throughout the office, the country, and the globe. Your hand-me-down might already include the hardware and software required for sharing information with others using your computer. Your system's previous owner may have installed the necessary equipment in an expansion slot or provided it as a separate unit. Some manufacturers include the hardware as part of a fully configured system, particularly with portable and laptop computers. If not, you might want to upgrade your hand-me-down for this capability. In this chapter, you'll learn how to use your hand-me-down to communicate with others.

Using Telecommunications

Since the world is already linked by telephone, it seems natural to use this system for communicating data. In fact, using inexpensive software and the telephone jack on your wall, you can send information to and receive information from almost anywhere in the world.

The key to this marvel is a device called the modem.

Understanding the Modem

Your hand-me-down's internal communications rely on *digital* signals, electronic states which are either on or off. But a telephone is capable of carrying a wide range of sound levels and tones—*analog* signals that have an infinite range of states between on and off.

To transmit information from your computer through the telephone lines, you must convert, or *modulate,* the digital signals into analog signals. In order to receive incoming data from the telephone network, you must reconvert, or *demodulate,* the signal back to digital. A *modem,* short for *modulator demodulator,* acts as a modulator when you send information, and as a demodulator when you receive information.

While all modems must be connected to a telephone network, not all need an actual telephone. Many modems can be plugged directly into a phone's wall jack because they provide auto-dial and auto-answer services.

An *auto-dial* modem can produce the signals necessary to connect with phone networks and dial numbers. With the right communications software, you can store phone numbers on disk and have the modem dial numbers and initiate communications at any time.

Auto-answer modems sense when the phone rings through voltage changes on the phone wires. They electronically "pick up" the phone and send a signal back indicating that the connection has been made.

With an auto-dial, auto-answer modem, you can send and receive messages even when you're asleep or away from home.

Connecting an Internal Modem

An *internal modem* is auto-dial and auto-answer. This type of modem is entirely contained on a circuit card that you plug into an empty expansion slot. Therefore, it does not take up any desk space or use a serial port that you might need for a mouse or printer. You connect the telephone line, usually with a modular jack, directly to a port on the back of the card. A *modular jack* is a connector that accepts the small plugs now commonly used for telephone equipment.

Of course, to use an internal modem you must have a card slot that is the correct size and type for the card on which the internal modem is mounted. Since they pull their power from the computer, internal modems may also drain the power supply of older or less expensive systems.

If there are two modular telephone jacks at the back of your computer, then you probably have an internal modem installed. (There are also some circuit cards for use with computer networks that also contain modular phone jacks. If you're not sure about the type of card installed in your hand-me-down, check with the previous owner.) Plug a length of telephone wire between the wall jack and the plug marked *line*. Then plug in your telephone to the jack marked *phone*. Some internal modems have one modular jack and a special cable that connects to both the wall jack and the telephone.

If you have an internal modem that is not yet installed, insert the card as explained in Chapter 7.

Connecting an External Modem

External modems sit on the desk outside of your computer and connect to a serial port. They plug into a wall outlet and can be easily moved to any computer that has a serial card. While newer external modems are auto-answer and auto-dial, some older ones require that you dial the phone manually. These older style modems will have a switch labeled *originate* and *answer.* You select the originate mode when you place the call, and the answer mode when someone calls you.

External modems have modular jacks labeled *line* and *phone,* and a serial connector, on the back. Use a serial cable to connect the modem's serial port to your computer's serial port. Plug a length of telephone wire between the wall jack and the plug marked *line*. Then plug in your telephone to the jack marked *phone*. Finally, plug in the modem's power cable.

Connecting Acoustic Couplers

Years ago, *acoustic coupler modems* were popular. These modems have rubber cups that hold the telephone handset and accept the transmission as sound waves. As the cups wear, however, extraneous noise can interfere with the transmission and degrade the signal. Most acoustic couplers will also not accept decorative phones with nonstandard handsets.

Connect the coupler by using a serial cable between the modem's serial port and the computer's serial port. There is no direct connection to the telephone system.

Acoustic coupler modems use a switch labeled *originate* and *answer* that is located either on the top or side.

Setting the Serial Protocol

All modems are serial devices. Like a serial printer, the modem accepts information as a series of individual bits, the ones and zeros that your hand-me-down uses to represent characters. If you have a serial printer, you know something about establishing the serial *protocol,* the correct communication setting between the printer and the computer through the serial port. When you're using a modem, the serial protocol must exactly match the protocol used by the computer you're communicating with.

Transmission Speed

Your computer and the computer you are communicating with must be set at the same speed so data can be transferred correctly.

Many people use the term *baud rate* to indicate speed, others use *BPS,* or bits per second. While these terms are not technically the same, you'll hear them used interchangeably. Common modem speeds are 300, 1200, 2400, and 9600. The higher the speed is, the more expensive the modem.

Data, Start, and Stop Bits

The computer you are communicating with must be prepared to accept your information when you transmit it. More expensive computer systems synchronize the transmission according to a fixed time period or clock rate. The receiving computer expects to receive a bit with each tick of the clock. Once the systems are synchronized, both systems use the clock rate to determine when each character starts and stops.

Modems capable of synchronizing the signals are rather expensive. So the typical PC modem transmits *asynchronously,* without synchronizing every character according to a clock rate. Instead of using the clock rate to keep track of when characters stop and start, asynchronous modems require three elements in the protocol. These elements inform the receiving computer which set of bits make up a character.

The *data bit* setting determines the number of bits that make up each character, usually between six and eight. A fixed number of *start bits* and *stop bits* are transmitted before and after each character. Since the bits themselves are transmitted at the determined baud rate, both computers can now determine when characters are being sent. The most commonly used serial protocols use stop bits but no start bits.

Parity

Data communications depend on the computer receiving each bit clearly and distinctly. The entire message may be ruined if just one bit is misinterpreted.

Parity inserts an extra bit into each character as a simple way of checking the accuracy of the communications. You can have even, odd, or no parity.

Each character consists of a certain number of data bits represented by either a one or a zero. With odd parity, the number of bits in each character must add up to an odd number. When they add up to an even number, the system adds a 1 parity bit to make the total odd. If they add up to an odd number, the system sends a 0 parity bit.

For example, suppose you transmit a character as the binary number

1000001

Since there are two 1 bits, the system would add a 1 parity bit, transmitting the character as

11000001

The character

0001011

would be transmitted as

00001011

with a 0 parity bit added to maintain the odd number.

The receiving computer adds up all of the bits it receives in each character. If set for odd parity, the computer assumes that each character is correct if the bits total an odd number, or faulty if they add up to an even number.

Controlling the Modem

Modems are rather sophisticated hardware that perform a variety of functions. Not only do they modulate and demodulate data, they also keep track of the condition of the telephone line, sensing whether the line is connected and whether there is a computer ready to accept data at the other end.

At one time, every manufacturer used its own method for controlling the modem. Today, however, most modems used with PC's understand a standard set of instructions called the *Hayes command set,* named for the company that developed it.

All Hayes commands start with the characters *AT,* telling the modem that you are sending it an instruction that you do not want transmitted through the network. In fact, the Hayes standard is often called the *AT command set.*

The instructions that follow *AT* tell the modem what to do. The instruction

    ATDT5559999

tells the modem to auto-dial the number 555-9999.

To use your calling card with a modem, you have to place some pauses after the number to wait for the network to catch up. Add a comma for each two-second interval you want the system to pause. For instance, the command

    ATDT0215559999,,21555511113333

dials the long-distance number, pauses for four seconds, and then enters the calling card number.

If you're calling a local number from an office phone that requires you to dial 9 for an outside line, the command is

    ATDT9,5559999

Unfortunately, not all modems that claim to be Hayes-compatible understand the full Hayes command set. Some recognize a limited group of instructions that were part of an earlier set before Hayes added a number of extensions.

Adding Communications Software

Having a modem is not enough—you need a communications program that channels messages to and from the serial port and handles the interface between the computer and the modem. Some software packages emulate a computer *terminal,* a basic input and output device for sending and receiving characters.

You can purchase a separate communications program, such as Crosstalk, or use one that comes with an integrated software program. PFS:First Choice, for example, includes a communications module already set up for connecting with several popular information services. You can add additional items to the menu or modify the default settings for your own hardware.

As an alternative to commercial software, you can purchase a public domain program for little more than the price of a disk. The shareware program QMODEM is a good example of the full range of functions that are available, and you can obtain it for free or for a minimal cost. If you like the program, you are requested to send a registration fee to the developer.

Compatible with the Hayes command set, QMODEM supports auto-dial, auto-answer modems and includes a dialing directory, record-keeping log, and automatic log-on macros. The extensive list of command keys presented in the help menu shows QMODEM's range of features (Figure 11.1).

Once you set up the dialing directory, for example, press Alt-D to display a list of phone numbers and protocols, including the transmission speed, type of parity, and the number of start bits (Figure 11.2). Press **D**, then select the menu number to auto-dial the number and make the connection.

You can change the protocol at any time before making contact using the Alt-P menu (Figure 11.3). If you're using a Hayes-compatible modem, enter **AT** to alert the modem to the change of protocol.

```
-[ Command Menu, Help and Status ]
 Alt-A Translate Table        Alt-J Function Key Set    Alt-S Split Scrn Toggle
 Alt-B Beeps and Bells        Alt-K Change Comm Port    Alt-T Screen Dump
 Alt-C Clear Screen           Alt-L Log Drive Change    Alt-U Scroll Back Toggle
 Alt-D Dial Phone             Alt-M ANSI Music Mode     Alt-V View/Edit File
 Alt-E Character Echo         Alt-N Invoke QINSTALL     Alt-W Disk Directory
 Alt-F SCRIPT Execution       Alt-O Change Sub-Dirs     Alt-X Exit Qmodem
 Alt-G Terminal Emulation     Alt-P Change Baud Rates   Alt-Y Delete a File
 Alt-H Hang-up Modem          Alt-Q Redial Last Number  Alt-Z Xon/Xoff Toggle
 Alt-I Program Info           Alt-R DOS Shell           Alt-Ø Session Log Toggle

 Alt-8    8 Bit Toggle        Alt-1 BS-DEL Switch       Ctrl-Home  Capture File
 Up-Arrow Scroll Back         PgDn  Download Files      Ctrl-End   BREAK Signal
 Shft-Tab Add Linefeed        PgUp  Upload Files        Ctrl-PrtSc Printer Echo
                              -[ EGA Modes ]
      Alt-2 80×25  Alt-3 80×35  Alt-4 80×43  Alt-5 80×50  Alt-6 80×57

    ------[ Qmodem Toggles ]------   -[ Time ]-    ------[ Copyright ]------
 Echo      Off  Capture      Off    16:17:31     The Forbin Project
 Linefeeds Off  ScrollBack   ON                  4945 Colfax Avenue S.
 Xon/Xoff  ON   Printer      Off                 Minneapolis, MN  55409
 Beeps     ON   LOG Session  Off                 Support # : 612-824-1451
 Music     Off  8th bit usage ON                 Data Line : 612-824-8167
 -------[ Qmodem SST Version 3.Ø Production. Compiled April 18, 1987 ]
        Press any key combination, [F1] for Help, or [ENTER] to return
```

Figure 11.1: *QMODEM help menu*

```
-[ Qmodem Phone Book ]
 Page  1 of A:\QMODEM.FON
[D]                    Name              Number      Comm      Script
 1  The Forbin Project, Home of Qmodem 1-612-824-8167  3ØØ-8-N-1  [blank]
 2  compuserve                            977-9758   12ØØ-7-E-1  [blank]
 3  genie                                 284-9343   12ØØ-7-E-1  [blank]
 4  hug                                16169823956   3ØØ-8-N-1  [blank]
 5                                                    3ØØ-7-N-1  [blank]
 6                                                    3ØØ-7-N-1  [blank]
 7                                                    3ØØ-7-N-1  [blank]
 8                                                    3ØØ 7-N-1  [blank]
 9                                                    3ØØ-7-N-1  [blank]
1Ø                                                    3ØØ-7-N-1  [blank]

-[ Options ]

         C - Clear Entry(s)          O - Other Information
         D - Dial Number(s)          R - Revise an Entry
         E - rEvise Prefix Codes   PgDn - Show Next Page
         L - Load new FON File     PgUp - Show Previous Page
         M - Manual Dial a Number

              Select ?

              Enter a Phone Book command, [Esc] to Exit
```

Figure 11.2: *QMODEM dialing directory*

```
Qmodem SST Version 3.0 Production. Compiled April 18, 1987.
Copyright (C) 1984,87 -- The Forbin Project and John Friel III
Initial screen size = 80 x 24
Scroll-Back lines available = 36
  ┌[ Set Modem Speed ]────────────────────────────────
Qmod│    Current setting is COM1:    300,E,7,1
    │  ┌──────────────Speed──────────────────────┐
    │   A) 300   B) 1200    C) 2400  D) 4800
    │   E) 9600  F) 19200    G) 38400
    │  ┌───────────────Parity─────────────────────┐
    │   H) Even        I) Odd         J) None
    │  ┌──Data Bits──────────Stop Bits──────┐
    │   K) 7    L) 8       M) 1     N) 2
    │
    │   Selection(s) [CR=Save ESC=Exit] ?
```

    [→←] Movement   [SpaceBar] Select Topic   [Letter] Immediate Selection

Figure 11.3: *Menu for changing protocol settings*

Using Your Modem

You're ready to communicate over the telephone line when your modem is installed and you have a communications program. Before starting, make sure that you have the telephone number of the person or service you want to contact, and the protocol that they use. If you're not sure, start by assuming 300 baud, no parity, 8 data bits, and 1 stop bit. (Although 1200 and 2400 baud modems are now common, it is safest to start with 300 baud, the baud rate that all modems and information services can recognize.)

Let's prepare your computer and software. We'll assume you have a communications program that configures the computer's serial port. If your program doesn't, use the DOS mode command

MODE COM1:300,N,8,1

to set the protocol.

Preparing Your Computer

Before making the call, follow these steps:

1. Start your computer.

2. Load your communications software.

3. Turn on your modem.

4. Set the protocol. Use your program's facility for setting the baud rate, parity, and the number of data and stop bits.

Now make the connection to go online.

Communicating with Auto-Dial, Auto-Answer Modems

Follow these steps to connect with an external or internal auto-dial, auto-answer modem using Hayes-compatible software.

1. Type **AT** and then press ◄─┘. The screen will display "OK," indicating that the modem is ready to communicate.

2. If you have a tone dialing system (TouchTone), type **ATDT** followed by the phone number; then press ◄─┘. (Type **ATDP** if you have pulse dialing.) The modem will dial the phone number and connect with the other phone. Most programs will report if the line is busy or didn't answer. If so, wait a while and try again.

3. Begin transmitting, or log on to the service according to the instructions provided.

Communicating with Manual-Dial Modems

To use a manual-dial modem, you must have a telephone near the modem. Follow these steps:

1. Dial the phone number.

2. When you hear a high-pitched sound, turn the modem's switch to the originate setting. Then hang up the receiver.

3. Begin transmitting, or log on to the service according to the instructions provided.

Communicating with Acoustic Couplers

To communicate with an acoustic coupler, you must have a telephone handset that fits snugly into the modem's rubber cups.

1. Dial the phone number.

2. When you hear a high-pitched sound, quickly insert the phone in the rubber cups and then turn the modem's switch to the originate setting.

3. Begin transmitting, or log on to the service according to the instructions provided.

Communicating over the telephone, to individuals or information services, can be exciting and educational. But because you're dealing with sophisticated hardware that must be set up to exact protocol, and because of the sometimes uncertain quality of the phone lines, there is always the possibility of errors. If you see garbage on the screen or are unable to connect, check your protocol settings and modem connections. Most services have a regular phone number you can call to speak with a service representative if you need help.

Exploring Information Services

Using a modem, you can communicate with any computer, anywhere in the world, as long as it too has a modem. You can call a friend, communicate with the office, or transmit proposals to clients and business associates. You can also use an information service to do research, make airline reservations, purchase stocks, or get the latest sports scores.

Information services provide a range of useful programs, databases, and products that you can access with your modem. You dial a local telephone number to connect to the service, and pay a connect charge for each minute you remain online. Some services charge more during prime-time business hours than they do for nights, weekends, and holidays, but rates range anywhere from $5 to $25 per hour. (Charges for specialty and professional databases can be substantially higher.)

CompuServe Information Service is a popular example. Although it is located in Ohio, you connect to it by dialing a local toll-free number. To log on to CompuServe, enter your ID number and password. Charges are based on hourly rates, but are applied per minute and are billed directly to your bank charge card. Because anyone with your ID and password can connect to CompuServe, make sure you keep them private.

Once on the service, you can go directly to the feature you want or work through a series of menus, starting with main menu shown in Figure 11.4. CompuServe menus change periodically as they bring new services and programs online.

```
  9 Order CompuServe Information Manager Upgrade
    (Above Articles are Free)
 10 Online Today
 11 Specials/Contests Menu (Free)

Enter choice !


CompuServe                    TOP

  1 Member Assistance (FREE)
  2 Find a Topic (FREE)
  3 Communications/Bulletin Bds.
  4 News/Weather/Sports
  5 Travel
  6 The Electronic MALL/Shopping
  7 Money Matters/Markets
  8 Entertainment/Games
  9 Hobbies/Lifestyles/Education
 10 Reference
 11 Computers/Technology
 12 Business/Other Interests

Enter choice number !
 TTY    ONLINE   1200-7-E-1   [Home]=?  ◄=◄ 8      X ♪        ↑      00:00:42
```

Figure 11.4: *CompuServe main menu*

For example, suppose you're planning a trip out of town and would like to find the weather conditions at your destination before packing. Select item 4 in the main menu—News/Weather/Sports—to display the menu shown in Figure 11.5. Press 4 to access the Weather menu that lists weather options (Figure 11.6). Finally, press 1 to select the NWS Public Weather service to reach the services that are available (Figure 11.7). Select the option that best suits your needs.

```
      5 Travel
      6 The Electronic MALL/Shopping
      7 Money Matters/Markets
      8 Entertainment/Games
      9 Hobbies/Lifestyles/Education
     10 Reference
     11 Computers/Technology
     12 Business/Other Interests

   Enter choice number !4

   News/Weather/Sports          NEWS

      1 Executive News Service (E$)
      2 NewsGrid
      3 AP Online
      4 Weather
      5 Sports
      6 The Business Wire
      7 Newspaper Library
      8 Entertainment News/Info
      9 Online Today Daily Edition

   Enter choice !
   TTY     ONLINE    1200-7-E-1     [Home]=?  ◀=◀ 8         X ♪          ↑'       00:03:28
```

Figure 11.5: *News and weather submenu*

```
   News/Weather/Sports          NEWS

      1 Executive News Service (E$)
      2 NewsGrid
      3 AP Online
      4 Weather
      5 Sports
      6 The Business Wire
      7 Newspaper Library
      8 Entertainment News/Info
      9 Online Today Daily Edition

   Enter choice !4

   News/Weather/Sports          WEATHER

   WEATHER

      1 NWS Public Weather
      2 AP Videotex Weather
      3 NWS Aviation Weather ($)
      4 Weather Maps

   Enter choice !
   TTY     ONLINE    1200-7-E-1     [Home]=?  ◀=◀ 8         X ♪          ↑       00:03:37
```

Figure 11.6: *Weather options*

```
         2 AP Videotex Weather
         3 NWS Aviation Weather ($)
         4 Weather Maps

     Enter choice !1

     CompuServe                  WEA-1


     PUBLIC WEATHER

         1 (SF) Short Term Forecasts
         2 (EF) Extended Forecasts
         3 (SW) Severe Weather Alerts
         4 (PP) Precipitation Probability
         5 (SS) State Summaries
         6 (CL) Daily Climatological Reports
         7 (SP) Sports and Recreation
         8 (MF) Marine Forecasts
         9 (AW) Aviation Weather
        10 (WM) Weather Maps

     Enter choice!
     TTY    ONLINE    1200-7-E-1   [Home]=?   ◀=◀ 8       X ♪              ↑      00:04:52
```

Figure 11.7: *Public Weather services*

Once you know the menu structure, you can go directly to the service you want in a few seconds. Your weather search would cost just a few cents.

Another nationwide information service is GEnie, sponsored by General Electric. You also navigate through GEnie by using a series of menus or by going directly to the service you want. GEnie excels in its diversity of interest groups, called *round tables,* for sharing your ideas and concerns (Figure 11.8).

Both CompuServe and GEnie include libraries of public domain programs that you can *download*—that is, transfer from the service to your own computer. Most of the programs have been written by interested users, like yourself, and who have donated them to the public. They also include *forums* sponsored by major software manufacturers. Through the forum, you can contact the manufacturer for information and assistance, or download the latest versions of printer drivers and other support programs.

Communicating in the Office

If you want to communicate with a computer right in your own office, you don't need a modem and phone line. Instead, you can connect your computers directly with a cable or through a network.

```
Enter #, or <H>elp?11

GEnie          PROFESSIONAL       Page 525
              Professional Services

 1. Public Forum..NonProfit Connection
 2. PhotoSource International
 3. Photography RT
 4. Desktop Publishers (DTP) RT
 5. LEGACY, The Law RoundTable
 6. Writers' RoundTable
 7. MIDI/WorldMusic RT
 8. Medical RT
 9. Religion & Ethics RT
1Ø. Home Office/Small Business RT
11. Education RoundTable
12. A Law Enforcement RoundTable
13. Aviation RoundTable
14. Japan RT
15. Jerry Pournelle RT

Item #, or <RETURN> for more?
 TTY    ONLINE   12ØØ-7-E-1    [Home]=?   ◄=◄ 8 EC    X ♪         ↑        ØØ:Ø1:5Ø
```

Figure 11.8: *The first of GEnie's professional interest options*

Hard-Wiring Computers

To share a file with another user, you could just give them a copy of your floppy disk. But this won't work when your disks don't fit the other user's disk drives. Most laptop computers, and many desktop computers, rely entirely on 3½-inch drives, so they can't use 5¼-inch floppies.

The solution is to *hard-wire* the two computers—connect them directly using a cable—and then transfer the files with a communications program.

As laptops become popular, the problem of incompatible drive sizes is more fre-quent, so special file-transfer software packages have become available. Such programs designate one machine as the *local* or *master* station, the other as the *remote* or *slave.* With both computers running the program, the master has direct access to the slave's disk, so the slave can run unattended once it is set up.

The master can list and change directories on the slave, transfer files to it, and initi-ate transmission of files from the slave to the master. Because transfer software packages are dedicated to direct file transfer, they are not limited to the baud rates of 300, 1200, or even 2400 found on modems, but can communicate at the highest speed possible over serial or parallel connections.

For example, one program, Fastlynx, can operate at up to 230,000 baud, transferring 1Mb of data per minute using a special *turbo* mode. It would take one hour to transfer a 1Mb file at 2400 baud.

All of the programs come packaged with both 5¹/₄-inch and 3¹/₂-inch disks, and most include a serial cable to connect the systems through their serial ports. Some of the cables include both 9-pin and 25-pin serial connectors on both ends so you do not need an adapter. A few transfer programs support communications through the parallel port, and include either a separate parallel cable or a combined serial/parallel cable with all of the connectors on each end.

Here's a brief review of several popular transfer packages:

The Brooklyn Bridge supports both serial and parallel transfers and includes both kinds of cables. The serial cable has both 9-pin and 25-pin connectors on both ends. In addition to transferring, the program can find, rename, delete, move, and view files on the slave. It is available from:

Fifth Generation Systems, Inc.
10049 N. Reiger Road
Baton Rouge, LA 70809
(800) 873-4384

DirecLink supports serial and parallel transfers and offers an optional cable package. The program can find, rename, delete, and move files, as well as compress them for faster transfer. It is available from:

Micro-Z, Inc.
4 Santa Bella Road
Rolling Hills, CA 90274
(213) 377-1640

Fastlynx supports both serial and parallel transfers and includes both cables. The serial cable has both 9-pin and 25-pin connectors on both ends. The program can rename, delete, and view files on the slave, but cannot move them in one operation. (*Moving* a file means automatically deleting the original file after transferring it to a new disk or system. With Fastlynx, you'd have to transfer the file and then delete it yourself.) It is available from:

> Rupp Corporation
> 7285 Franklin Avenue
> Los Angeles, CA 90046
> (800) 852-7877

Hotwire uses serial transfers and includes a cable with both 9-pin and 25-pin connectors on both ends. It can find, rename, delete, move, and print files on the slave. It also supports transfer of files over a modem. It is available from:

> Datastorm Technologies, Inc.
> P. O. Box 1471
> Columbia, MO 65205
> (314) 443-3282

Laplink III includes a combined serial and parallel cable for transfers through either port. The cable includes a parallel connector and both 9-pin and 25-pin serial connectors on each end. It can rename, delete, and view files on the slave, but cannot print them or move them. To print a file, you have to exit Laplink and then use the DOS command PRINT or a word processing program. It is available from:

> Traveling Software, Inc.
> 18702 N. Creek Parkway
> Bothell, WA 98011
> (800) 662-2652

Paranet Turbo only supports communications through parallel ports and includes an 8-foot parallel cable. It can find, rename, delete, and move files, but cannot print them. Paranet also includes a utility to back up files from your hard disk. It is available from:

> Nicat Development Corporation
> 207-788 Beatty Street
> Vancouver, British Columbia V6B M1
> (604) 681-3421

PC-Hookup allows for serial and parallel communications and supports transfers over a modem. It includes a serial cable with both 9-pin and 25-pin connectors, and can find, move, delete, and rename files. It is available from:

Brown Bag Software
2155 South Bascom Avenue
Campbell, CA 95008
(800) 523-0764

Using a DOS Alternative

Your version of DOS might have its own transfer program provided as a service by the manufacturer. For example, Zenith Data Systems includes with DOS its own program, ZCOM, for transferring files over the serial port. While it lacks the file-management functions of the commercial programs, it can transmit files to the slave and initiate transmission of files from the slave.

With the program installed in two computers, you can transfer files at speeds of up to 115,200 baud, although speeds higher than 9600 are not recommended. At higher speeds, even minor communication problems, such as electrical interference, result in a large number of transmission errors.

You can have one computer run ZCOM in the server (or slave) mode by entering

ZCOM SERVER

at the DOS prompt. That computer can then be left unattended since all file transfers are controlled by the other system—the master.

You should use the MODE command to set both computers at the same baud rate. If you do not, the *scan* option will detect the baud rate of the server and set the master's rate to match.

You must have your own cables and be able to get the program on disks formatted for each machine. But ZCOM is easy to use with just the fundamental options for transferring files (see Table 11.1).

Table 11.1: *ZCOM Options*

ZCOM Option	Function
Receive <*file name*>	Directs the server to transmit the named file
Transmit <*file name*>	Sends the named file to the server
Files *.*	Lists the files on the server's disk; other wildcards and file specifications can be used
Baud	Sets the baud rate on both computers
Scan	Scans the server to determine the baud rate
Password	Sends an optional password to the server to initiate contact
Connect	Connects to a Hayes-compatible modem
Disconnect	Disconnects from the modem
Quit	Ends ZCOM at the user end; the server remains in ZCOM
Abort	Ends ZCOM at both computers
Ldrv	Changes the server's default drive
CDir	Changes the server's default directory

Solving Problems with Full-Featured Networking

Hard-wiring two computers is fine if you only want to transfer files. In order to use a program on the other computer, however, you'd have to transfer it to your machine, disconnect, and then run the program from DOS. You may also have to contend with different versions of data files on both machines. You might transfer a data file, make changes to it, and forget to copy the edited file back to the original computer.

Networking is the solution to these problems. When you *network* two or more computers, each can share the resources of the other. You can read and write files directly on the other machine's disk without transferring those files to your own storage. You can also use a printer that's connected to another computer.

Building a network is often a complicated process, however. Some networking systems are just software programs that use cables connected to the serial ports of the machines. But most networks require a network card installed in an empty expansion slot as well as software that supplements DOS and controls the flow of data through the network.

The way networks operate varies. Some use a central computer, called the *file server,* for storing applications and shared files, and for acting as the network controller. The server can also include file areas for electronic mail messages for other computers on the network. The computers that access the server are called *workstations.* This configuration allows for tight security of programs and files. For example, the Novell Netware network allows you to determine which directories and files each workstation can access.

Other networks let each computer access files in all other computers without a central server. The TOPS network, for example, provides two general types of functions: file service for sharing files and printer service for sharing printers. Each computer on the network can start up as a server, a client, or both. A *server* makes files and printers available to others on the network in a procedure called *publishing.* A directory that's been published is called a *volume.* A *client* accesses the published files and printers of the server in a procedure called *mounting.* When you mount a volume, you are telling your computer to treat the published volume as a new disk drive. If you mount a volume as drive E, you can log on to the server's directory by typing **E:**, just as if it were a disk in your own computer. You can be a server and client at the same time, letting others use your resources while you use those of others.

Security is provided several ways. If you do not publish any disks as a server, no one can access your files. You can also establish a password that clients need in order to access your files, or you can "hide" your files from others on the network.

You print over the network in three ways:

Local	You are using a printer directly connected to your station.
Remote	You are using a printer connected to some other station in the network. The printer must first have been published by the computer, and you must mount it on yours.
Network	You are using a printer connected directly to the network, not to any one station.

Because versions of the TOPS hardware and software are available for non-DOS machines, the network can be used in offices with both IBM and Apple Macintosh computers. You can even copy files between IBM and Macintosh systems using the network's TCOPY command, its own version of the DOS program XCOPY. For example, the command

TCOPY D: * .DAT C: /T

copies and converts Macintosh files on the network drive D to DOS format on your own drive C.

Because of the complexity of networks, most organizations assign one person as the *network administrator.* This person assigns passwords and security levels, sets up the physical hardware, and advises network users.

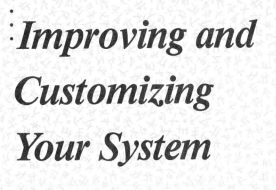

Part Three

Improving and Customizing Your System

Chapter Twelve

Enhancing DOS

*M*any computer users find DOS cumbersome and limited. DOS is not user-friendly—to work with DOS you must plod through the directory structure, keeping track of the location of your files and the paths to subdirectories. While you'll be more comfortable with DOS commands once you're familiar with them and your hand-me-down, the commands are not intuitive. You have to memorize them, remember their syntax and punctuation, and always return to the DOS prompt to access DOS.

To overcome the limitations of DOS, your hand-me-down's previous owner might have installed a DOS shell on your hard disk or supplied one on a floppy disk. A DOS *shell* is a program that replaces the DOS prompt as a means of communicating with the operating system.

In this chapter, you'll learn about DOS shells, programs that back up your disk, and utilities that can recover deleted files. If your hand-me-down does not include a DOS shell or utility software, you'll learn how these can be valuable additions to your software library.

Working with DOS Shells

DOS provides a full range of functions for dealing with your files. Unfortunately, if you're not familiar with DOS commands, looking at a screen that just displays an A> or C> may be intimidating. DOS error messages that are not helpful and do not accurately explain the cause of the problem are also alarming. For example, the error message "Bad command or file name" could appear when you enter the incorrect path, misspell a file name, use the incorrect syntax, or try to run a program that doesn't exist. When you see this error message, it's up to you to determine what you did wrong. In addition, while subdirectories can make it easier to deal with files, they can also result in inordinately long and complex commands, easily prone to errors. DOS shells provide a new way of working with DOS, making it easier for you to manage files and directories.

Different shells have different ranges of features. However, all shells have some basic benefits. Instead of discussing all of the features available in each shell program, this chapter focuses on functions found in popular DOS shells.

Most shells are TSR (terminate-and-stay-resident) programs. TSR programs load into your computer's memory and stay active while you work on another application. When you start a program from within the DOS shell, the shell *collapses,* or tucks itself away in memory. When you exit the application, the shell reappears in full on your screen.

Managing Your Files

DOS shells provide an easy way to manipulate individual files or groups of files. Most use a point-and-shoot method, letting you copy, delete, rename, or move a file to another disk or directory by pointing to its name on the screen using the mouse pointer or cursor movement keys.

Figure 12.1 shows the file management screen from the program QDOS II. To erase a file, for instance, you press the up or down arrow key to highlight its name in the directory on the right side of the screen. Then you press the right arrow key to select Erase from the top command line.

DOS shells often provide functions that aren't available in DOS. Most shells, for example, provide the move, find, and edit functions, and let you rename directories.

The Move function copies a file to another location and deletes the original in one step. The Find function reports the directory in which a file is located. The Edit function displays the highlighted file in a built-in word processor, making it easy to create or modify files such as AUTOEXEC.BAT or CONFIG.SYS without first having to load a word processing program. The Rename function, used to change the name of files, also allows you to change the name of a directory without transferring all of its files.

In place of wildcards, most shells let you *tag* files in the point-and-shoot display—designating groups of files that you want to copy, erase, rename, or move at one time.

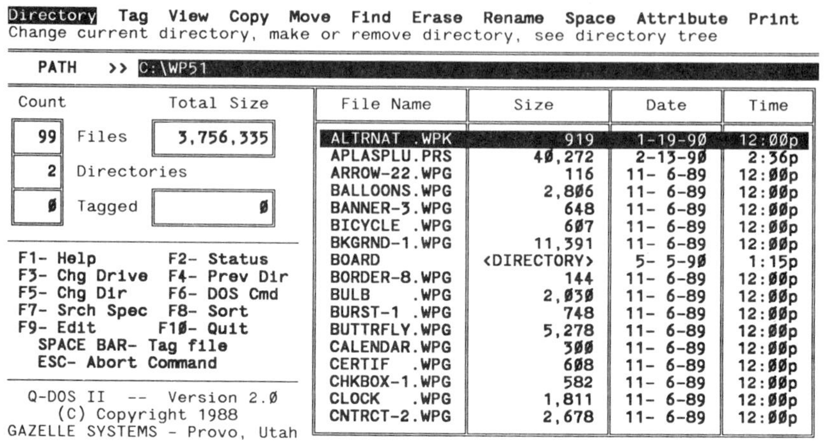

```
┌──────────────────────────────────────────────────────────────────────┐
│ Directory  Tag  View  Copy  Move  Find  Erase  Rename  Space  Attribute  Print │
│ Change current directory, make or remove directory, see directory tree │
│                                                                        │
│   PATH   >> C:\WP51                                                    │
│  ┌──────────────────────────────┐  ┌──────────────────────────────────┐ │
│  │ Count        Total Size      │  │ File Name    Size    Date   Time │ │
│  │ ┌──┐                         │  │ ALTRNAT .WPK     919  1-19-90 12:00p│ │
│  │ │99│ Files    3,756,335      │  │ APLASPLU.PRS  40,272  2-13-90  2:36p│ │
│  │ └──┘                         │  │ ARROW-22.WPG     116 11- 6-89 12:00p│ │
│  │ ┌─┐                          │  │ BALLOONS.WPG   2,806 11- 6-89 12:00p│ │
│  │ │2│ Directories              │  │ BANNER-3.WPG     648 11- 6-89 12:00p│ │
│  │ └─┘                          │  │ BICYCLE .WPG     607 11- 6-89 12:00p│ │
│  │ ┌─┐          ┌──────────┐    │  │ BKGRND-1.WPG  11,391 11- 6-89 12:00p│ │
│  │ │0│ Tagged   │        0 │    │  │ BOARD        <DIRECTORY>  5- 5-90 1:15p│ │
│  │ └─┘          └──────────┘    │  │ BORDER-8.WPG     144 11- 6-89 12:00p│ │
│  │                              │  │ BULB    .WPG   2,030 11- 6-89 12:00p│ │
│  │ F1- Help       F2- Status    │  │ BURST-1 .WPG     748 11- 6-89 12:00p│ │
│  │ F3- Chg Drive  F4- Prev Dir  │  │ BUTTRFLY.WPG   5,278 11- 6-89 12:00p│ │
│  │ F5- Chg Dir    F6- DOS Cmd   │  │ CALENDAR.WPG     300 11- 6-89 12:00p│ │
│  │ F7- Srch Spec  F8- Sort      │  │ CERTIF  .WPG     608 11- 6-89 12:00p│ │
│  │ F9- Edit       F10- Quit     │  │ CHKBOX-1.WPG     582 11- 6-89 12:00p│ │
│  │   SPACE BAR- Tag file        │  │ CLOCK   .WPG   1,811 11- 6-89 12:00p│ │
│  │   ESC- Abort Command         │  │ CNTRCT-2.WPG   2,678 11- 6-89 12:00p│ │
│  │                              │  └──────────────────────────────────┘ │
│  │ Q-DOS II  --  Version 2.0    │                                      │
│  │    (C) Copyright 1988        │                                      │
│  │ GAZELLE SYSTEMS - Provo, Utah│                                      │
│  └──────────────────────────────┘                                     │
└──────────────────────────────────────────────────────────────────────┘
```

Figure 12.1: *File management screen of QDOS II*

One of the greatest benefits of shells, however, is that they display the disk tree structure graphically, letting you see at a glance the relationships between directories and subdirectories (Figure 12.2). This feature should help you navigate DOS's potentially complex directory structure. List the files in any subdirectory or log on to one by pointing to its name on the screen.

Viewing Your Files

The DOS command TYPE lets you view the contents of a file as long as it is in ASCII format. You get nonsense characters and symbols when you try to display a file that contains control codes.

Using a *file viewer,* the DOS shell displays application files as ASCII text, ignoring formatting and other codes that would garble the display. File viewing lets you quickly review the contents of a file from the directory listing so you can make sure you have the proper file highlighted before taking any action.

Norton Commander, for example, has a powerful View command that can display files from a wide range of programs, including eight databases, nine spreadsheets, nine word processing programs, and graphic files in the PCX format.

You can also split the screen into two windows, the directory list on the left and a view window on the right. As you point to a file in the directory list, its contents appear automatically in the view window (Figure 12.3).

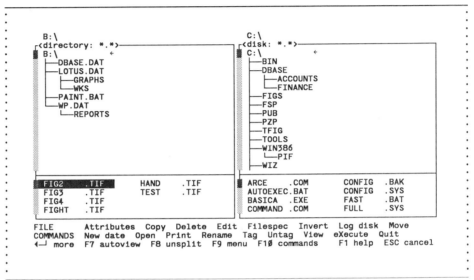

Figure 12.2: *XTreePro Gold displaying two disk tree structures*

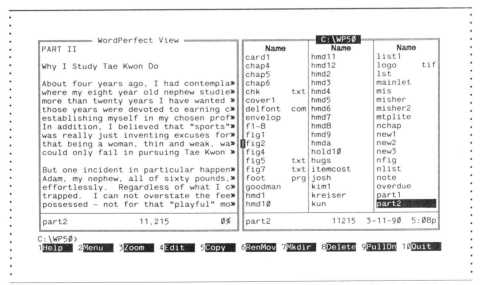

Figure 12.3: *Norton Commander's View mode with the contents of the highlighted file in the other window*

Unfortunately, several shells are limited in the number of viewers they have available. Some only display ASCII files, for example. If you use many application programs, look for a DOS shell with more file viewers.

Launching an Application

The methods used to start an application from within a shell vary. Many shells use a point-and-shoot approach—you highlight the application you want to run on the directory listing and then press a specific function key.

DOS Partner uses a menu approach. When you install the program, it scans your disk, looking for executable applications. When you select Applications from the program's main menu, it displays a point-and-shoot menu listing your major programs (Figure 12.4).

DOS Partner has a different way of organizing your files. You log on to a drive using a drive management screen that simulates the front panel of your computer (Figure 12.5). The file management screen then displays directories, and groups files into *folders* according to their extensions (Figure 12.6). This feature is useful when you

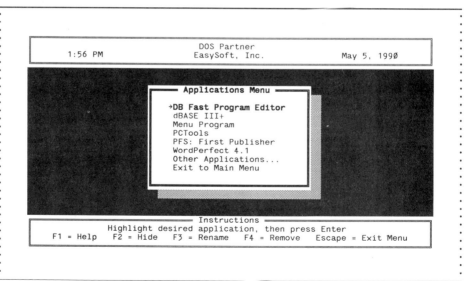

Figure 12.4: *DOS Partner automatically creates a menu of your applications*

are working with applications that use specific file extensions for user data files. You can configure DOS Partner to use the "file cabinet metaphor" referring to folders, drawers, and subdrawers, or to the traditional files, directories, and subdirectories.

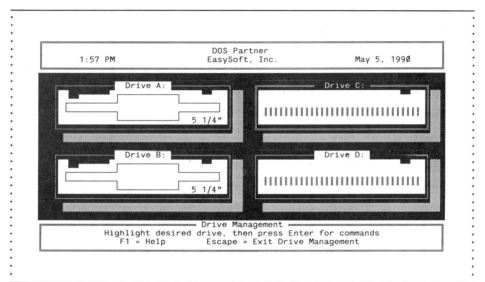

Figure 12.5: *Logging on to drives in DOS Partner*

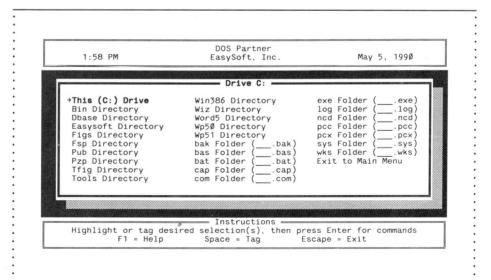

Figure 12.6: *Files grouped by extension in DOS Partner*

Making Your Own Menus

When you use your computer primarily for running just a few applications, you might not want to be bothered with the full directory listing. Many DOS shells let you create custom point-and-shoot menus that list just selected applications.

Bourbaki's 1dir +, for example, includes the traditional directory, with the function key commands shown at the bottom of the screen (Figure 12.7). However, you can customize the bottom command line to include your favorite applications instead of the shell commands. Run the application from the command line simply by pressing the function key shown over its name (Figure 12.8).

Other DOS shells let you create custom menus that are not associated with the function keys. User menus in Norton Commander, for instance, use a single letter to activate an application (Figure 12.9).

Securing Your Data

Some users worry that menu shells invite unauthorized access. They believe that hiding important files in deep levels of subdirectories, and using unrelated directory names, will discourage, or at least slow down, prying eyes and hands.

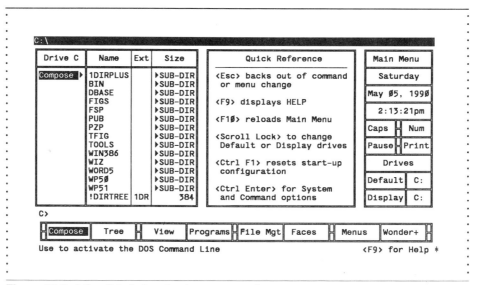

Figure 12.7: *1dir + lists its function key commands*

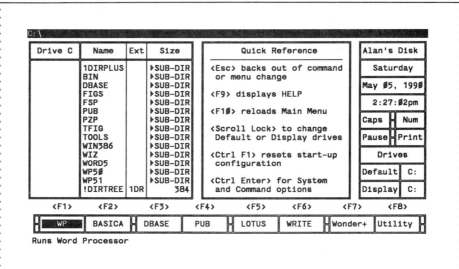

Figure 12.8: *Modifying the command line to your needs*

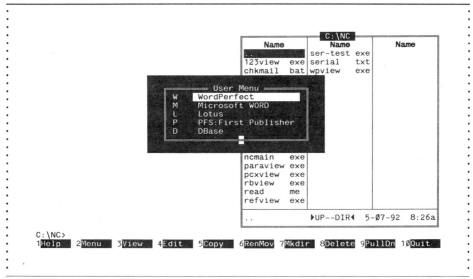

Figure 12.9: *Custom menu created with Norton Commander*

However, 1dir+ allows optional password protection on several levels. You can have system-level security by requiring a password to log on to the computer at bootup. Once you set up the password in 1dir+, you add the command

DEVICE = C:\1DIRPLUS\USERON.SYS

to CONFIG.SYS, and the command

USERON

to AUTOEXEC.BAT.

The system file disables the use of Ctrl-Break to terminate AUTOEXEC.BAT so the batch file will continue to run until the proper password is entered. (This does not, however, prevent booting from a separate system disk in drive A.) You can also add password protection to individual menus and commands.

Streamlining Hard-Disk Backup

You can perform full or incremental backups with many general-purpose DOS shells by using their COPY command. For example, QDOSII can make an incremental backup of files with the archive flag on, turning the flag off when done. DOS Partner's COPY command will even format the destination disk and prompt you to insert a disk when one becomes full. Nevertheless, independent backup programs can make backups faster and more convenient.

Some backup programs save files in their own special format. Like DOS Backup, Point-and-Shoot PC-Fullback and Perfect Backup use a non-DOS format and require their own restoration programs. Other programs, such as BackEZ, Backpak, and Fullback, save files in a format that you can restore using the commands COPY or XCOPY.

Let's take a closer look at two backup programs that use different approaches.

Using Intelligent Backup

Intelligent Backup is a menu-driven program from Sterling Software that provides some unique features for making backups. You select options from a main menu that lets you back up and restore files, configure the system, and perform some file management tasks normally found in DOS shells (Figure 12.10).

You can have the program back up files using its default parameters, or you can customize the process in the Backup Level Selection menu (Figure 12.11). If you have not yet made a full backup, the FULL option will be highlighted automatically in the menu. Because most of the files will have to be backed up, the settings under

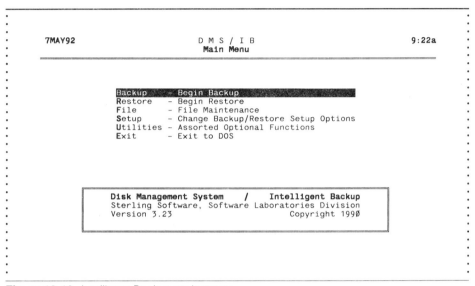

Figure 12.10: *Intelligent Backup main menu*

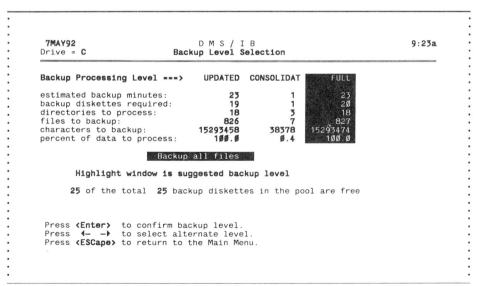

Figure 12.11: *Backup Level Selection menu*

the UPDATED column, normally used for an incremental backup, will be almost identical to the full backup options. Use the consolidated backup option to organize your incremental backup disks.

Intelligent Backup reports its progress during the actual backup, estimating how long the backup will take, the number of directories, files, and characters that have been backed up, and how many remain (Figure 12.12). You can cancel the backup at any time.

It is just as easy to restore files. You can designate directories or files to be restored using the ? and * wildcards, or you can tag specific files in a restore directory (Figure 12.13). Several advanced options let you customize your restore operation even further.

If you want to reduce the number of floppy disks required for backup, you can choose between two methods of data compression. Using standard compression reduces file size up to 40%. You can also select super compression, which reduces file size up to 80% but increases backup time by about 50%.

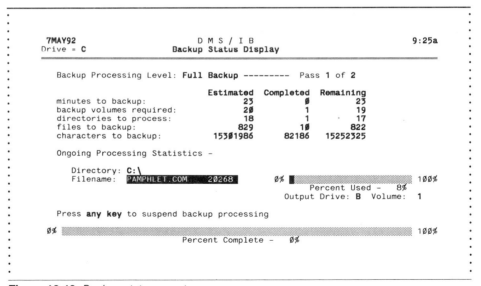

Figure 12.12: *Backup status report*

```
 7MAY92                        D M S / I B                          9:28a
                         Restore - Filename Selection List

                                Last Update          Backup
    Sel --Filename--    Size    Date/Time           Date/Time    Dir Name
    ****** Top ******
       ARCE.COM         5710   30MAY87 12:00p    7MAY92   9:26a   C:\
       AUTOEXEC.BAT       39    5MAY90  2:43p    7MAY92   9:26a   C:\
       BASICA.EXE      70848   15JUL85 12:09p    7MAY92   9:25a   C:\
       COMMAND.COM     23948    4SEP87  2:37p    7MAY92   9:25a   C:\
       CONFIG.BAK        146   15MAR90  2:53p    7MAY92   9:26a   C:\
       CONFIG.SYS         44   20MAR90  9:07a    7MAY92   9:26a   C:\
       FAST.BAT           17   10JUL88  9:14a    7MAY92   9:25a   C:\
       FULL.SYS           91   30AUG88  4:50p    7MAY92   9:25a   C:\
       FUNDS.BAT          23   20NOV88  3:15p    7MAY92   9:26a   C:\
       HPPS.COM         1669   26FEB88 12:35a    7MAY92   9:25a   C:\
       IB.BAT             43   30MAR88 11:08a    7MAY92   9:25a   C:\
       IBCHK.BAT          84   15DEC87  9:06a    7MAY92   9:26a   C:\
       IMCAP.COM        9566   15MAY86  5:14p    7MAY92   9:25a   C:\
       MARK.COM          256   27MAR88  6:57p    7MAY92   9:26a   C:\
       MORT.BAS         3724   14SEP89  5:51p    7MAY92   9:26a   C:\

    Mark         Unmark    Restore   Print    Show     Quit
    Mark file to be restored
```

Figure 12.13: *Restore directory*

Using SitBack

If you want the security of backups but don't want to spend the time making them, consider SitBack from SitBack Technologies. SitBack is a memory-resident program that automatically backs up your files during periods of inactivity. When the program senses that you haven't pressed a key for about two minutes, it scans your disk to back up new or updated files. It will even continue the backup in the background as you work with your application.

When you install the program, you designate the disk drive to use for the backup. As you work, keep a backup disk loaded and ready. SitBack will only back up files to a disk with a volume label beginning *SB,* so it will not destroy an application or data disk that you have inserted in the target drive. This type of backup is particularly useful for incremental backups that can be made to one disk, or for backing up a hard disk to another hard disk.

As with most backup programs, you can tell SitBack to exclude certain files and you can customize it in a number of ways. For example, you can inactivate the keyboard delay option or set it to an interval between 20 and 60,000 seconds. You can also designate specific times of the day to back up files. For example, you can activate SitBack during lunch or dinner breaks.

Recovering Lost Files

Shell and backup programs may be extremely useful and time saving, but you could always just use DOS. File-recovery programs, on the other hand, are worth their price even if you only have to use them once.

When you delete a file, DOS doesn't erase the data from the disk; it just alters the first character of the file's name in the directory. As long as you don't save another file that takes up the directory space of the deleted file, or any of the sectors in that file's chain, as explained in Chapter 7, the deleted file can be completely recovered.

MACE Utilities and Norton Utilities are perhaps the most well-known data-recovery packages. As an example of data recovery, let's consider several programs that are part of MACE Utilities. If you have a hard-disk drive, you can set up MACE Utilities to work from a main menu.

Undeleting a File

To recover a deleted file, type **UNDELETE** followed by the drive and path in which the file was located. MACE searches the directory, prompting you to restore each deleted file that it finds. When you enter the first letter of the file name, the utility inserts it into the directory and confirms that the file was successfully restored.

You can use the program to restore an entire subdirectory at once. For example, suppose that you deleted all of the files in the Games directory, and then deleted the directory itself.

From the root directory, enter

   UNDELETE GAMES

to restore the directory entry, and then undelete all of the files that the directory originally contained by entering the first letter of each file.

Once you save a file that uses the directory space of a deleted file, the deleted file is lost forever. You also won't be able to recover executable program files whose sectors have been partially overwritten, even if the directory space was untouched. However, you may be able to salvage parts of deleted ASCII files as long as the directory listing is intact. Many recovery programs let you undelete files in a *manual* mode by searching the disk sector by sector for data you'd like to save to a new file. Most programs will display the contents of the sectors listed in the file's chain and let you confirm whether you want them restored. This option is only useful with ASCII or other text files, not with executable programs.

DOS version 3.3 Plus, distributed by Zenith Data Systems, includes the program GDU (general disk utilities). The program includes options for undeleting files and performing other disk services. Check your own version of DOS for utilities the manufacturer might have supplied.

Recovering a Formatted Disk

By regularly using special utility programs, you might be able to restore the files on a hard disk that you accidentally formatted. These utilities save a copy of the directory and FAT in a special file. As long as you didn't save any new files on the disk, the program can reconstruct the entire disk. Imagine the time this can save if you accidentally reformat your hard disk.

RXBAK is a MACE utility that saves key disk information. Run it every day to update the information with any changes you make. If you accidentally format your hard disk with the DOS command FORMAT, boot your computer with a floppy disk, insert the MACE Utility disk that contains the program UNFORMAT, and then enter

    UNFORMAT C:

The program searches the disk until it locates the data saved by RXBAK. Then it asks you to confirm the restoration.

Restoring a formatted floppy disk is slightly more difficult. When you use the DOS command FORMAT on a floppy disk, both low- and high-level formats are performed and any information saved by RXBAK will be lost. However, MACE comes with two alternate format programs: FORMATH for hard disks and FORMATF for floppy disks. Delete the DOS program FORMAT and install these MACE alternatives. Both programs format the disk by erasing only the FAT and root directory, not the data elsewhere on the disk. UNFORMAT will be able to recover your files without a problem.

Compressing a Disk

As your disk becomes full, it may not be possible for DOS to store your files in consecutive clusters. Files stored in nonconsecutive clusters are called *fragmented*, and the more fragmented files on your disk, the more time DOS needs to load and save files. In order to cut down on access time and extend the life of your drive, you can *compress*, or *unfragment*, your disk.

When you compress a disk, the computer rewrites every file so its data is contiguous. Since compression rewrites the entire disk, don't start the process until you're sure you don't want to restore any deleted files.

The amount of time it takes to compress a disk depends on its capacity and the number of unfragmented files. MACE Utilities includes the program FRAGCHK, which reports the number of fragmented files (Figure 12.14). If application or data files that you use often are fragmented, it pays to compress the disk.

Most compression programs display a cluster map showing the operation's progress. The map indicates where the program is moving files as the program makes them contiguous starting at the beginning of the disk or disk partition (Figure 12.15).

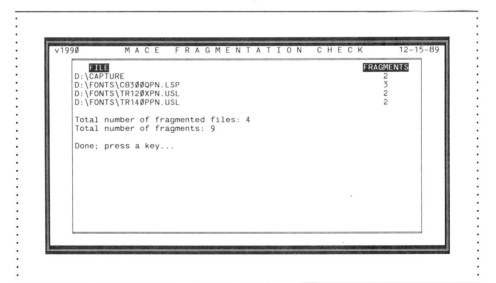

Figure 12.14: *FRAGCHK reports on the number of fragmented files*

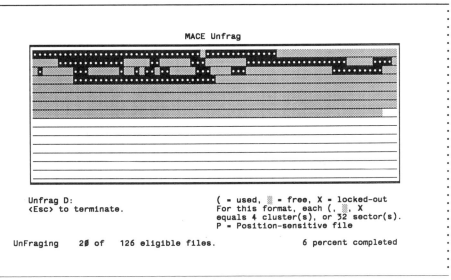

Figure 12.15: *Disk compression map of MACE Utilities*

Although compressing a large hard disk can take some time, the wait is worthwhile. If you were using a large application that was fragmented, you'll notice a definite increase in performance after compression.

Supercharging DOS

You can improve DOS one step further with programs that provide an integrated environment in which to work. These programs take the *desktop* approach, seeking to combine all of the tools you need in one package, figuratively putting everything on your desktop.

We'll look at two different approaches: a resident DOS utility, and Windows, a graphical user interface.

TSR Desktops

Take Charge! (the exclamation point is part of the name) is a TSR program that combines a DOS shell, custom menus, a communications program, and undelete, compression, and other disk utilities in one package.

Its menu program allows you to list up to 26 applications. But its real power lies in the utility menu that you can display instantly from the DOS prompt or while running an application by pressing Alt-spacebar (Figure 12.16).

From the utility menu, you can perform all of the customary DOS shell functions by selecting Disk Services or File Services. You can display a graphic tree of your directory structure, or perform point-and-shoot functions on individual files and groups of files (Figure 12.17).

The utility menu also lets you access the desktop utilities of a calculator, calendar, alarm clock, and database. For example, the calculator provides a "tape" output that you can send to your printer. You can even transfer the total into an application. For instance, suppose you're writing an invoice with a word processing program and have to total the items and subtract a discount. You can pop up the Take Charge! calculator, perform the math, and then move the total directly into the document.

Using the Alt-Shift key combination along with a function key, you can pop up any of the utility options directly without displaying the menu. For instance, with Take Charge! loaded, you can press Alt-Shift-F3 to use the calculator, or Alt-Shift-F7 to perform file services. When you're using an application program, the TSR portion of Take Charge! uses less than 20K of memory.

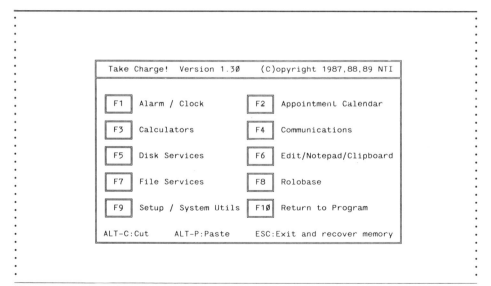

Figure 12.16: *Take Charge! utility menu*

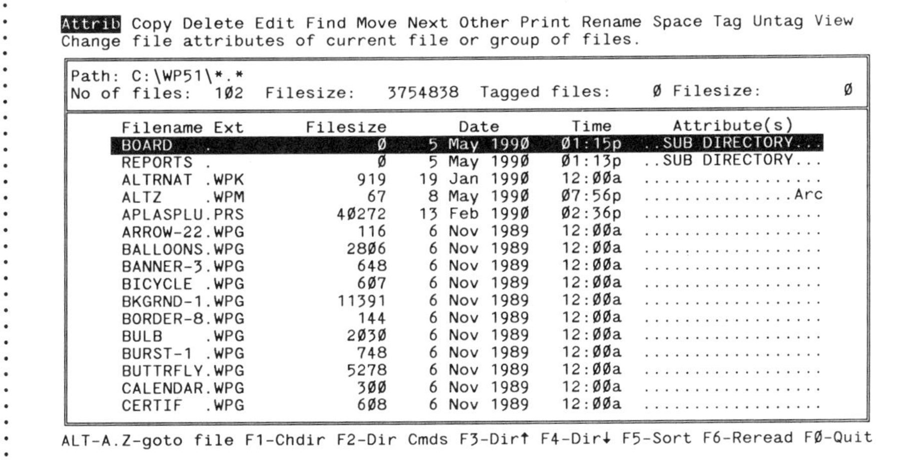

```
┌─────────────────────────────────────────────────────────────────────┐
│ Attrib Copy Delete Edit Find Move Next Other Print Rename Space Tag Untag View│
│ Change file attributes of current file or group of files.            │
│ ┌─────────────────────────────────────────────────────────────────┐ │
│ │ Path: C:\WP51\*.*                                                 │ │
│ │ No of files:  102  Filesize:   3754838  Tagged files:   0 Filesize:      0│ │
│ │                                                                   │ │
│ │   Filename Ext    Filesize      Date      Time    Attribute(s)    │ │
│ │   BOARD    .           0     5 May 1990  01:15p  ..SUB DIRECTORY...│ │
│ │   REPORTS  .           0     5 May 1990  01:13p  ..SUB DIRECTORY...│ │
│ │   ALTRNAT .WPK       919    19 Jan 1990  12:00a  ................. │ │
│ │   ALTZ    .WPM        67     8 May 1990  07:56p  ..............Arc  │ │
│ │   APLASPLU.PRS     40272    13 Feb 1990  02:36p  ................. │ │
│ │   ARROW-22.WPG       116     6 Nov 1989  12:00a  ................. │ │
│ │   BALLOONS.WPG      2806     6 Nov 1989  12:00a  ................. │ │
│ │   BANNER-3.WPG       648     6 Nov 1989  12:00a  ................. │ │
│ │   BICYCLE .WPG       607     6 Nov 1989  12:00a  ................. │ │
│ │   BKGRND-1.WPG     11391     6 Nov 1989  12:00a  ................. │ │
│ │   BORDER-8.WPG       144     6 Nov 1989  12:00a  ................. │ │
│ │   BULB    .WPG      2030     6 Nov 1989  12:00a  ................. │ │
│ │   BURST-1 .WPG       748     6 Nov 1989  12:00a  ................. │ │
│ │   BUTTRFLY.WPG      5278     6 Nov 1989  12:00a  ................. │ │
│ │   CALENDAR.WPG       300     6 Nov 1989  12:00a  ................. │ │
│ │   CERTIF  .WPG       608     6 Nov 1989  12:00a  ................. │ │
│ └─────────────────────────────────────────────────────────────────┘ │
│ ALT-A.Z-goto file F1-Chdir F2-Dir Cmds F3-Dir↑ F4-Dir↓ F5-Sort F6-Reread F0-Quit│
└─────────────────────────────────────────────────────────────────────┘
```

Figure 12.17: *Take Charge! file services menu*

PC Tools is another TSR desktop program. Version 6 of the program includes a DOS shell, a communications program, and hard-disk backup, recovery, and desktop utilities.

Microsoft Windows

While shells and TSR utilities use the basic framework provided by DOS, Windows provides a *GUI,* or graphical user interface. A GUI offers point-and-shoot capabilities for all functions using graphic symbols (*icons*) that represent DOS concepts, and full mouse support.

A typical Windows screen is shown in Figure 12.18. You can execute a program or select one of the commands on the top line through point-and-shoot. The icons at the bottom of the screen represent three desktop programs that are waiting in the background—a calculator, calendar, and simple database called the *cardfile.* Notice that the icons visually represent the functions of the programs.

Because of its graphic nature, Windows can display text characters using *screen fonts,* files that match the bit pattern of your printed characters (Figure 12.19). This provides a WYSIWYG (what you see is what you get) display so you can see exactly how your document will appear on paper.

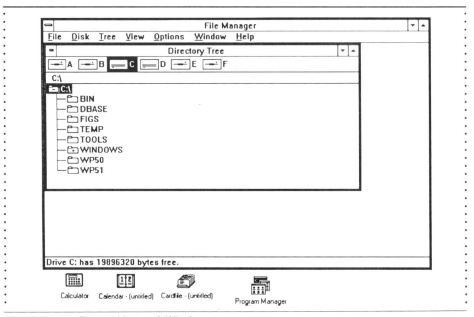

Figure 12.18: *Typical Microsoft Windows screen*

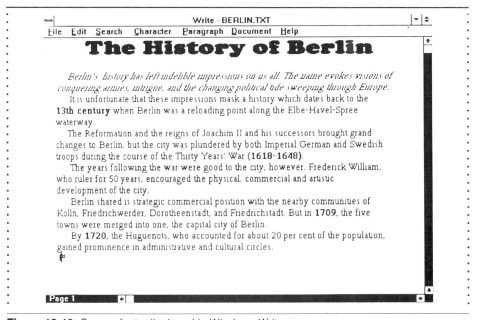

Figure 12.19: *Screen fonts displayed in Windows Write*

Windows also allows multitasking when you are using software specially designed for Windows. *Multitasking* is the capability to run more than one program or perform more than one function at a time.

Figure 12.20 shows two applications being used together—Paintbrush on the left and Windows Write on the right. The drawing of the keyboard lock was created in Paintbrush and was then transferred into a document being prepared by Windows Write.

Programs that are designated as *Windows applications* are designed to use the GUI that the environment provides. They can display screen fonts and can be held in the background when you pop up a desktop utility. Windows provides the printer and display drivers, which are shared by all applications.

While many non-Windows programs can be launched from within Windows, they cannot use the graphic environment or share the screen with other applications. They must have their own printer and display drivers. If you have enough computer memory, however, you can switch from one application to another, keeping one in the background.

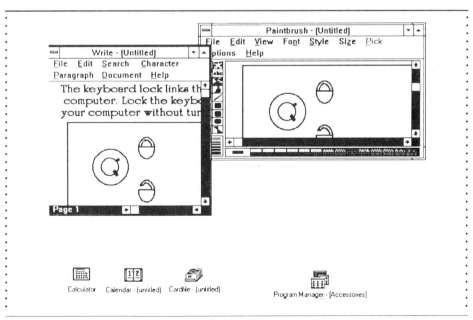

Figure 12.20: *Multiple applications running in Microsoft Windows*

Using Diagnostic Software

Now we'll look at diagnostic programs that go beyond the limited resources of CHKDSK. These programs analyze your system, report on its status, and often try to correct system problems. (You'll find information on obtaining these programs at the end of the chapter.)

First, let's examine two programs designed to maintain and improve the performance of disk drives. We'll then review some general-purpose diagnostic programs.

Spinrite II

Each time you add or change a disk file, fresh magnetic information is recorded on the disk and within the directory and FAT. This reinforces those areas of the disk but not the sector header, which is written only during the low-level format. The *sector headers* contain the address of the sector used by the FAT to locate a file.

Over a period of time, the sector header can fade until it is too weak to be read by DOS and is reported as a "Sector not found." Spinrite II, from Gibson Research, performs a low-level format of your hard disk, reenergizing the headers without destroying the data on the disk.

The program has two main options: a Quick Surface Scan and an Analysis that performs the actual low-level format.

The Surface Scan first checks the condition of key system components and then reads every track on the disk, looking for faulty sectors and displaying its progress on a track map.

While the Scan doesn't correct any bad sectors, it alerts you to potential problems and indicates that you should perform a low-level format.

The Analysis option evaluates the performance of your hard disk and then reports system parameters, as illustrated in Figure 12.21. It next determines if the current sector interleave is optimal for your system's actual performance, giving you the option of selecting a new interleave setting (Figure 12.22).

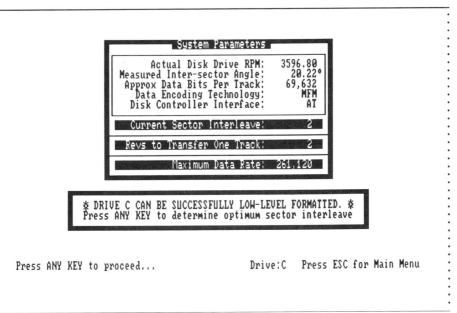

Figure 12.21: *Spinrite displays system parameters before beginning the low-level format*

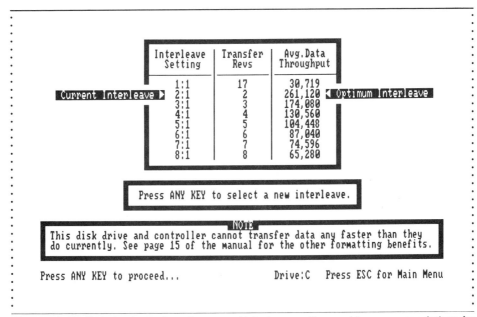

Figure 12.22: *Spinrite determines the current interleave setting and its recommendations for optimum performance*

Consecutively numbered sectors are not necessarily next to each other on the track. It takes time for the computer to process the information that it reads from a sector. If the sectors were actually consecutive, the system might read one sector, and then spin past the next sector before the computer was ready to read it. The system would then have to wait until the disk had spun all the way around again before reading the data from that sector, slowing down the time it would take to load files and run programs.

To prevent this from occurring, consecutively addressed sectors are often spaced apart to maintain a steady pace for reading or writing. By the time the system is ready to use the next sector, it is properly positioned under the read/write mechanism. The number of sectors between two "consecutive" ones is referred to as the *interleave.* If Spinrite II determines that the interleave setting is not efficient, it suggests a new one to use during the low-level format. Spinrite II completes the low-level format, changing the interleave if you choose to do so.

The time it takes to complete a low-level format depends on the *pattern testing depth* that you select. Each sector of the disk can be tested with a number of bit patterns. The larger the number of patterns, the longer the process takes but the more certain you can be of the disk's integrity. You can select 0, 5, 42, or 84 patterns. The most thorough test with 84 patterns could take all night.

MACE Utilities

MACE Utilities is a collection of some 25 programs aimed at diagnosing and fixing disk problems. The SYSTAT program, for example, displays statistics about your system's processor, disks, interfaces, and memory (Figure 12.23).

REMEDY performs a surface scan, looking for bad sectors. It transfers any data in bad sectors to good sectors, changing the file's chain in the FAT and marking the bad cluster as unusable. Results of the scan are displayed on a sector map that shows the location of system files and reports the number of sectors per cluster (Figure 12.24).

The ER program (short for *emergency room*) repairs damaged FAT's, directories, and boot sectors. It saves the original boot, FAT, or directory data to another disk, and then attempts to repair the damage. If the changes do not improve the drive's condition, you can restore the original structure using an UNDO command.

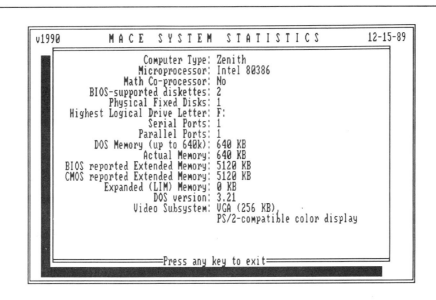

Figure 12.23: *MACE Utilities SYSTAT programs reports system resources*

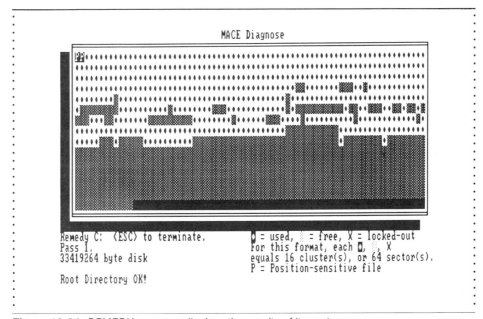

Figure 12.24: *REMEDY program displays the results of its sector scan*

Diagnostic Programs

While Spinrite II and MACE deal primarily with disks, there are programs that treat a wide range of system components. Here are summaries of four popular diagnostic programs:

Check It, from Touchstone Software, analyzes your system's speed and efficiency. It tests memory, disk drives, interface ports, video circuits, and printers. If it locates a memory error, it reports the bank in which the faulty integrated circuit is located.

Manifest, from Quarterdeck Office Systems, reports your system's type and amount of memory, CPU, interface ports, video adapter, disk drives, and CMOS settings. It displays the contents of AUTOEXEC.BAT and CONFIG.SYS, and even suggests configuration changes to improve overall performance.

Service Diagnostics, from Supersoft, tests your CPU, coprocessor, interface ports, video display, keyboard, memory, and disk drives. It can perform low-level formatting and diagnose performance of floppy-disk drives.

System Sleuth, from Dariana Technology Group, describes your system's CPU, interface ports, memory, and hard disk, reporting any bad sectors. It also saves your CMOS information in a special file for use after replacing the battery.

Software Source Guide

For more information on software discussed in this chapter, contact the following companies:

Bourbaki, Inc.
615 West Hays Street
Boise, ID 83701
1dir+

Central Point Software, Inc.
15220 N. W. Greenbriar Parkway, Suite 200
Beaverton, OR 97006
PC Tools

California Software, Inc.
525 N. Cabrillo Park Drive
Santa Ana, CA 92701
Backpak

Dariana Technology Group
7439 La Palma Avenue, Suite 278
Buena Park, CA 90620
System Sleuth

Departmental Technologies, Inc.
P. O. Box 645
Andover, NJ 07821
Take Charge!

EasySoft, Inc.
1215 Hightower Trail, Suite B100
Atlanta, GA 30350
DOS Partner

EZ-Logic
315 S. El Monte
Los Altos, CA 94022
BackEZ

Fifth Generation Software
10049 North Reiger Road
Baton Rouge, LA 70809
MACE Utilities

Gazelle Systems
42 N. University Avenue, Suite 10
Provo, UT 84601
Q-DOS II

Gibson Research
22991 La Cadena
Laguna Hills, CA 92653
Spinrite II

Peter Norton Computing
2210 Wilshire Blvd. #186
Santa Monica, CA 90403
Norton Commander

Quarterdeck Office Systems
150 Pico Blvd.
Santa Monica, CA 90405
Manifest

Second Ring Publishers
P. O. Box 82400
Phoenix, AZ 85071
Bakup

SitBack Technologies, Inc.
7219 W. 95th Street, #301
Overland Park, KS 66212
SitBack

Sterling Software, Inc.
202 E. Airport Drive, #280
San Bernardino, CA 92408
Intelligent Backup

Supersoft
P. O. Box 611328
San Jose, CA 95161
Service Diagnostics

Touchstone Software
909 Electric Avenue
Seal Beach, CA 90740
Check It

XTree Company
4330 Santa Fe Road
San Luis Obispo, CA 93401
XTreePro

Chapter Thirteen

*Adding
and Using
Memory*

Your hand-me-down is constantly transferring bits of information at high speeds between input and output devices and its memory. *Memory* is where your computer stores information—the application you are running, the data you're working on, the results of processing performed by computer circuits, and even the image that appears on your screen. Unlike disk drives, which store your files when not in use, memory holds information you and your computer are using at the time.

The amount of memory already in your hand-me-down, however, might not be enough to run some applications that you have or plan to acquire. Your hand-me-down might also have types of memory that require special techniques to use.

In this chapter, you will learn about the various types of computer memory, how to install additional memory in your computer, and how to use memory for maximum productivity and efficiency.

How Computer Memory Works

The computer's memory is a series of electronic storage areas that each hold one bit of information. The presence or absence of an electrical charge in the area is interpreted as the one or zero of binary data. Eight individual storage areas combine to make one byte (that is, one character) of information.

Most memory is *volatile,* meaning that once you turn off your computer, the electric charges dissipate and the memory is lost. You need an internal battery, as in a clock/calendar circuit, to maintain the memory when the machine is off. Some laptop computers also have a battery that powers the memory when the machine is off, so you don't have to save data on a disk. Other memory is *nonvolatile*—that is, it does not forget the binary information when the machine is off, even when there is no battery. This type of memory can be compared to a series of switches. For example, if you turned off the power supply to your house, all of the lights and electrical appliances would go off. But when you turn the power back on, the devices that were switched on previously would be on again. When you turn on your computer, the position of the "switches" in nonvolatile memory automatically returns the memory to its previous state.

Types of Memory

The variety of terms used to describe memory often makes memory difficult to understand and use. So let's define memory in two ways—in terms of the type of data it stores and how it is used by DOS and application programs.

Understanding ROM and RAM

ROM, short for *read-only memory,* is permanent, nonvolatile memory that cannot be changed. Think of ROM as a one-way street: the binary information in ROM can be transferred to elsewhere in your system, but no new information can be stored in ROM. ROM stores the boot information, your system's self-test program, and other valuable information that is required for the computer to operate. The information stored in ROM is built into your computer.

Your system might have a variation of ROM called *PROM,* or *programmable read-only memory.* PROM's are memory devices that can be written to, or programmed, one time. Rather than being entered during the manufacturing process, the binary information is added later in a process called *burning.* But once written, the device serves as permanent ROM.

One other variation of ROM is the *EPROM,* for *erasable programmable read-only memory.* While this sounds like a contradiction, EPROM's in your computer are nonvolatile, read-only memory. The data can only be erased and programmed using special equipment. The device has a clear plastic window on top. When exposed to high-intensity ultraviolet light, the memory is erased and the EPROM can be programmed with other data. Once installed in your computer, both PROM's and EPROM's are nonvolatile read-only memory.

RAM is memory that you write to, as well as read from. While RAM stands for *random access memory,* the term *read-write memory* more clearly defines it. Most

RAM is volatile memory that is erased when you turn off your computer. You might hear RAM called *user memory,* since it is where your application is stored when it is loaded from disk and where your data is stored on its way between the keyboard, screen, and disk drive. When an application specifies its minimum memory requirements, it is referring to RAM, and it is RAM that you can add to your system.

RAM can be either dynamic or static. *Dynamic RAM (DRAM)* can only store the electrical charges for a short time. To maintain the data while the machine is on, the circuits are periodically *refreshed,* applied with a new charge of current to maintain the data. *Static RAM (SRAM),* on the other hand, maintains the on or off state without being refreshed.

How Memory Is Used

In order to read from or write to a memory storage area, the computer has to know the area's *address,* or where it is located in relation to the total memory in your system. When we say that a computer can address 1024K, we mean that it can locate a maximum of 1,024,000 memory locations. However, just because the computer circuits can address that many locations doesn't mean that DOS can use them. To understand this phenomenon, let's look at the three types of memory: conventional, expanded, and extended.

Conventional Memory

When DOS was first written, hardware such as the IBM PC, XT, and compatibles could only address 1024K, or 1Mb, of memory. But only a section of that memory, called *conventional memory,* could be used by DOS applications.

Look at the *memory map* in Figure 13.1. The numbers along the side of the map indicate the addresses that start each section. As you can see, the first 640K (minus a small area for storing DOS BIOS information) is conventional memory. The other areas are reserved by DOS and your computer for storing other types of information. For example, in the original IBM memory scheme, the area from 832K to 960K was reserved for use by the IBM PC Jr.

Because memory addresses above 640K were required for the system, or reserved for some future use, DOS was written to use only conventional memory

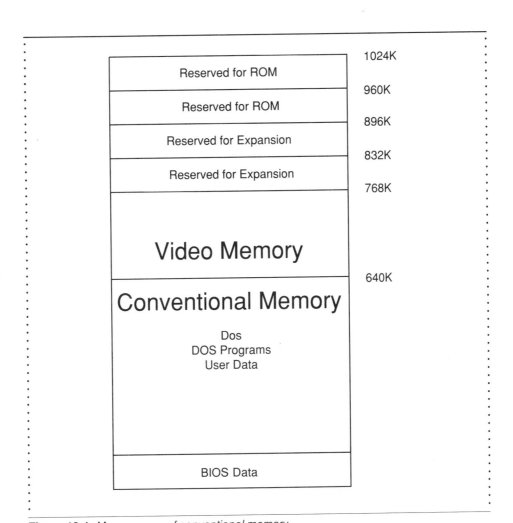

Figure 13.1: *Memory map of conventional memory*

for your programs. So even though your computer is advertised as having 1Mb or more of RAM, you'll only be able to use 640K of this memory, and some of that is used by DOS and device drivers. That's why CHKDSK will report something like

655360 bytes total memory
580768 bytes free

on systems that have 1Mb and more or memory.

Expanded Memory

To overcome the limitations of conventional memory, Lotus, Intel, and Microsoft joined to break the 640K limit. They developed *expanded memory,* a system for using additional memory that the computer itself cannot address physically. The system, called the *LIM specification,* or *EMS memory,* uses a separate area of memory that is linked to addressable memory through an EMS window (Figure 13.2).

With special drivers and compatible software, blocks of expanded memory are switched back and forth between the EMS hardware and the window where the memory can be addressed by your computer. This technique is known as *bank switching.*

For example, suppose that you're working on a spreadsheet too large to fit in conventional memory. Parts of the spreadsheet will be stored in EMS memory and swapped into the EMS window when needed. EMS-compatible software can address the EMS window and thus use the area as it would use conventional RAM.

The EMS specification has been refined over the years, with changes made to the EMS driver.

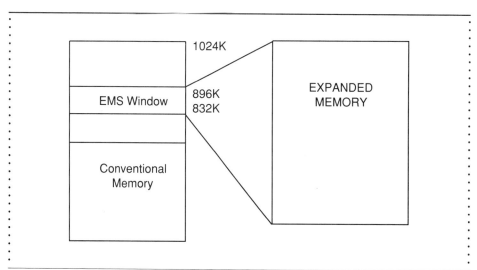

Figure 13.2: *Map showing expanded memory*

Extended Memory

Computers using 286, 386, and 486 microprocessors can physically address more than 1Mb of memory. AT and compatibles can address up to 16Mb, and 386 and 486 machines can address up to 4Gb (gigabytes), or 4 billion bytes. Memory above 1Mb that can be addressed directly is called *extended memory* (Figure 13.3).

It might seem that extended memory would displace the need for expanded memory. Unfortunately, the operating system written with the 640K limitation cannot use

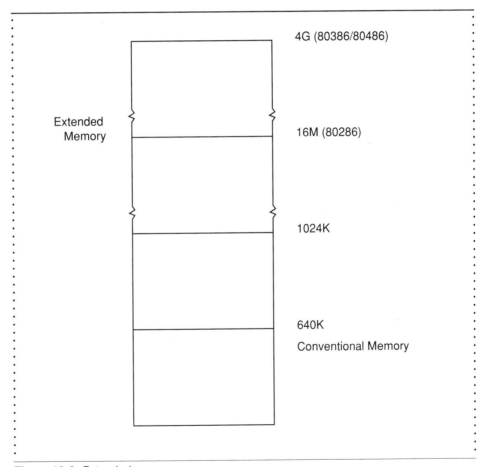

Figure 13.3: *Extended memory*

extended memory unless you have special driver software or programs written especially to handle it. In addition, expanded memory is still the only option for PC- and XT-compatibles that cannot address extended memory.

Memory Hardware

RAM is physically located in either a computer chip, a memory module, or a combination of both.

RAM *chips* are integrated circuits that can store volatile electrical charges. They are classified by the number of bits they can store—a 64K chip can store 64,000 bits. While the first IBM PC used 16K chips, 64K, 256K, and now 1 megabit chips are available.

Chips are also distinguished by the way they hold data. Most are *bit-wide,* meaning that you need eight chips to store data, each chip holding one bit of each character. A 256K x 1 chip can store 256,000 bits; you need eight of them to store 256,000 characters.

There is also a ninth chip for parity, the system for checking data explained in Chapter 12. If you see a parity error when starting your computer, an error was detected in memory by the self-test program. So for each block of memory, you need nine chips—eight to store the data and one for parity. You'd need nine 1 megabyte 1024K x 1 chips, for example, to hold 1 megabyte of data.

While bit-wide chips are the most common, there are 64 x 4, 256 x 4, and 1024 x 4 chips in which each of the eight chips stores 4 bits per address.

Chips are also classified by the speed by which they can accept and remember data, measured in nanoseconds (billionths of a second). The chip must be fast enough to handle the data sent to it by the microprocessor. Earlier memory chips could not keep up with the first 80286 computers, so a system of *wait states* was developed. During a wait state, the computer pauses to give memory a chance to catch up. A system that has no wait states has memory fast enough to keep up without pausing.

A memory module contains a complete set of chips in one package that stores 256K or 1Mb of RAM. So instead of needing nine chips to store 256K or 1Mb, you'd need one 9-bit wide module.

There are two types of modules: SIMM's and SIPP's. *Single inline memory modules,* or *SIMM's,* are the most common, and they use edge card connectors that fit into a socket that's on another card. *Single inline pin packages,* or *SIPP's,* use pins that fit into matching holes.

There are systems, like the ALR Powerflex, that use both chips and SIMM's. The Powerflex uses eight 265K x 4 chips for the first 1Mb of memory, and additional memory is added in SIMM's.

Adding Memory

My first personal computer, a Radio Shack Model I, had 4K of RAM, and I remember my excitement when I increased it to 16K. I couldn't imagine needing any more, even though I soon expanded it to its maximum of 64K.

In those days, before the IBM PC, all software—word processors, spreadsheets, databases, communications programs—worked in 64K. But added features, graphics, and advanced printer support started to demand more and more RAM. The minimum of 64K quickly rose, and today most software requires at least 512K or more.

If all of your programs work with the memory you have, and you are pleased with your system's performance, there is really no reason to add memory. However, you might have to add memory to use more powerful applications or to make your system more efficient.

Adding RAM can be expensive, since its cost has fluctuated widely over the years, sometimes rising as much as 500%. But in most cases, you can quickly add memory yourself or replace defective memory, without paying for a service call or repair bill.

Before you make the decision to add memory, you first have to identify the type of memory you have.

Identifying Your Memory

Memory chips or modules can be located on the system's motherboard, on a separate memory card, or both. The *motherboard* is the main circuit board that contains most of the computer circuits, and in many systems, the board also contains RAM.

When the board has as much memory as it can fit, it is *fully populated.* At this point, additional memory must be installed on a separate *memory card,* a circuit board that contains RAM and that you insert in an empty card slot. You add memory to the motherboard until it is fully populated, and can then add a memory card if you still need more memory.

Other systems have all of their RAM on memory cards, and none on the motherboard. When the memory card is fully populated, the only way to add memory is to install another card if you have an empty card slot. Some memory cards only contain RAM, while others are *multifunction boards* that also include a clock/calendar and one or two interface ports.

If you have your system's documentation, look for specifications on adding memory. You might find a list of the recommended chips, SIMM's, or circuit cards that can be installed. Don't purchase any memory until you are certain that it is appropriate for your machine.

If you don't have the documentation, consult a computer store or the manufacturer, or follow these steps:

1. Unplug your computer and remove its cover.

2. Identify the type of memory. Look for chips in neat rows of nine. While the identifying numbers of the chips vary, look for rows of chips that all have the same number. If you don't see chips, look for a SIMM, a small circuit board inserted at a right angle to another card. The SIMM will have a row of nine rectangular boxes mounted to its surface (Figure 13.4).

3. Copy the numbers that are on the chips or SIMM's.

4. Identify the capacity and speed of your memory. With chips, you'll usually see 64, 256, 1000, or 1024 near the end of the ID number printed on top, identifying the number of bits each stores. The ID number will end with a number indicating the speed: 8 or 80 for 80 nanoseconds, 12 or 120 for 120 nanoseconds, and 15 or 150 for 150 nanoseconds. For example, this number on a chip

   P21256-15

   identifies a 150-nanosecond 256K-bit RAM chip.

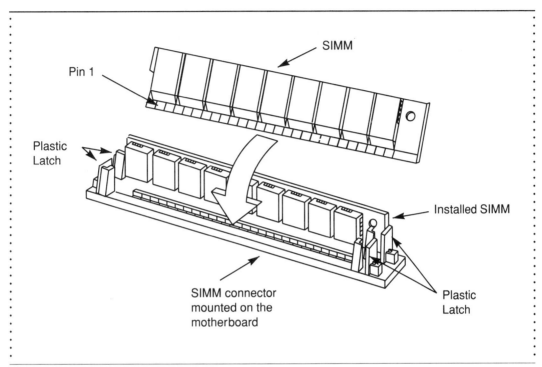

Figure 13.4: *A SIMM (single inline.memory module)*

Most SIMM's also end with a number identifying their speed, but many do not clearly show their capacity. Some will include 256 or 1000 to indicate a 256K or 1Mb device. In any case, write down the entire number so you are prepared to order more memory.

5. Determine if your card is fully populated. If your motherboard or memory board can take more memory, you'll see empty rows of chip sockets or an empty card edge next to installed RAM. If there are no empty chip or SIMM sockets, you have to purchase a memory card.

Planning Your Additional Memory

How much memory you add depends on how much money you want to spend. Before purchasing additional memory, take these precautions:

▶ Add memory one bank or section at a time. A *bank* contains enough RAM to store memory at an address location, so you must add all nine chips at once. If a bank holds two SIMM's, both must be inserted.

▶ All RAM in the same bank must match. You can usually use a chip or SIMM that's faster than memory already installed, but not one that's slower. Just make sure that all of the RAM in the same bank is the same speed.

▶ Some computers can accept banks of either 256K or 1024K SIMM's. For example, the Powerflex accepts either size SIMM in bank 3 and 4, so the memory configuration extends from 1Mb to 5Mb (Table 13.1). Each bank holds two SIMM's, and both must be the same type.

Table 13.1: *Memory Configuration in ALR Powerflex*

Total Memory	Bank 1	Bank 2	Bank 3	Bank 4
1Mb	4 - 256K x 4	4 - 256K x 4		
1.5Mb	4 - 256K x 4	4 - 256K x 4	2 - 256K x 9	
2Mb	4 - 256K x 4	4 - 256K x 4	2 - 256K x 9	2 - 256K x 9
3Mb	4 - 256K x 4	4 - 256K x 4	2 - 1024K x 9	
5Mb	4 - 256K x 4	4 - 256K x 4	2 - 1024K x 9	2 - 1024K x 9

▶ Static electricity can destroy a memory chip or SIMM. To be safe, keep the memory in its protective sleeve or wrapper until you are ready to install it. Touch the computer's case to ground yourself before picking up the memory. This discharges any static electricity in your body.

Once you pick up the memory device, don't put it back down. If you *have* to put down a chip or SIMM, place it back in its original container or lay it down on a nonconductive material such as wood or plastic, with the metal pins facing up.

Purchasing Memory

Decide how much memory you want to add, and then contact a computer store or mail-order company. Describe your system in detail to the salesperson—the make and model of the computer, the amount and type of memory it currently has, and how much memory you want to add.

Do not purchase memory that is slower than what is already installed or what is recommended by the manufacturer. It may not work with your system, resulting in errors during the self-test program at bootup or unpredictable behavior of your applications.

Many systems use a generic type of memory, either 256K or 1024K bit-wide DRAM chips. But there are systems that use special chips or require specific speeds.

Be particularly careful when purchasing a memory card, making sure the board will fit in one of your available card slots. Find out how much memory comes on the card and its total capacity—a card advertised as 4Mb might be able to store that much when fully populated, but may be sold without memory. Make sure you get a price that includes the memory. Explain that you'd like a card that can be configured as either extended or expanded, so you can decide later how you want to use the memory.

Finally, plan ahead. Even if you cannot afford a fully populated card, consider a card that has room for expansion. The difference in price between a fully populated 1Mb card and a 2Mb card with only 1Mb installed might be minimal. The 2Mb card might be a better buy, however, especially if you have add more memory later.

Inserting Chips

Follow these steps when you are ready to insert memory chips:

1. Make sure you have access to the chip sockets. Remove the card only if necessary and place it on a nonconductive surface.

2. Ground yourself.

3. Check that the pins of the chip are at a right angle to the body of the chip. If you have to straighten them, place one row of pins against a hard wood or plastic surface and gently press the chip body until the pins are at a right angle. Turn the chip over and straighten the other set.

4. Gently insert all of the pins into the socket. There is nothing to prevent you from inserting a chip in the wrong direction, ruining the

chip and possibly other components when you turn on your machine. However, all chips have a groove or other *index mark* that indicates the position of pin number 1 (Figure 13.5). Pin number 1 of the chip must be inserted in pin 1 of the socket. You'll see a small 1, or an outline of the index mark printed on the circuit board.

5. Apply even pressure until the chip is fully seated in the socket. Some sockets are rather tight and you might have to press quite hard to seat the chip fully. If you have trouble, tilt the chip toward one end, push that end half way in, and then push in the other end halfway. Finally, apply pressure to seat the entire chip fully.

6. Check that no pins are bent, either under the chip or towards the outside of the socket. If they are, remove the chip by prying it off with a thin-blade screwdriver or a special chip remover, which is available at many computer and electronic stores. Ground yourself and carefully straighten the pins. Do not bend the pins any more than absolutely necessary. If bent too much and too often, the pins will break and the chip will be worthless.

7. Insert all of the chips, a full bank at a time.

8. Check again to make sure that all of the chips are inserted and are properly oriented toward pin 1.

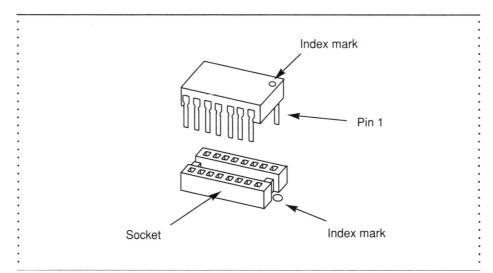

Figure 13.5: *The index mark indicates pin number 1*

9. Set up your computer to recognize the memory as explained in the section "Recognizing Additional Memory."

Inserting SIMM's

Follow these steps to insert a SIMM:

1. Make sure you have access to the SIMM sockets. Remove the card only if necessary and place it on a nonconductive surface.

2. Ground yourself.

3. Align the card edge of the SIMM with the socket.

4. Press the SIMM down until two latches on the socket snap into place in holes in the SIMM. If you have difficulty, pull the latches outward as you insert the SIMM. When the SIMM is in place, release the latches so they click into place.

5. Insert all of the SIMM's, a full bank at a time.

6. Set up your computer to recognize the memory as explained in the section "Recognizing Additional Memory."

Adding Memory Boards

When your motherboard or memory card is fully populated, you have to insert another card. (There are a few memory expansion systems, primarily for Zenith computers, that fit *piggyback,* or directly on top of existing memory.)

Before inserting a memory card, decide if you want the memory configured as extended or expanded. Many cards have switches or jumpers that set them as extended or expanded, or that set their *base address*—where they fit into the system's memory map. While you can always reopen the machine and change the switches, setting the board before you install it will save time. Check the documentation to see how your board is set up.

Insert the memory board following the instructions in Chapter 7 for inserting circuit cards.

Recognizing Additional Memory

Your computer will not recognize the additional memory until you tell it that the memory is there. On most systems you must set switches or jumpers on the motherboard before you can use added memory. A number of other machines, usually AT's and above, must also include total system memory in CMOS. You should have a setup or configuration disk, a program on your DOS disk for setting CMOS, or a setup program built into ROM.

Sometimes the CMOS and switch settings do not match. You set the switch settings to total memory, and the CMOS to extended memory. Expanded memory is controlled by the EMS driver and is not considered during the setup procedure of many systems. However, since every system configures memory differently, you must have the proper documentation.

Look in your system's documentation for instructions on configuring it for memory. If you don't have the documentation, check with a computer store that handles your machine, or call or write the manufacturer.

The Expanded Memory Driver

In order to use expanded memory, you must load the EMS driver, a file called EMM.SYS, EMS.DRV, or something similar. The driver swaps blocks of memory between the EMS board and the EMS window.

Add a device command to CONFIG.SYS, as specified in your system documentation, such as

DEVICE = C:/DOS/EMS.DRV

and then reboot your system. The name of your driver may be different or in the root or other directory.

Your system or memory board might come with its own version of the driver. If it does, use that version instead of the one supplied with DOS. In some cases, a generic driver supplied with DOS will not work.

Using Added Memory

Once the EMS device driver is loaded, many applications, such as Lotus 1-2-3, can automatically use expanded memory. Other applications, like Microsoft Windows, can access extended memory because they handle memory management internally.

Aside from specially written programs, the added memory is not available to DOS and other applications that are still restricted to 640K. Fortunately, you can take advantage of the added memory in several ways.

Each of these methods use device driver commands in CONFIG.SYS. For you to use any of these features with expanded memory, the EMS device driver must be the first device command in CONFIG.SYS.

Using a RAM Disk

Next to your printer, your disk drive is the slowest part of your computer system. Even the fastest drives take much longer to read and write data when compared to the speed of RAM.

A RAM disk, also known as a *virtual disk,* is an area of high-speed RAM used to store programs and data that would take longer to access on a disk drive. When you set up a RAM disk, the system treats the memory area was it were a real disk drive. You log on to a RAM disk as you would log on to a disk drive. You can copy files to it, and even divide it into subdirectories. If you're using a program that requires frequent disk access, copy the entire program into the RAM disk, log on to it, and then run the application. Retrieving and saving files to the RAM disk is much faster than using a real disk.

Create a RAM disk using the DOS device driver VDISK.SYS (supplied with PC-DOS) or RAMDRIVE.SYS (provided with many versions of MS-DOS) in CONFIG.SYS. The syntax of the command is

    DEVICE = <*path*>\VDISK.SYS <*options*>

For example, add the command

    DEVICE = C:\DOS\VDISK.SYS

to create a RAM disk with no options using a driver in the DOS directory. When you reboot or start your computer, you'll see a message similar to

```
VDISK Version 3.08 virtual disk G:
Buffer size:      64K
Sector size:      128
Directory entries:  64
Transfer size:     511
```

Enter **G:** to log on to the RAM disk. At this point, you can use it as you would any real disk in your system. Unlike a real disk drive, however, the RAM disk is volatile; its contents will be erased completely when you turn off or reboot your computer. For this reason, you should copy your new or updated files to a real disk before turning off the machine.

The options determine the disk's capacity, the size of its sectors, the number of directory entries, and the type of memory to use.

The syntax for the options is

DEVICE = <*path*>\VDISK.SYS <*xxx*> <*yyy*> <*zzz*> </E or /A>

where

xxx	Determines the total size of the disk in bytes
yyy	Sets the size of each sector—512 is the recommended value
zzz	Specifies the maximum number of root directory entries
/E	Creates the RAM disk in extended memory
/A	Creates the RAM disk in expanded memory, as long as the EMS driver is loaded

If you're not sure of the settings, enter the device driver command without options, or enter the command setting only the total drive size.

Using a Disk Cache

While a RAM disk can speed up your work, shutting off your system before saving data in a RAM disk to a real disk can be disastrous. A compromise solution is to use a disk cache. A *disk cache* is a program that automatically stores frequently used disk sectors in RAM. When DOS needs the sectors, the cache program retrieves them from RAM instead of the slower disk.

The sectors are stored only for read operations. No new data or programs are stored there so you won't lose any data if you accidentally turn off your computer or have to reboot.

There are many different cache programs; some are included in versions of DOS, others available in shell or utility programs. Most let you specify the amount of memory to set aside, and whether to use extended or expanded memory.

SMARTDRV, for example, is a disk-cache device driver supplied with Microsoft Windows. The version supplied with Windows 3.0 includes several options for configuring how memory is used. The syntax to include in CONFIG.SYS is

> DEVICE = *<path>*\SMARTDRV.SYS *<xxx>* *<yyy>* /A

where

xxx	Determines the size of the cache in kilobytes when Windows is not running
yyy	Sets the size of the cache in kilobytes when Windows is running—called the minimum cache size
/A	Uses expanded memory—extended memory will be used if this option is not included

Without options, the driver sets aside a 256K cache in extended memory.

As an example, the command for creating a 1Mb disk cache using expanded memory is

> DEVICE = C:\WIN\SMARTDRV.SYS 1024 /A

The SMARTDRV driver supplied with earlier versions of Windows does not include the minimum cache size option.

Print Spooling

The slowest part of a computer system is the printer. Even the fastest printer can't keep up with the speed at which data is transmitted through a serial or parallel port.

For this reason, the computer sends as much data as the printer can handle, and then waits until it can accept more.

Some applications make you wait until one document or publication is completely printed before you can begin working on another. Other applications can print in the *background,* dividing the computer's processing time into sections so it appears you can work with one job while it prints another. But you won't be able to leave the application until all of the printing is completed, and your display may seem to lag slightly behind your typing.

A *print spooler* is a program that intercepts data being sent to the printer and stores it in high-speed RAM as fast as your application transmits it. As far as the application is concerned, the entire job is printed once all of the data is in the spooler. The spooler then handles background printing on its own, moving data from RAM as the printer becomes available. You can work on another job, change applications, and even send other jobs to the spooler. However, any print jobs still in the spooler will be terminated when you turn off the computer.

The DOS command PRINT acts as a print spooler that uses conventional memory for storing data. It does not use extended or expanded memory, and can only print ASCII text files, or special print files, from the DOS prompt.

However, general-purpose print spoolers such as PrintCache from LaserTools can accept data from within your applications, print any type of file, and work with expanded or extended memory.

Your version of DOS might even include a spool driver or program. Zenith Data Systems, for instance, includes the program ZSPOOL.COM with its versions of DOS. Activate it from the DOS prompt or include it in AUTOEXEC.BAT. The syntax is

    ZSPOOL *<xxx>* /A /P:X /C

where

xxx	Sets aside RAM space in kilobytes
/A	Uses expanded rather than conventional memory
/P:X	Designates printer priority, or the number of characters to print for each clock cycle
/C	Clears the print buffer

For example, to establish a 1Mb print spooler in expanded memory, enter this command at the DOS prompt

    ZSPOOL 1025 /A

By using RAM disks, caches, and spoolers, you can take advantage of extended or expanded memory even when your applications cannot.

Other Memory Managers

A number of companies offer hardware or software that help to manage your memory in several ways. Most memory managers trick DOS into using some of the extended memory above the 640K address, making up to an additional 384K of memory available for your applications and data files. This is called *relocation*.

Memory managers also convert extended memory, which few applications can access, into more commonly used expanded memory. The conversion is useful with extended memory boards that cannot be switched to expanded memory. Even with boards that can be configured, converting memory saves you the trouble of opening the computer to make the change manually. You can leave the board configured as extended for programs that do use it, such as Windows, and then quickly change it to expanded memory when needed.

For example, TC! Power from Departmental Technologies converts memory between 640K and 1Mb into extended or expanded memory, even on PC- and XT-compatible machines. It can emulate the version 4.0 EMS driver by swapping extended memory in and out of the EMS window so you don't need a separate EMS board to use expanded memory programs. The program can even use space on your hard disk in place of expanded or extended memory, although swapping disk space takes longer than using RAM.

The ALL ChargeCard is a hardware alternative. This small card fits between the 80286 processor chip and the motherboard—remove the processor, insert the ChargeCard, and then plug the processor into a waiting slot. The card comes with a special device driver called ALLEMM4 that makes your system's extended memory available as expanded memory and allows DOS to address conventional memory up to 960K directly. The driver makes more conventional memory available to your applications by moving some of DOS's BIOS and other data into higher areas of memory.

You should also check your system documentation. Some systems have their own relocation option built into the ROM setup program that converts memory between 640K and 1024K into expanded memory.

For more information, contact:

ALL Computers, Inc.
1220 Yonge Street, 2nd Floor
Toronto, Ontario
Canada M4T 1W1
ALL ChargeCard

Departmental Technologies
P. O. Box 645
Andover, NJ 07821
TC! Power

LaserTools
5900 Hollis Street
Emeryville, CA 94608
PrintCache

Quarterdeck Office Systems
150 Pico Blvd.
Santa Monica, CA 90405
QEMM Memory Manager

Chapter Fourteen

Adding
Disk Drives

14

*I*f you're working on a computer network, you may be using a diskless workstation. A *diskless workstation* is a computer system without disk drives of its own; it uses the disks in the network server. The rest of us, however, need disk drives to store our programs and data. Even laptop computers lose their battery charge eventually, and systems with enough nonvolatile RAM to replace drives are well into the future. Technology may someday make our disk drives obsolete. But for now, floppy- and hard-disk drives will be our principal way of storing data.

The disk drives in your hand-me-down must be able to run your application programs. Many programs require a hard-disk drive, or a special number, size, and capacity of floppy-disk drives. In previous chapters, you examined your software to determine its required hardware, and you learned how to use your disk drives. In this chapter, you'll learn how to add new drives or replace existing drives to meet your software's basic needs and improve your hand-me-down's performance. You'll also learn how to prepare your hard-disk drive, and how to salvage some drives that seem damaged beyond repair.

Inserting new disk drives is easy but requires some mechanical ability. If you are unsure about working on the inside of your computer, consult a computer store or repair shop. Even if you don't want to insert a disk drive yourself, read this chapter so you can learn how to prepare your hard disk and correct problems. If you decide to install your own disk drive, purchase it new from a reliable dealer. While a hand-me-down computer can be an excellent investment, used disk drives are not recommended.

Replacing Damaged Disk Drives

Actually, your computer system has few moving parts. Aside from the keyboard, a fan, and perhaps a mechanical mouse, the only mechanical parts that may suffer from use are the disk drives. In other words, your disk drives are the part of the system most likely to fail. Every time you start your system, you wear down the drives. Every read and write operation your computer performs damages them a little more.

We rely so much on our drives that when they do fail or even lose performance, the entire system suffers. Some computers will let you boot from alternate drives, either from the hard disk or one of the floppy disks, if your normal boot disk fails. But other systems won't start at all if the hard disk crashes or if floppy drive A is inoperable. With proper care and maintenance, your drives can last as long as your system. Nevertheless, drives do fail and must then be replaced.

Floppy-disk drives are usually cheaper and easier to replace than to repair. Fixing a broken latch knob will cost more than a new floppy drive. However, some hard-disk problems can be repaired for less than the cost of replacement. In fact, you can usually correct most hard-disk problems yourself using DOS and other utilities, although you'll probably lose the data stored on your disk. When more serious problems arise, you might repair instead of replace in order to try to salvage the data, not necessarily to save money. But if the hard disk is physically damaged, high repair costs make replacing a damaged disk a viable option.

Adding Storage Capacity

The disk drives in your hand-me-down may be operable, but not sufficient to store or run your application programs. Some of the most popular application programs won't even run on floppy-disk drives, or may require high-capacity drives in AT-class machines.

You might also have software on disk formats that are incompatible with those in your hand-me-down, such as 1.2Mb disks when you have 360K drives, or 5$\frac{1}{4}$-inch disks when you have 3$\frac{1}{2}$-inch drives. It's likely that you've run into a disk size problem if you have a laptop or desktop computer with only 3$\frac{1}{2}$-inch drives.

When your disk drives cannot accommodate your software, you have to add a floppy or hard disk to your system, or replace an existing drive with one of a different size or capacity.

Understanding Disk Controllers

A disk system consists of two parts, the transport mechanism and the controller. (Some very early systems, and some non-PC-compatible machines, incorporate the transport and controller in one unit.) The *transport* is the disk drive itself (where you insert a floppy disk), the mechanical components that turn and handle the disk, and electronic circuits that run it. It is the transport that you hear when your drive is accessed. The *controller* is an electronic circuit that converts the commands and data from the computer into the signals required by the transport. In most cases, the controller is on a separate circuit board. Some systems, however, have the drive controller built into the motherboard or a general-purpose I/O (Input/Output) circuit card.

Controllers vary in the number and types of drives they support. Most controllers support two floppy and two hard disks. To add a hard drive, you just have to purchase the drive itself and connect it to the existing controller. Some older systems, however, support only floppy drives (usually two, although the original IBM could support four floppies). To add a hard drive to these systems, you have to purchase and insert a separate hard-disk controller.

Many controllers in PC- and XT-compatibles cannot accept 1.44Mb 3½-inch disks. You can install such drives, but you'll have to purchase a separate controller as well.

Maintaining Drive Compatibility

Before installing the disk drive, make sure that it is compatible with your system. It has to be compatible with the interface of your controller, and its format has to be compatible with the hardware and BIOS. It also must be physically compatible to fit into the computer.

Data Coding

Data is recorded on a disk by electrical impulses that alter the magnetic field on bit-size portions of the disk's surface. The most frequently used system for recording is *Modified Frequency Modulation,* or *MFM.* Each change in the magnetic field, called a *flux transition,* is interpreted as either a binary one or zero.

Run Length Limited, or *RLL,* is a system that can store up to twice as much data on the same disk by converting the data into RLL own format. A technique called *2,7 RLL* stores 50% more data than MFM. *Advanced RLL,* or *3,9 RLL,* doubles the MFM capacity.

Interface

The disk interface controls the movement of read/write heads from sector to sector, and the transfer of data to and from the disk's surface. While all floppy drives interface in exactly the same way, there are several types of hard-disk interfaces.

The earliest interface used by IBM, and still used frequently with drives of less than 40Mb, is called *ST506*. ST506 connects the drive to the controller with two flat ribbon cables. A *data cable* with 20 wires carries binary information to be recorded on or read from the disk. A wider 34-wire *control cable* carries the signals that regulate the drive and its operations. The computer stores a record of the drive's parameters, including the number of bad sectors, either in its BIOS or CMOS. The controller checks the record before writing to the disk.

A newer interface, the *Enhanced Small Device Interface,* or *ESDI,* also connects with two cables but allows data to be transmitted faster than ST506. While ESDI can be used by low-capacity drives, it is more frequently used for larger drives, up to 600Mb. ESDI systems store parameter and bad sector information on the drive itself. The controller accesses the information from the drive rather than CMOS.

Drives supported by the ST506 and ESDI interfaces are basically mechanical devices that require their own unique type of controller. You shouldn't purchase a drive until you are sure that it is compatible with the controller.

The *Small Computer Standard Interface* (*SCSI*) offers a generic approach to interfacing. Instead of installing a separate controller card for each device, you install one SCSI host adapter. The *host adapter* converts the computer's signals to a format acceptable to all SCSI devices, which have their own built-in controller. Once you have the host adapter installed, you can purchase and use any SCSI device without worrying about compatibility.

SCSI drives use a single 50-wire cable. You can connect up to seven SCSI devices on one host adapter, connecting one after the other on the same cable. Each device controls itself, so theoretically several SCSI devices can be running simultaneously.

Physical Compatibility

Disk drives (except hard-disk cards that you'll learn about later) are installed in *recesses,* or drive bays, behind your hand-me-down's front panel. The size and number of the bays determine how many drives you can install in your system. Obviously, you cannot fit 5¼-inch drives in a bay designed for 3½-inch drives. In addition, your disk drive bays may be full height or half height. A full-height bay can accept either one full-height drive about 3½-inches high or two half-height 1 ¾-inch-high drives.

If you have two full-height bays, you can store several combinations of hardware, up to two half-height floppies and two half-height hard disks. If you already have two full-height floppies, you have to remove one to install a hard-disk drive. Of course, you could replace the floppy with one half-height hard disk and one half-height floppy. You might need a special adapter to place one or more half-height devices in a full-height bay.

Many computers have four half-height bays, although in some, only two bays are *exposed,* or visible from the outside. The exposed bays are designed for floppy drives, the hidden bays for hard drives. You can install any combination of half-height devices in these units. However, a combination of two floppy and two hard drives is the most common maximum setup (Figure 14.1).

Installing a 3½-inch drive, which is about 1½ inches high, in a half-height 5¼-inch drive bay also requires a special adapter, a small half-height cage that holds the drive and covers the bay window (Figure 14.2).

System Compatibility

Beside physically fitting into the bay, the drive must be compatible with DOS and BIOS. High-capacity 5¼-inch drives require versions of DOS 3.0 and later. Version 3.2 is required for 720Mb 3½-inch drives and version 3.3 or later is required for high-capacity 1.44Mb drives. Some versions of DOS 3.21 can also support 1.44Mb disks.

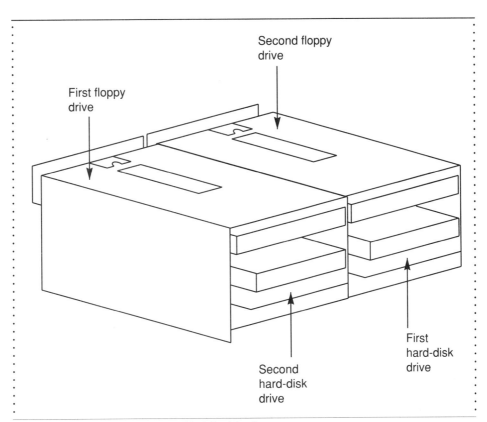

Figure 14.1: *System with four half-height drive bays*

In addition, the BIOS of some earlier PC and XT models cannot support 1.2Mb disks, and some AT and PS/2 models cannot use 1.44Mb disks. To overcome these limitations, you must purchase a special disk controller with the BIOS functions built in. You can also use the device drivers DRIVER.SYS or DRIVEPARM included in DOS 3.2 and later. It allows you to use drives, both internal and external, that are not supported by the BIOS. Check your DOS manual if you have questions.

Understanding Drive Hardware

To install a drive, you have to use the proper cables. Drives connect to the computer's internal power supply and to the disk controller. If the connectors on the drive are the incorrect type to attach to the cables already in the system, you'll have to purchase new cables or special adapters that make them fit together.

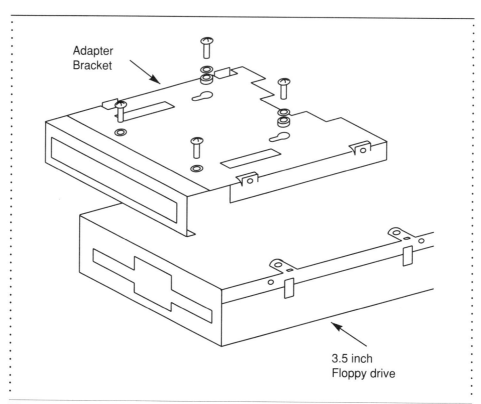

Figure 14.2: *Adapter for holding 3¹/₂-inch drive in 5¹/₄-inch drive bay*

You also might have to make some adjustments to the drive's hardware and to the switches inside the hand-me-down itself. While many of these adjustments are easy to make, it is best if you have the documentation for both the drive and your computer. If you don't have the documentation, have a professional install the drive for you.

Let's take a detailed look at these hardware considerations.

Making Power Connections

Most power supplies have four 4-wire connectors that can be used for any combination of floppy and hard disks (Figure 14.3). The connectors can only fit in one way. If you have only two connectors, you can install a third drive using a Y-connector, an adapter that divides one power connector into two (Figure 14.4).

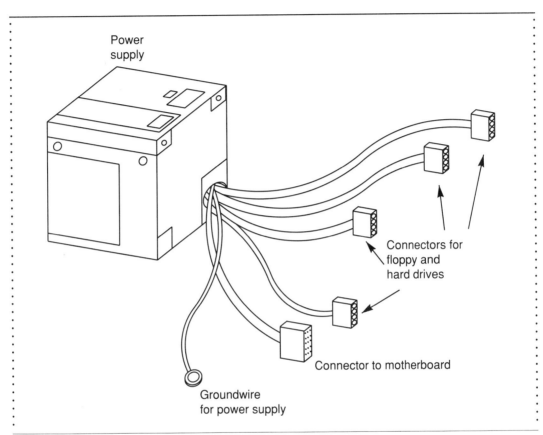

Figure 14.3: *Power supply drive connectors*

If you are installing a hard disk with a Y-connector, however, make sure the system's power supply is adequate. Early model PC's have a small 63.5- or 100-watt power supply, too low to be safely divided between two half-height floppies and a full-height hard disk. Most XT models have 130-watt supplies, and AT's have up to 200 watts—both more than adequate for additional hard drives.

Some 3½-inch disk drives have smaller power connectors than those used in 5¼-inch systems. To install a 3½-inch drive in a computer designed for 5¼-inch drives, you need a power supply adapter. The adapter converts the power supply cable to attach to a smaller power connector in 3½-inch drives. Many 3½-inch drives come with the adapter. If you need a Y-connector, you can purchase one with both 5¼-inch and 3½-inch plugs.

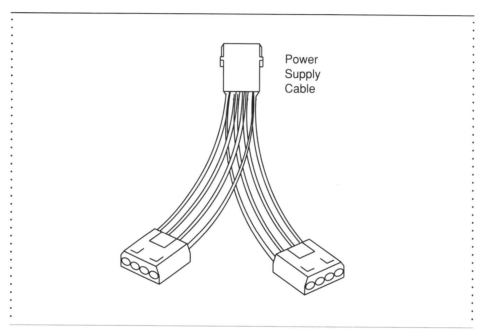

Power
Supply
Cable

Figure 14.4: *Y-connector for power supply*

Matching Connectors and Cables

Floppy disks connect to the controller with one 34-wire cable. The end attached to the controller has a female pin-type connector.

Most cables have two other connectors—one at the opposite end that connects to drive A, and one in the center for drive B. The end for drive A has a group of twisted wires, so you can always distinguish this end from the controller connector. (There are some drive cables that do not have twisted wires. You'll learn about these in the next section "Setting Drive Select Jumpers.")

Card-edge connectors are used for 5¼-inch and many 3½-inch drives. However, some 3½-inch drives use a pin-type connector. If you are adding a second disk drive with a different type of connector from the existing drive, you'll need a new cable since most cables have two of the same connectors.

Always plug in the end with the twisted wires to drive A, and plug in the center connector to drive B. Table 14.1 shows the type of connectors you'll need for various combinations of drives that have different types of connectors. For example, to install a 3½-inch drive in a system that already has one 5¼-inch drive, you'll need a cable with a card-edge connector on one end and a pin-type connector in the center.

Table 14.1: *Cable Configurations for Disk Drives Using Different Connectors*

Drive A	Drive B	End Connector (Twisted Wires)	Center Connector	Controller End
5¼	5¼	Card edge	Card edge	Pin
3½	3½	Pin	Pin	Pin
5¼	3½	Card edge	Pin	Pin
3½	5¼	Pin	Card edge	Pin

Card-edge connectors are keyed so they can only go in one way. Pin-type connectors on 3¼-inch drives, however, can physically connect in either direction, but only one way is correct. One side of the cable will be striped, painted red or black. The striped side represents pin number 1. Attach the connector so the striped side is aligned with pin number 1 of the drive's socket. With the drive mounted horizontally, pin number 1 is usually on the left of the card edge.

Hard-disk drives connect with either one or two cables. The data cable of ST412 and ESDI drives is a 20-wire cable with a pin-type connector that fits onto the controller and a card-edge socket for the drive.

The controller cable is identical to a 5¼-inch floppy-disk cable. It has a 34-pin connector for the controller and two edge connectors for the drives. Plug in the end with the twisted wires to drive C, and plug in the center connector to drive D.

Setting Drive Select Jumpers

Disk drives are made with a *drive select jumper* that some systems use to determine the drive's letter. The jumper is either a jumper block near the back of the drive or small slide switch on the side of 3½-inch drives that must be set to indicate the drive's letter (Figure 14.5).

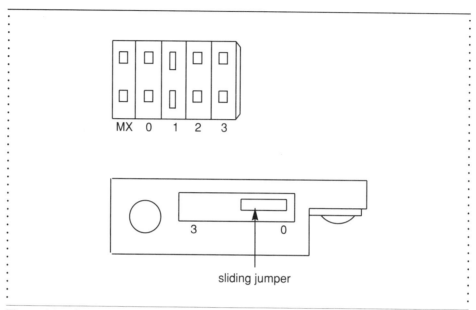

Figure 14.5: *Drive select jumpers*

With IBM and compatible systems, you should always set the jumper to the second drive position, since the twist on the cable distinguishes the first and second drive— the drive at the twisted end is either drive A or C. Set jumpers numbered 0 to 3 to number 1, jumpers numbered 1 to 4 to number 2. With jumper blocks that have five sets of pins, ignore the one labeled with the letters *MX* or other letters.

There are some hard-disk cables that do not have a group of twisted wires. With these cables, the drive select jumpers determine drives C and D. If your cable is *straight-through,* it has no twisted wires. Set the jumper on the lower drive (drive C) to the first drive position, and set the jumper on the higher drive (drive D) to the second drive position. In most floppy-disk systems, the twisted wires are necessary since they not only determine the drive number, but they also carry the motor control signals.

Terminating Resisters

Drive controller cables are designed so the electrical charges flow through them from one end to the other. But when the charges hit the end of the cable, they could reflect back toward the controller, possibly causing errors or damaging your disks.

To prevent this, the drive on the end of the cable—drive A or C—has a terminating resister that absorbs the charges before they can reflect back. The resister is usually located near the back of the drive, close to the controller cable connector. It can be shaped like an integrated circuit with two rows of pins plugged into a socket, or like a SIPP (*single in-line pin package*), a thin rectangular object with one row of pins.

If you are installing drive B or D, you must remove the resister pack. Pull it straight out but save it in case you want to switch the drive for A or C. If you are installing a new drive A or C, make sure the resister pack is in place.

Removing a Disk Drive

The steps for removing floppy disks and hard disks are almost identical. You'll need a Phillips screwdriver and some masking or adhesive tape. Depending on your computer, you might also need a thin blade screwdriver.

When you have to replace or remove your drive for service, follow these steps:

1. Park the hard-disk drive, if you have one, as explained in Chapter 5.

2. Unplug the power cords.

3. Remove the cover.

4. Gain access to the drive. How you do this depends on the location of the disk you want to remove and how it is attached inside the computer.

   ▶ Some machines have a metal shield covering the drive bays that you must first remove to gain access to the drives.

   ▶ Other systems secure one or more drives to a metal housing which is in turn connected to the cabinet. In this case, you have to unscrew and remove the housing to access the drives. There are usually retaining screws on the front of the cabinet and at the bottom of the housing that secures it to the case.

   ▶ You might have to remove one disk to access the one you really want to take out. For instance, to remove the bottom of two vertically mounted drives, you might have to remove the top drive first. Continue following the steps to remove the drives.

5. Remove the controller and power cables connected to the drive. Before disconnecting a cable, mark it to indicate the drive it was attached to. You should do this even if you are removing only one drive, since some machines have extra power supply cables for additional drives. Mark the cable by writing the drive's letter on a piece of adhesive tape and wrapping the tape tightly around the end of the cable.

6. Remove the screws that secure the drive to the drive bay. There are usually two screws on each side, although a few systems mount the drives on the top or bottom.

7. Lift out the drive. Place the drive on a nonconductive surface, being careful not to bend any of the electrical or mechanical components.

Installing Your First Hard Disk

If you have a floppy-disk system, your first hard-disk drive will completely change the way you use your hand-me-down. You'll no longer have to search for a DOS disk to boot your computer, or shuffle stacks of floppy disks looking for a program or file. Because hard-disk drives access information faster than floppy disks, you'll see a dramatic increase in overall performance.

In this section, you'll learn how to install a hard-disk drive in a floppy-disk system. Don't attempt to install your own hard disk unless you feel confident about your abilities. Although installing a hard disk is a simple task in many systems, it can be quite complicated in others. Hard disks are not as susceptible to damage as circuit cards, but they can be damaged if inserted incorrectly or handled roughly.

Determining Needed Hardware

In addition to the drive and cables, you might need a controller card and a power supply adapter. Check your system documentation, or contact a computer store or the manufacturer. If you cannot get a satisfactory answer, follow these steps:

1. Unplug the power cords.

2. Remove the cover.

3. Follow the wide ribbon-cable from the floppy disks to the floppy-disk controller card. If there is an unused 34-pin connector, the controller supports a hard disk. One connector is for the floppy drives; the other is for the hard disk. Purchase a drive and cable but not a controller card. Just describe the make and model of your system to the salesperson.

   If you need to purchase a controller as well, buy it along with the drive so you know they are compatible. Since most early model controllers cannot handle 1.44Mb 3½-inch disk drives, check your documentation or contact the manufacturer to see if you need a special controller card.

4. Follow the floppy-disk power connectors to the power supply. If there is not an unused 4-wire connector, you'll need a Y-connector.

Preparing the Drive Bay

When you have all of the parts you need to install the drive, start by preparing the drive bay.

1. Unplug the power cords.

2. Remove the cover.

3. Gain access to the bay where you will insert the drive, taking out and marking any cables that you have to remove.

Many hard disks are embedded, meaning that they fit entirely in the bay and are not exposed on the front panel. If the front of the drive has an indicator light and a finished front panel, the panel will take the place of a bay cover. Remove the cover from the bay but save it in case you want to remove a drive later (Figure 14.6).

Installing the Controller

Follow these steps if you are also installing a hard-disk controller:

1. Remove the plate covering an unused expansion slot.

2. Insert the controller card as explained in Chapter 9.

3. Connect the cables to the controller (Figure 14.7).

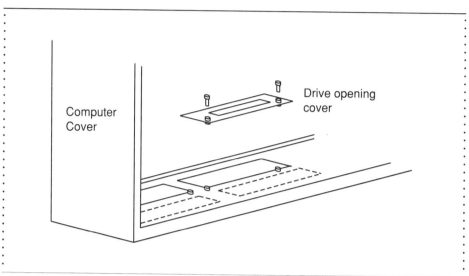

Figure 14.6: *Removing the bay cover*

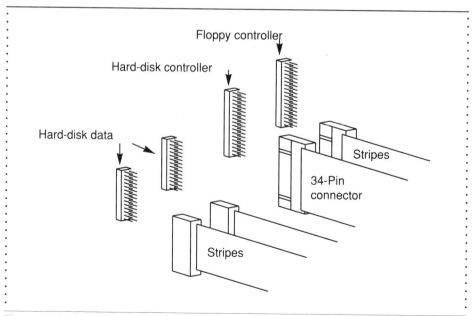

Figure 14.7: *Drive controller and data cables attached to controller card*

If you have two ribbon cables, one is 20 wires wide, and the other is 34 wires wide. Both have pin-type connectors and must be installed so the striped edge aligns with pin 1 on the card.

Inserting the Drive

Finally, install the drive and connect its cables. Check to make sure the drive came with mounting screws, usually four 6-32 Phillips-head screws.

1. Set the drive select jumper according to the manufacturer's instructions. If you don't have instructions, set the jumper to position 2 with a cable with twisted wires, or position 1 for a straight cable.

2. Make sure the terminal resister pack is installed.

3. Attach the drive to the housing using the small screws supplied.

4. Connect the cables to the drive. Be sure to connect the end of the controller cable with the twisted wires to the card-edge connector on the drive.

5. Connect the power supply, either directly or using the Y-connector.

6. Reinstall other drives, cables, or housings that you removed and check carefully for any lost screws.

7. Replace the cover.

Refer to "Setting Up Your Hard Disk" later in this chapter.

Installing Your Second Hard Disk

As you add software to your system and your data files grow, you might start to run out of room on your hard disk. If you have an available bay, you can add a second hard disk with a larger capacity instead of replacing the one you have.

Depending on how you set up your system, one hard disk can be drive C, the other drive D. You can even use the second hard disk as a convenient place to back up files from the first.

Follow these steps to install a second hard-disk drive:

1. Park your hard disk and then unplug the power cords.

2. Remove the cover.

3. Gain access to the bay where you will insert the drive, taking out and marking any cables that you have to remove.

4. Set the drive select jumper according to the manufacturer's instructions for installing the drive as drive D—the second hard disk. If you don't have instructions, set the jumper to position 2.

5. Remove the terminating resister on the drive you are installing. A terminating resister should already be installed on the first drive on the end of the cable.

6. Attach the drive to the housing using the small screws supplied.

7. Connect the pin-type plug of the 20-wire data cable to the controller card.

8. Connect the other end of the data cable to the drive.

9. Connect the center plug on the controller cable to the card-edge on the drive. On systems with only one floppy drive, make sure you use the cable that is already attached to the first hard drive, not the floppy-disk cable.

10. Connect the power supply, either directly or by using the Y-connector.

11. Reinstall the other drives, cables, or housings that you removed, and check carefully for lost screws.

12. Replace the cover.

Refer to "Setting Up a Hard Disk" later in this chapter.

Installing a Second Floppy-Disk Drive

Hard disks are invaluable, but there's nothing like having two floppy-disk drives for making disk copies. It's easy to insert a second floppy-disk drive, or replace drive B with one of a different size or capacity. Since all floppy-disk controllers support at least two drives, you just need the drive itself. Refer back to the section "Connectors and Cables" to make sure you have the proper hardware. Then follow these steps to insert a second floppy disk that is the same size as the first:

1. Park your hard disk, if you have one, and then unplug the power cords.

2. Remove the cover.

3. Gain access to the bay in which you will insert the drive. Remove and mark any cables that are in the way, and remove the blank bay cover.

4. Set the drive select jumper according to the manufacturer's instructions. If you don't have instructions, set the jumper to position 2 for a twisted wire cable, or position 1 for a straight cable.

5. Remove the terminal resister pack.

6. Attach the drive to the housing using the small screws supplied.

7. Connect the center plug on the controller cable to the drive (Figure 14.8).

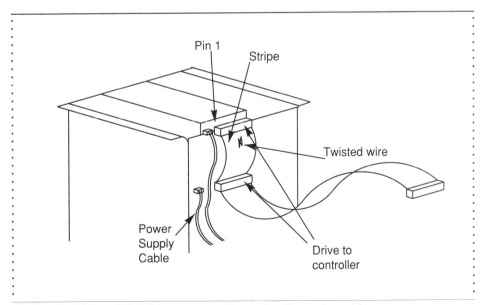

Figure 14.8: *Second disk drive connected to center plug on the cable*

8. Connect the power supply, either directly or by using the Y-connector.

9. Reinstall the other drives, cables, or housings that you removed and check for lost screws.

10. On XT systems you must set switches located on the motherboard so the computer recognizes the additional drive. Set the switches according to Table 14.2. With two floppy drives, switch 7 should be down (in the 0 or "off" position), and switch 8 up (in the 1 or "on" position).

11. Replace the cover.

Table 14.2: *On XT systems, Set Motherboard Switches to Recognize the Number of Installed Floppy-Disk Drives*

Number of Floppy Drives	Switch 7	Switch 8
1	down (0)	down (0)
2	down (0)	up (1)
3	up (1)	down (0)
4	up (1)	up (1)

Mixing Drive Sizes

You need some special hardware to insert a second drive that's a different size than the first.

Since $3^1/_2$-inch drives are becoming more popular in the PC world, many users want to add a $3^1/_2$-inch drive to $5^1/_4$-inch systems. Some $3^1/_2$-inch drives come installed in an adapter to fit into a $5^1/_4$-inch drive bay. If not, you'll need a housing adapter to install the drive. Also, check the size and type of connectors on the rear of the drive. If the drive uses a pin-type connector, you'll need a special controller cable and probably a power-connector adapter, as explained previously.

When you have all of the necessary hardware, you need to follow these steps.

1. Park your hard disk, if you have one, and then unplug the power cords.

2. Remove the cover.

3. Gain access to the bay in which you will insert the drive. Remove and mark any cables that are in the way, and remove the blank bay cover.

4. Set the drive select jumper according to the manufacturer's instructions. If you don't have instructions, set the jumper to position 2 for cables with twisted wires. If the cable is straight and you are installing the drive at the end of the cable as drive A, set the drive select jumper to position 1.

5. Remove the terminal resister pack on the drive in the middle of the cable.

6. Insert the drive into its housing adapter, and then attach the adapter to the drive bay.

Some drives come with a separate drive indicator light that plugs into a hole in the drive adapter or the front of the computer. Push the light through the hole into a plastic retainer that holds it in place (Figure 14.9).

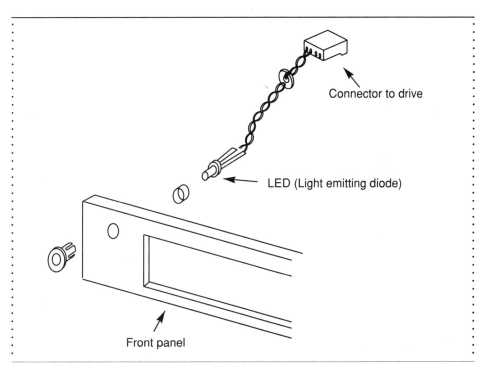

Figure 14.9: *Inserting a drive indicator light*

7. If you have to install a new controller cable, remove the cable that's already installed and insert the new one. Insert into the controller card the end that does not have the twisted wires.

8. Connect the center plug on the controller cable to the new drive.

9. Insert into the existing drive the end of the cable with the twisted wires.

10. Connect the power supply. If there is an unused power supply connector, attach it to the larger end of the power supply adapter that came with the drive, and then connect the other end of the adapter to the drive. If you have to use a Y-connector, disconnect the power connector from the other floppy-disk drive, attach the Y-connector, and then connect it to both drives.

11. Reinstall other drives, cables, or housings that you removed and check carefully for lost screws.

12. On XT systems, you must set switches located on the motherboard so the computer recognizes the floppy-disk drives. Set the switches according to Table 14.2. With two floppy drives, switch 7 should be down (in the 0 or "off" position), and switch 8 should be up (in the 1 or "on" position).

13. Replace the cover.

To install a 1.44Mb drive in an older system, you might have to install and purchase a special controller card.

Systems designed for 3½-inch drives usually have small drive bays that cannot accept a 5¼-inch drive. For other alternatives, refer to the section "Other Drive Options" later in this chapter.

Replacing a Drive

If a disk drive breaks down, purchase and install a new one of the same size and capacity. Make sure the drive select jumper is set to the second position (if the cable has twisted wires) and the terminating resister pack is installed or removed, as on the original.

You may, however, want to replace drive A with a drive of a different size or capacity. Some AT users with one floppy drive prefer to replace their 1.2Mb disk drive with a 360K disk drive, so their computers are disk-compatible with earlier machines. The controllers in AT machines can run 360K drives with no problems. You would also have no problem changing from a 1.44Mb disk drive to a 720K disk drive.

If you want to change to a higher capacity disk or to a different sized disk, make sure your system is compatible in all ways before purchasing any hardware. If your system is not compatible, you can always switch to a newer version of DOS or purchase a separate controller card. Consult a repair shop or the manufacturer if you are not sure.

Configuring Your System

With some systems, you can use a second floppy-disk drive once it is installed, or a hard disk as soon as you set it up. If you have an IBM XT or compatible system, you must set the switches on the motherboard as shown in Table 14.2. The CMOS of some AT machines and above, however, must be configured to access a new floppy disk, and all AT and above systems must be configured to recognize a new hard disk.

You should have a setup or configuration disk, a program on your DOS disk for setting CMOS, or a setup program built into ROM. While floppy disks are identified just by size and capacity, the wide range of hard disks makes configuration more difficult. To make it somewhat easier, CMOS setup routines identify common hard disks by type number. When you enter the type number of your drive, CMOS records the technical information associated with it. Since using the wrong ID number can damage your hard disk, check your system or hard-disk manual, or consult the manufacturer, for the drive's type number.

If you can't get the type number, or the hard disk is not included in your machine's built-in drive types, you may be able to configure the system manually. In addition to knowing the drive's capacity, however, you'll need some technical information about how the drive is constructed (Figure 14.10).

A hard-disk drive may contain one or more disk *platters,* a flat circular disk that stores magnetic information. Each platter's surface is divided into a series of concentric rings, called *tracks,* numbered consecutively from the outer edge, starting with 0. Each track is divided into *sectors,* or individual segments.

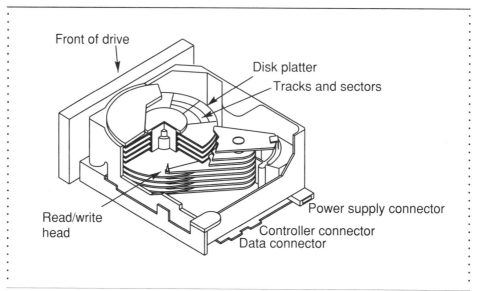

Figure 14.10: *Typical hard-disk construction*

The collection of all similarly numbered tracks is called a *cylinder*. Cylinder 1, for example, consists of the number 1 track on every platter. As the disk drive rotates, the disk sectors pass beneath a *read/write head* that records information on or reads information from the disk surface.

As the tracks get closer to the center of the disk, bits must be recorded more densely to maintain a constant bits-per-sector ratio. This higher density can result in a weaker magnetic field and more chance for errors. To overcome this problem, many systems automatically increase the current in the read/write head starting at a certain cylinder. This process is called *write precompensation*.

When you configure a hard disk manually in CMOS, you have to know the number of sectors on a track, the number of cylinders, the number of read/write heads, and the starting precompensation cylinder number, if your disk has one. You'll also need to know the *landing* or *shipping zone*—the area of the disk to place the heads when a PARK, SHIP, SHIPDISK, or similar command is given. You should be able to find this information in your system or hard-disk manual. If not, contact the manufacturer.

Many CMOS setup routines let you enter this specific information in place of a type number. When you are not given that option, select a type number for a drive with no more than the number of cylinders and heads in your drive. You might lose some capacity, but at least you'll be able to use the drive. Selecting a type number of a drive with more cylinders and heads can damage your hard disk.

Other Drive Options

There are ways to expand your hand-me-down's disk storage in ways besides installing standard drives. Some of these options, however, are rather expensive or may not be compatible with your hardware.

In this section, you'll learn about special high-capacity storage devices, disk drives that do not fit in your system's drive bays, and installation of more than two floppy-disk drives. If you decide to add one of the storage devices discussed here, check first with your system's manufacturer or an authorized repair shop. Make sure the addition will not void any warranty or repair contract, and that your system is capable of operating with the hardware installed.

Hard-Disk Cards

When you have no drive bays available and don't want to remove one of your floppies, you can add a *hard-disk card*—a circuit card that contains both the controller and hard disk and that slips into an empty card slot. Most hard-disk cards get their power directly from the computer's bus, but a few connect to the power supply with a Y-connector. Because hard-disk cards don't take up a drive bay, you can still have two full-height floppies for copying disks.

The physical size of the hard-disk card may be a limiting factor. While they all plug into one card slot, some hard-disk cards are so thick that they take up an adjacent slot. In some cases, only the end of the card containing the drive is thick, so you can still use a shorter card in the next slot.

External Drives

With laptops and many smaller systems, an external drive is the only way to add extra drives. An *external drive* is a floppy- or hard-disk drive that sits on the desktop next to your computer. It has its own power supply, which plugs into a wall outlet, and a controller cable that connects to an adapter card that you install in an unused expansion slot. Always use a surge protector between the drive and the wall outlet to protect your drive.

External drives are commonly used to connect drives that are a different size than those in the computer. If your computer has 3½-inch built-in drives, you would need an external drive to run 5¼-inch disks.

Because they have their own power supply, external hard-disk drives are an option for older machines with power supplies of 100 watts or less. However, they do take up desk space and you have to contend with the extra power switch and cable running across your table.

Special Drives and Configurations

Some unique drive configurations are possible, depending on how adventurous you feel. For example, Eastman Kodak Company markets a 5.5Mb floppy drive that uses special 5¼-inch diskettes. The drive is rated at 6.6Mb but diskettes only store 5.5Mb after being formatted with Kodak's special software. Nonetheless, with 5.5Mb per disk, you could back up a 20Mb hard disk with *only* four disks. These disks are more expensive than ordinary floppies, but the cost of about $3 per disk is well worth it. The drive comes with its own controller and a device driver that tricks DOS into treating it as a hard disk in drive D. It can read, but not write to, standard 360K disks.

You can also add additional controller cards to operate more than two floppy drives or two hard drives. The Compaticard from Micro Solutions, for example, comes complete with a variety of connectors that let you run up to four additional drives in your system, both internal and external. Combined with your system's standard controller, you can have any combination of six 5¼-inch or 3½-inch drives.

Setting Up a Hard Disk

When you install a new hard disk, you have to prepare it for use with your system, taking care of the low-level formatting, partitioning, and high-level DOS formatting.

Low-level formatting divides the disk into tracks and sectors, writing a *header* that DOS will use to locate files at the start of each sector. *Partitioning* allows you to divide the hard disk into more than one "logical" drive, such as making one hard disk appear as drives C and D to the operating system. The *high-level* DOS format creates the directory and FAT's for storing file information.

Low-Level Formatting

Many hard disks come already low-level formatted by the manufacturer. This is useful since the low-level format process can take some time and requires knowledge of the technical specifications of the disk.

Check your documentation to see if the disk has been formatted. If not, you should have received a floppy disk that includes a low-level format program. The program might be called DISK, DM, PREP, INSTALL, LFORMAT, or any number of names, so check your documentation carefully.

IBM does not include a low-level format program with DOS, although it is available on the optional Advanced Diagnostics Disk. But don't use the IBM program if your hard disk comes with a low-level format program. Because of special techniques to store data, particularly with hard-disk cards, the IBM version might actually damage the disk.

Always use the low-level formatting program that comes with your hard disk. Some manufacturer's versions of DOS do come with low-level format programs, so check your DOS manual.

Partitioning the Hard Disk

Once it is low-level formatted, the hard disk is physically ready to be used by your system. The next step, partitioning, divides the hard-disk platters into the disk drives associated with drive letters such as C and D.

Except for versions 4.0 and later, DOS can only address up to 32Mb of disk space because of the limitations of the file allocation table scheme. So if you have a disk that stores 32Mb or less, DOS can use the entire drive as one partition, or one logical drive.

If you have a disk larger than 32Mb and configure it as one partition, all space above 32Mb will be ignored. Running CHKDSK on a 40Mb drive, for example, will show only 32Mb of disk space—quite a waste of resources.

To get the maximum use of a hard disk larger than 32 Mb, partition it into several drives. On a 40Mb disk, for instance, you can have one 30Mb partition as drive C and another 10Mb partition as drive D. You can allocate your disk space any way you want, even divide the disk into smaller partitions such as drives C, D, E, and F.

One of the partitions, however, must be the DOS boot partition, the logical drive from which DOS will boot when you start your computer. The other partitions can serve as nonbootable data disks or, depending on your system, non-DOS partitions for other operating systems, such as XENIX and CP/M-86.

The partitioning program supplied with most versions of DOS is called FDISK. (Some manufacturers call this program PART.) It allows you to designate how much of the disk you want to allocate to each partition and which will be bootable, or active. The active partition is the only one that DOS recognizes automatically, and is the one used to boot the computer.

You must run FDISK or some other partitioning program to designate the bootable partition, even if you're not dividing the hard drive into more than one logical disk. When the FDISK menu appears, select option 1, Create DOS Partition (Figure 14.11). You'll be asked to enter the starting and ending cylinders of the partition and whether or not you want the partition to be the active one.

```
IBM Personal Computer
Fixed Disk Setup Program Version 3.20
(C)Copyright IBM Corp. 1983,1986

FDISK Options


Choose one of the following:

     1.   Create DOS partition
     2.   Change Active Partition
     3.   Delete DOS Partition
     4.   Display Partition Data


Enter choice: [1]




Press Esc to return to DOS
```

Figure 14.11: *FDISK menu*

Figure 14.12 shows the partition information for a 42Mb hard disk divided into two partitions, about 32Mb and 10Mb, respectively. Both are DOS partitions—they are used for DOS, not another operating system—and partition 1 is active.

Formatting the Active Partition

Once you create an active DOS partition, you must format it using the DOS command FORMAT with the /S option to make the disk bootable.

Follow these steps:

1. Start your computer with the DOS system disk in drive A.

2. Type **FORMAT C:/S/V**, and then press ⏎ to format the active partition and install the system files. The /V option will prompt you to enter a volume label, or disk name. Using the /V option when you format a drive prevents you from accidentally formatting the hard disk. You can now log on to and use drive C.

3. If you partitioned your hard drive into more than one disk, format each of them now. You do not have to transfer the system files to

```
Display Partition Information


Partition Status    Type  Start  End Size
     1        A     DOS      Ø   769  77Ø
     2        N     DOS    77Ø   985  216


Total disk space is   987 cylinders.







Press Esc to return to FDISK Options
```

Figure 14.12: *Partition table*

inactive partitions, so format drive D, for instance, with the command **FORMAT D:/V**.

Partitioning Zenith Computers

In most systems, the partitioning program assigns each inactive partition a drive letter. However, there are some computers and DOS versions, such as those manufactured by Zenith Data Systems, in which the drive letters must be assigned by DOS when you start your computer. If you are unable to format an inactive partition, such as drive D, then you have to include a special command in AUTOEXEC.BAT before you can format or otherwise access the nonboot drive.

With Zenith computers, add the command ASGNPART to your batch file using this syntax

ASGNPART *<drive number:> <partition> <drive letter:>*

where

<drive number:>	Designates the number of the disk drive—your first drive is number 0, the second is number 1, and so on
<partition:>	Designates the partition number
<drive letter:>	Is the DOS drive designator

For example, if your first hard disk is divided into two partitions, the first is drive C, the active partition. Before you can format or otherwise use the second partition, enter the command

ASGNPART 0:2 D:

This command links the second partition on the first (0) drive, to the DOS drive D.

Make sure ASGNPART is on your root directory, or the path is set to the directory storing DOS files, such as

PATH C:\DOS\
ASGNPART 0:2 D:

Once you boot your system and assign drive letters to nonactive partitions, format them with the FORMAT command. To format the second partition assigned to drive D, use the command

FORMAT D:

Because there are quite a few steps involved in preparing a hard-disk drive, let's summarize the procedure for your first hard disk:

1. If necessary, low-level format the hard disk.

2. Partition the drive, creating an active DOS partition and optional inactive DOS partitions.

3. Format the active partition as a system disk.

4. Format the inactive partitions, if any. (With Zenith computers, assign the drive letters using the ASGNPART command.)

Solving Hard-Disk Problems

When you're experiencing problems with your hard disk, you might be able avoid repair or replacement costs. Here are some common hard-disk problems that you can usually correct yourself. If these suggestions do not work, consult a repair shop or consider replacing the drive.

You can log on to, but not boot from, the hard disk.

▶ The disk is formatted but not as a system disk. Use the SYS command to copy the system from a DOS disk in drive A to the hard disk. If that doesn't work, back up any files on the hard disk and then reformat it as a system disk with the command **FORMAT C:/S/V**. Restore the backup files.

You can't log on to the hard disk.

▶ If you cannot log on to the active hard disk (drive C), the disk should be reformatted. First, try using a nondestructive low-level format program such as Spinrite II or Disk Technician. If that doesn't work, format the disk with the FORMAT command. If the disk won't format, run FDISK to see if the disk has been partitioned. If FDISK doesn't recognize the disk, it has to be low-level formatted.

If you cannot log on to an inactive partition, it may not be formatted. (If you have a Zenith computer, check for the proper ASGNPART command in AUTOEXEC.BAT before formatting the drive.)

There are excessive bad sectors.

▶ If the disk is usable but you get an excessive number of bad sector errors, back up the entire disk and then try using a nondestructive low-level format program. If that doesn't work, the disk has to be formatted again.

However, bad sectors are isolated during the low-level format process and just recorded on the FAT during the high-level format. If reformatting doesn't correct the problem, you have sectors that went bad after the disk was low-level formatted. There are a number of utility programs that can make DOS aware of bad sectors without performing another low-level format. With Norton Utilities, for example, use the command **DT/M/B**. Your version of DOS might have a similar program. For example, Zenith Data Systems includes the program DETECT with DOS, which scans your hard disk and adds any new bad sectors to those recorded during the last low-level format. Once new bad sectors are detected, run FORMAT to place an accurate record of bad sectors in the FAT. If you don't have DETECT or a similar program, perform a low-level format.

Some Storage Alternatives

Finally, let's look briefly at two alternatives to traditional disks drives—tape and removable media. Both of these provide high-capacity storage primarily designed for backups, for long-term archival storage, or for transporting data from one location to another.

There are a few systems that were sold with tape or removable devices installed by the manufacturer. Your hand-me-down might also include one of these devices added by the previous owner. If not, you still might find these alternatives worth-while additions.

Tape Storage

Some of the earliest microcomputers on the market relied on tape for storing data and programs. The original IBM PC had a cassette tape interface port that connected with a special cable to a regular audio cassette tape recorder. Although they are no longer viewed as an alternative for primary storage, tape devices are quite popular as backup media since a single tape can store 10Mb or more of data.

Like disk drives, tape systems can be internal (fitting into a disk drive bay) or external. Some require their own controller cards, others connect directly to the standard floppy-disk controller cable.

The earlier tape devices worked in the start-stop mode. Data was recorded in blocks, with the tape stopping after each block was written. This method is fine for saving files or programs individually as you would on a disk.

For making backups of your hard disk, there are streaming tape drives. A *streaming tape* records data continuously without stopping between blocks of data. However, you can still make file-by-file as well as complete image backups of your disk. Some image backups can even handle copy-protected software on your hard disk, restoring the program to running condition after a hard-disk crash.

Removable Storage

If you use more than one computer, you might be able to transfer data from one computer to another with a floppy disk. If the drives in both machines are compatible, you can save your work in the office on a disk, and then take it home to finish at night. However, you would be out of luck if the machines had different sized drives, or if you were working with a single hard-disk file too large to fit on a floppy disk.

You might also run out of room on your hard disk. When you back up data to floppy disks or even tapes, you still have to restore the backed up files before using them again. For example, perhaps you save all 20Mb of last year's budget information on a tape, and then delete it from the hard disk. In the middle of this year, you need to access last year's data but there is not enough room on your drive for the current year and last year's 20Mb. Your only option is to

1. Back up and then remove the current year's data.

2. Restore and access last year's data.

3. Remove last year's data, backing it up if you make any changes.

4. Restore the current year's data.

This is quite a lot of work.

Removable storage systems overcome these problems by using high-capacity hard-disk-like cartridges that you can take in and out of the drive transport. With some of the systems, you write data to and read it from the device just as if it were a hard disk installed in your computer. So while you can use removable storage systems as secondary storage for backups, they are fast enough to be used as primary storage, or to replace your main drive mechanism. In the case of the 20Mb of budget data, you'd just have to pull out the cartridge containing the current year and plug in the cartridge with the last year. Other systems use slower devices that are more suitable for backup and long-term data storage.

If you want to add a removable storage device to your hand-me-down, keep in mind that they can be rather expensive, although the cost depends on how the device is configured. One type of system uses a relatively inexpensive base housing that connects to your computer but requires removable disk packs that can cost up to $800 each. This type of system is preferable if you want removable storage but do not intend to save a number of disk packs.

If you want to use the removable media for long-term storage, systems that cost more initially but use less expensive media might be preferable. Once you install the system, additional packs might cost less than $150 each.

When shopping for a removable media system, calculate the cost per megabyte of storage. A system with an $800 base unit and three $800 40Mb packs would cost $26.66 per megabyte for the 120Mb setup. A $2000 system with three $150 40Mb packs costs only $20 per megabyte.

Before deciding to add a tape or removable media system to your hand-me-down, check with the manufacturer or a knowledgeable salesperson to determine if it is compatible with your computer and your expectations.

Product Reference

For information on the products mentioned in this chapter, contact:

Eastman Kodak Company
Mass Memory Division
343 State Street
Rochester, NY 14650
(619) 587-4831
6.6Mb floppy disk

Micro Solutions
132 West Lincoln Highway
DeKalb, IL 60115
(815) 756-3411
Compaticard controller

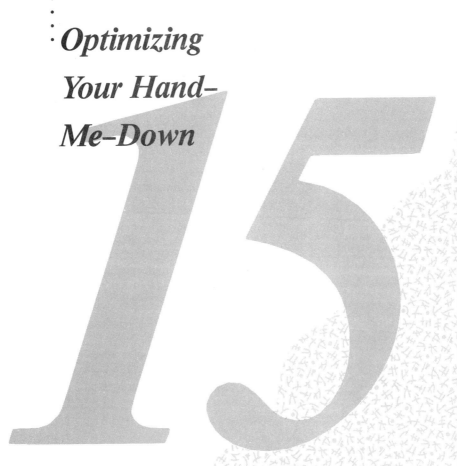

Chapter Fifteen

Optimizing Your Hand-Me-Down

15

Your hand-me-down computer might not be as ideal as one you would select yourself. After all, if you had the resources you could choose the most powerful system complete with all of the peripherals you'd need for maximum productivity. Still, your hand-me-down can serve as a base that you can build upon with purchases from a retailer or mail-order company.

Adding a hard-disk drive, using a disk cache, and periodically compressing fragmented files will make dramatic improvements to your hand-me-down's performance. So will adding and using expanded or extended memory for RAM disks and print spoolers. However, these efforts may still not make your hand-me-down the ideal system.

This chapter reviews more sophisticated ways to upgrade your system. You'll learn the benefits of multitasking software, and about hardware designed to raise your system to new levels of performance.

Improving Efficiency with Multitasking

If you have several megabytes of extended or expanded memory, much of it will be sitting idle a great deal of the time. While the number of programs using expansion memory is growing, most DOS applications fit nicely within the limits of conventional memory. But you can use that extra memory to run more than one program at a time, called *multitasking*.

Since most of us are accustomed to running one application at a time, the benefits of multitasking might not immediately be evident—but just imagine the capabilities.

Suppose you have to get a proposal completed before the staff meeting but you still have to write the text and print a database report that requires time-consuming calculations. Without multitasking, you have to wait for one task to finish before starting the next. With multitasking, you load the database program and start it generating the report; then you switch to the word processing application to write the text. By the time you're done with the text, the report is calculated and printed.

With multitasking, the two programs are not actually running at the same time. Instead, your system's processing time is divided into *time slices,* small periods of time. The system devotes a few time slices to one application, and then switches to the other application for a few time slices.

The program that you are working with and that is displayed on the screen is called the *foreground* application. The other program being run is called the *background* application. Multitasking switches between the two so fast that your work with the foreground application is undisturbed when the time slices are spent on the background program, giving the illusion that both programs are functioning simultaneously. With the right hardware, you can use your system as if you had several computers attached to one keyboard and screen, even passing information from one program to the other as you work.

In Chapter 12 you briefly saw how the Windows graphic environment can be used for multitasking. Let's take a look at some other approaches.

Multitasking on PC-Compatibles

Practical multitasking requires more than conventional memory and at least an AT-class computer, preferably a 386. However, it is possible to perform multitasking on PC- and XT-compatibles.

DoubleDOS from Softlogic Solutions, for example, offers multitasking capabilities on PC-compatible computers with conventional memory, even though it can take advantage of any expanded memory you have. DoubleDOS can run on a floppy-disk system without a hard disk. The program divides your memory into a top and bottom section, letting you set the amount of memory devoted to each (Figure 15.1). Each section now operates as a separate computer, with one in the foreground and one in the background.

```
DoubleDOS version 4.ØØ is now resident

Total memory available is 597K

Enter size for TOP memory section (in K):

All remaining memory will be assigned to the BOTTOM memory section.

Type the enter ◄┘ key to assign 298K to each memory section.
```

Figure 15.1: *DoubleDOS opening options*

For example, suppose you create two memory sections of 298K each. After starting DoubleDOS, you'll see the message

DoubleDOS Top Memory Section (298K)
C>

showing the amount of memory allocated to that section. You can now run an application program or work with DOS as you would normally. When you want to run another application, press Alt-Esc to place the first section in the background—what DoubleDOS calls the *invisible memory section*—and display the prompt

DoubleDOS Bottom Memory Section (298K)
C>

With the background program still running, you can now execute another application or DOS command, and switch back and forth between the two sections by pressing Alt-Esc.

You can exchange areas, change the size of the sections, or reboot your computer from the DoubleDOS menu, which you display by pressing Alt-Del (Figure 15.2).

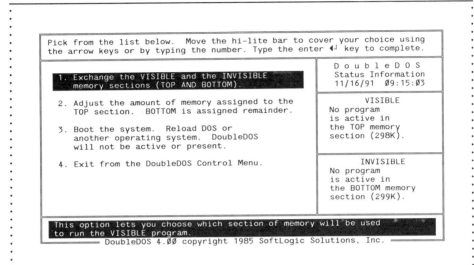

```
Pick from the list below.  Move the hi-lite bar to cover your choice using
the arrow keys or by typing the number. Type the enter ◀┘ key to complete.

                                              D o u b l e D O S
  1. Exchange the VISIBLE and the INVISIBLE    Status Information
     memory sections (TOP AND BOTTOM).         11/16/91  Ø9:15:Ø3

  2. Adjust the amount of memory assigned to the        VISIBLE
     TOP section.  BOTTOM is assigned remainder.   No program
                                                    is active in
  3. Boot the system.  Reload DOS or                 the TOP memory
     another operating system.  DoubleDOS           section (298K).
     will not be active or present.
                                                       INVISIBLE
  4. Exit from the DoubleDOS Control Menu.        No program
                                                    is active in
                                                    the BOTTOM memory
                                                    section (299K).

  This option lets you choose which section of memory will be used
  to run the VISIBLE program.
          ═══════ DoubleDOS 4.ØØ copyright 1985 SoftLogic Solutions, Inc. ═══════
```

Figure 15.2: *DoubleDOS menu*

If you have two printer ports and two printers, both applications can be printing at the same time. In fact, DoubleDOS supports up to four printers simultaneously. You can even have both programs displayed at the same time if you have two video adapters and two monitors. One monitor will be assigned to the top section, the other to the bottom section.

Multitasking on AT Computers and Above

If you're lucky enough to have a hand-me-down that is an AT-class or above computer, you have a wide range of multitasking DOS environments available.

For instance, Omniview, from Sunny Hill Software, runs on 286 and 386 class machines using DOS version 2.0 or later. When you run a program, you designate the minimum amount of memory it requires as well as the maximum amount of expanded memory you want allocated to it. You can also specify if you want the program to run in the background or to be temporarily suspended when you switch out of it. Suspending a program allows you to free up the computer's processing power for another application while maintaining the background program and its data in memory.

Like most multitasking programs, Omniview lets you set the priority between background and foreground tasks. The priority determines how many time slices are devoted to each task. A program with higher priority will be given more time slices in which to operate. To use Omniview on a 386 computer, you should also use the company's 386-To-The-MAX memory manager.

Desqview 386 is a multitasking program from Quarterdeck Systems. It comes with the QEMM memory manager that, among other things, converts extended memory into expanded memory to be used for swapping between applications.

Like other 386 multitasking programs, Desqview takes advantage of the 386's *virtual mode.* In this mode, the 386 can run programs larger than available memory and can run several DOS programs in their own *virtual machine.* The 386 manages memory so each application runs as if it were on a separate computer—a virtual machine—independent from the others. Like Microsoft Windows, Desqview can display several applications at the same time in their own windows.

Versions of Desqview are available for PC-, XT-, and AT-class machines. They allow multitasking but without the virtual machine feature of the 386 processor.

Taking the virtual machine concept even further is VM/386, from IGC, Inc. When you use this program, each virtual machine can run its own version of DOS and use individual AUTOEXEC.BAT and CONFIG.SYS files. This is useful if you have to run an older application that requires an early version of DOS and a newer application that needs the latest version.

Saving Time by Program Switching

If you don't have enough hardware for multitasking, you might still be able to use program switching. *Program switching* allows you to load more than one application, but only run the one in the foreground. The background applications stop running yet remain in memory so your data is not lost and you can switch back to them with a few keystrokes.

Even though only one program is actually running at a time, program switching can be quite efficient. In many cases, you want the flexibility to refer to a file from one application when you work with another. It's not important that the background application is suspended, just that you can switch into it without exiting the foreground application.

Program switching can be performed on all computers but is often limited to the number of programs that can fit in your memory at one time. If you have only 512K of conventional memory, you can load several smaller programs at the same time, but not larger ones like WordPerfect and Lotus 1-2-3.

You can accomplish some degree of program switching from applications that have a DOS command function. While running WordPerfect, for example, press Ctrl-F1 and then 1 to select the Go to DOS option. You'll see the message

Enter 'EXIT' to return to WordPerfect

followed by the DOS prompt. WordPerfect is still in memory—it's just suspended. You can now execute a DOS command or run another program. Since WordPerfect is still in memory, however, you must have enough memory to hold it and the other application at the same time. If not, you'll see the message

program too big to fit in memory

when you try to run the second program.

However, some specialized program-switching software let you load more programs than your memory can store. When you switch between programs, the status of the background program is recorded on your hard disk, allocating as much memory as possible to the foreground task. Software Carousel, for instance, can load up to twelve programs at a time, swapping programs in and out of the hard disk while maintaining the current condition of each.

The key difference between multitasking and program switching is that in multitasking, the background application is still executing. This is primarily important when you want the background program to continue printing, calculating, or transmitting characters.

Enhancing Your System with Coprocessors

The combined demands of multitasking software, device drivers, and application programs require every bit of processing speed and power you have available. A fully loaded system pushes the processor to its limits, especially when using expanded memory and running programs that require complex calculations.

One way to ease the burden on your computer is to divide its work between more than one *microprocessor,* the integrated circuit that controls the computer's operations and performs most of its basic functions. *Multiprocessing* is a hardware technique in which several microprocessors work together. Because these microprocessors share the burdens of the system, overall performance is faster and more advanced functions can be performed. However, multiprocessing systems are expensive and not likely to show up as hand-me-downs for many years.

A less expensive alternative to multiprocessing is coprocessing. A *coprocessor* is a microprocessor circuit dedicated to a specific or specialized task. It takes some of the burden from your system's central processor, allowing it to devote optimum power to general-purpose computing tasks.

Unlike the system's central processor, which is used by every DOS program, coprocessors are only used by software designed for them. Coprocessors created for specialized printing, for example, need special device drivers and font files to be used with application programs.

Using Numeric Coprocessors

The most frequently used coprocessor is the *numeric coprocessor,* a circuit dedicated to performing high-speed complex calculations required by statistical and engineering applications and programs that are graphic-intensive. While displaying text images and low-resolution graphics demands little of your system, high-resolution and high-speed graphics require vigorous computations.

Numeric coprocessors are so widely used that many application programs support them and will perform their calculations in the coprocessor rather than the general-purpose microprocessor. Most of these programs automatically sense when the coprocessor is present and require no additional setup or configuration.

The *87* family of numeric coprocessors from Intel Corporation is the industry-wide standard for PC-compatible computers. Each member of the family is matched with a microprocessor. The 8087 coprocessor is designed for the 8086 and 8088 CPU's, the 80287 for the 80286 CPU, the 80387 for the 80386 CPU, and the 80387SX for the 80386SX CPU. There is also an 80C287 coprocessor used in many laptop computers.

Coprocessors come in various speeds to match the microprocessor. The speed in indicated after the chip number in megahertz, so a 80287-6 coprocessor can be used in systems running up to 6 MHz. (The exceptions are the 8087-2 rated at 8 MHz, and the 8087-1 at 10 MHz.) If no speed number is given, the chip can run at speeds of up to 5 MHz.

Many AT and compatible computers can use any speed 80287 chip. Since most 386 computers are more demanding, however, they need an 80387 that matches the 386's processing speed. A few 386 machines can use any 80387 that's not faster than the processor, and some can even use 80287's.

Weitek Corporation makes an alternative numeric coprocessor for 386 systems— the WTL 1167. The coprocessor consists of several integrated circuits on a small circuit board that plugs into a 121-pin socket. It will not fit into a socket designed for the Intel 80387. Because the WTL 1167 offers better performance in some areas than the Intel 80387, some manufacturers include a Weitek-compatible socket in their high-end computers.

The WTL 1167 works only with applications written specifically for it, not with programs designed for the Intel 80387. But the circuit board has an 80387 socket where you can install an Intel chip for use with programs that require an 80387.

Adding a Coprocessor

The 8087 and 80287 coprocessors are packaged as 40-pin integrated circuits. The 80387 and 80387SX are square devices with 68 pins (Figure 15.3). If your computer can accept a coprocessor, it will have an empty chip socket on the motherboard. Some 386 computers will have two empty sockets, one for a 80387 and one for an 80287—but you only use one.

As with any chip, static electricity can destroy a coprocessor, so keep the coprocessor in its protective wrapper until you are ready to install it. Touch the computer's case to ground yourself before picking it up and, if possible, don't put it down until you install it. Here are the steps involved in adding a coprocessor:

1. Park your hard disk, if you have one.
2. Unplug your computer and remove the cover.

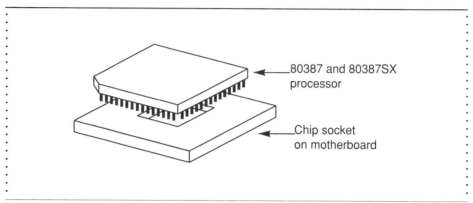

Figure 15.3: *80387 and 80387SX numeric coprocessor*

3. Identify the coprocessor socket. Look for an empty 40-pin or 68-pin socket on the motherboard or CPU card.

4. Ground yourself by touching the computer's case.

5. Check that the pins of the chip are at a right angle to the body of the chip. If you have to straighten them, place one row of pins against a hard wood or plastic surface, and then gently press the chip body until the pins are at a right angle.

6. Align pin number 1 of the chip toward pin 1 of the socket. Don't assume that the coprocessor is oriented like other chips around it. The notch on the chip must face the same direction as the notch printed under the socket on the circuit board.

7. Gently insert all of the pins into the socket.

8. Apply even pressure until the chip is fully seated in the socket.

9. Check that no pins are bent, either under the chip or towards the outside of the socket. If they are, remove the chip by prying it up with a thin-blade screwdriver or special chip remover. Ground yourself and carefully straighten the pin. Do not bend the pin any more than absolutely necessary. If bent too much and too often, the pin will break and the chip will be worthless.

10. Check again to make sure the coprocessor is properly oriented toward pin 1 and all of the pins are inserted.

Configuring Your Computer

Check your system documentation for details on configuring your computer to recognize the coprocessor. On most PC and XT models, there are a series of switches on the motherboard. The coprocessor can be used when the second switch of the first bank of switches (with a PC) or the second switch of the only bank of switches (with an XT) is in the off position—toward the left.

AT models and above are usually set to recognize the coprocessor through CMOS. Run your setup program or other CMOS routine to change CMOS settings. If you don't have documentation for your system, contact the manufacturer or a computer retailer that handles your model.

Increasing Speed with a Memory Cache

You know that a disk cache stores frequently needed disk sectors in high-speed RAM. This improves performance because the data can be retrieved faster from RAM than from the disk drive. Slow memory can hamper overall performance just as a slow disk drive can. Because high-speed memory chips are expensive, many systems use slower chips and make your system catch up during idle wait states. A memory cache can overcome this problem and create a zero wait state computer. A *memory cache* is a small section of high-speed memory that stores frequently used data in place of slower RAM.

When a program needs data, the system first looks for it in cache memory without needing a wait state. The percentage of times the data is found in cache is called the *hit rate.* The higher the hit rate, the larger the increase in system performance. If the data is not found in the cache—called a *miss*—the system then looks in regular RAM subject to the normal wait state.

Many 386 systems have cache memory already built in to the motherboard to achieve an advertised zero wait state. If your system does not, you can add a cache memory card in an expansion slot. But before buying the card, consider how you might best use your existing memory.

High-speed cache memory is expensive but the cost isn't prohibitive because cache memory is usually from 32K to 128K. What's important is the method used by the system to decide what data should go into the cache. The more the system can anticipate what data the program will need in order to operate, the higher the hit rate.

Some programs use data in a very predictable pattern, making it easy for the cache to anticipate what instructions will be used and to place them in its memory. However, programs that use complicated switching routines with extended or expanded memory might have a higher miss rate and won't realize a dramatic increase in speed.

If you're not pleased with a program's speed, try using a RAM disk or disk cache if you have extended or expanded memory. These might make enough of an improvement. If you still want to increase performance, check with your system's manufacturer for recommended cache cards.

Maximizing Your System with CPU Surgery

The ultimate upgrade without buying a new system is to replace your processor with a newer and faster model. You can possibly upgrade your XT to an AT, your AT to a 386, or your 386 to a 486. You perform this major transformation by either inserting an accelerator board or by replacing your entire motherboard with a new one.

An *accelerator board* is a CPU card that fits into an expansion slot and replaces your existing processor. The Intel Inboard 386/PC, for example, is a plug-in expansion card that can transform most computers—even some PC and XT models—into 386's. (Intel has a list of computers the board is guaranteed to work with.) Its 1Mb of RAM can be expanded to 5Mb, and it has a socket to hold a 80387 coprocessor. You insert the card into a slot, remove your existing CPU chip, and connect a cable between the chip socket and the Inboard card.

Fastcache-SX, from Microway, is a similar card designed to upgrade an AT or compatible to a 386SX machine. It comes in both 16 and 20 MHz versions, with either 32K or 64K of high-speed cache memory.

A few computers are even designed with CPU expansion built in to the motherboard. The AT-compatible ALR Powerflex, for instance, includes a Feature Connector designed to hold the company's 386SX or 486 upgrade board. Just plug in the board, reconfigure CMOS, and you have a 386SX or 486 computer system. Both upgrade boards have a socket for the 80387 coprocessor.

If you have a 286 machine and want to upgrade without using an expansion slot, you can install an Evergreen 386 Superchip. This is a small 2¼-inch square card that directly replaces the 286 CPU chip in most systems, upgrading it to a 386SX. You pull out the 286 chip and insert the Superchip in its socket. It is compatible with your existing 286 expansion boards, ROM, and RAM, and works with a 80287 coprocessor. The only systems not suitable for the Superchip are those with the 286 soldered permanently in place or with tightly packed boards that don't have enough clearance for the Superchip, which is slightly larger than the 286 chip.

While you have to access and remove your CPU chip carefully, accelerator boards are designed for easy installation. Before accelerator boards were developed, the only option for upgrading the CPU was a total transplant—the removal of your entire motherboard and the insertion of a new one.

The procedure is more difficult than inserting an accelerator card, and some replacement motherboards are not totally compatible with existing 286 hardware. In a few cases, you have to change RAM chips, replace your 80287 with an 80387, and reroute other cables and connectors. Motherboard replacement is best left to the adventurous and technically experienced.

As with any hardware expenditure, consider an upgrade path carefully. Make sure the upgrade will give you the performance and hardware and software compatibility that you want. Get enough documentation and a guarantee that the upgrade will work with your system, making sure that it is totally compatible with your memory and other hardware. If the upgrade is not compatible, you might need to purchase new memory, a disk controller, a video card, and even a keyboard—making the final cost of your upgrade many times the cost of the accelerator card or motherboard itself.

If you purchase an accelerator board, select the vendor with as much care as you select the board itself. Because of its technical nature, you might have questions about the board's installation, setup, and compatibility. A supportive and knowledgeable dealer will be able to recommend the best accelerator card for your system and guide you through its use. Many dealers will even install the card for free or for a small fee. If you're not experienced with working inside your computer, it pays to have the card professionally installed and tested.

There are mail-order companies that sell accelerator boards and other hardware for less than most retail stores. While some of the companies provide after-sale support, mail-order businesses can afford to charge less because they don't provide the same level of personal attention and assistance that you may get from a local store. If you're confident of your choice of an accelerator board and your ability to install it, purchasing through a mail-order source could save you money. Select vendors that guarantee their products and preferably have toll-free support lines if you do have questions.

Looking Before You Leap to Upgrade

Each upgrade requires a financial commitment, and if you select all of the upgrades discussed here you'll have a virtually new computer system. But at some point, you have to consider the cost effectiveness of upgrading compared to buying a new computer.

That's not to say you should never upgrade. If you have a solid AT-compatible, purchasing an accelerator card is an inexpensive path to 386 processing power. Upgrading an XT to a basic AT could also be cost effective. But the extreme upgrade from an inexpensive PC hand-me-down to a full-fledged 386 would involve more than an accelerator card. You might also need additional memory, a new power supply, a VGA video card and monitor, and a hard-disk drive. To be fully compatible with new 386 machines, you might also purchase a high-capacity floppy-disk drive.

Where do you take your new hybrid computer when it needs repairs? You might have to ship the individual components back to their manufacturers. Even if the original machine was a name-brand computer, many authorized repair centers won't even look at a machine if it has a single third-party part. I had a friend who had to remove his upgraded hard-disk drive whenever he took his computer in for repair. Otherwise, the shop wouldn't honor the service contract.

Yet, for the cost of the total upgrade, you can purchase a new 386SX computer, complete with warranty. Adding a disk drive and additional memory is a reasonable expense if your system is otherwise sound and suitable. But think twice before gutting the machine and starting over.

In the next chapter, you'll consider some additional reasons to upgrade and learn how to plan your upgrades for maximum value. You'll also learn what to do if your hand-me-down cannot be upgraded any further.

There are many other accelerator boards besides those mentioned here. But for more information about the products discussed in this chapter, contact

Evergreen Technologies, Inc.
1325 N. W. 9th Street
Corvallis, OR 97330
(800) 733-0934
Evergreen 386 Superchip

Softlogic Solutions, Inc.
P. O. Box 6221
Manchester, NH 03108
(603) 644-5555
DoubleDOS, Software Carousel

IGC, Inc.
4800 Great America Parkway
Santa Clara, CA 95054
(408) 986-8373
VM/386

Sunny Hill Software
P. O. Box 55278
Seattle, WA 98155
(800) 367-0651
Omniview

Microway, Inc.
P. O. Box 79
Kingston, MA 02364
(508) 746-7341
Fastcache-SX

Quarterdeck Office Systems
150 Pico Blvd.
Santa Monica, CA 90405
(213) 392-9851
Desqview, QEMM

Chapter Sixteen

Planning Your Hand–Me–Down's Upgrade

16

*S*everal chapters in this book have been devoted to upgrading your hand-me-down. We've looked at high-resolution video adapters, expanded and extended memory, pointing devices, disk drives, coprocessors, and accelerator boards.

Your upgrade decisions should be based on your needs and should be cost effective. Select an upgrade only if you need additional resources, increased speed, or improved performance. On the other hand, you should consider future needs and not settle for a less expensive option that will later have to be replaced. For example, adding a hard-disk drive to a basic PC system may be wasteful if you really need an AT to run one of your applications. Likewise, while installing an accelerator card may enable an XT to run software designed for a 386, the resulting system may still not perform with the speed and power of a full-fledged 386.

This chapter looks at some possible reasons to upgrade your hand-me-down, and what actions to take when it seems economically inefficient to optimize your hand-me-down any further.

Upgrading for Speed

Computer speed, measured in megahertz, is based on the speed with which the microprocessor can process instructions. The earliest PC's ran at about 4 MHz; then advancements in microprocessor technology made 8, 12, 16, 20, and even 33 MHz chips a reality.

Speed is one of the selling points we see in advertisements, with manufacturers vying for the fastest machine on the market. But the important issue is actually performance, and not microprocessor speed.

For instance, in certain configurations, a 20 MHz processor might not perform better than a 16 MHz processor. The 20 MHz machine may use slower memory chips and require one or two wait states, while a zero wait state 16 MHz system runs at almost the same rate, for less money.

If you're using a program that requires frequent disk access, the speed of your hard disk will have more effect on performance than the speed of the microprocessor. A machine with a slow processor and a fast hard drive will often perform better than a system with a faster processor and a sluggish drive.

Depending on how you use your computer, its speed might be of little importance. A high-speed system will make dramatic differences in graphic- and computation-intensive applications, but little in text-oriented programs such as word processors. Before upgrading for speed alone, try exhausting less expensive alternatives such as RAM disks, spoolers, disk caches, or adding or upgrading a hard-disk drive.

There are several paths to take if you still want more speed. You can purchase a faster system, replace your CPU or motherboard as explained in Chapter 15, or install a clock speed-up kit that is available for some machines. The kit replaces your computer's clock circuit, the electronics that time and synchronize the system's operations. The kits are most popular with owners of older model systems that run at 4 MHz—they often double the effective speed.

Moving to the 486

Some users might like to upgrade to the newest microprocessor, now the Intel 80486. The 80486 combines an 80386 microprocessor, a numeric coprocessor, and a 8K memory cache in one chip. Available in either 25 MHz or 33 MHz versions, it is ideal for high-speed applications.

With all of its speed and power, the 80486 does have some drawbacks. Most vendors package the 486 in expensive high-end systems suitable for network servers or workstations, thinking that only power users with a lot of money would consider the chip. While the built-in cache is convenient, it is generally considered not sufficient for major applications, so many manufacturers include an additional external memory cache card as well, adding to the cost.

There are also some hardware and software compatibility problems. The high-speed systems have trouble running some software designed for slower PC's,

XT's, and AT's. While some 486 systems can be switched into slower speeds to increase compatibility, there are still programs and expansion boards that will not operate correctly.

The decision to buy a 486 system or a 486 accelerator board should be based on the software you're using and its need for speed and power. While you wouldn't need a 486 for basic word processing, for example, its advanced capabilities would be ideal for large and complex spreadsheets, high-resolution graphics, and other computation-intensive applications.

Upgrading to Use New Applications

Some programs, such as version 3 of Lotus 1-2-3 and the Oracle database manager, require an AT-class and above computer. But because of the tremendous base of PC and XT systems, a vast majority of application programs run on PC and XT models. There are still plenty of applications that need nothing more than a two-floppy PC system.

To keep up with newer versions of software, however, adding memory and a hard-disk drive might be more important than the microprocessor itself. Upgrade to at least 640K or to whatever your motherboard can accept, or add expanded memory.

If you want to run a program that specifies an AT-class machine, check the fine print for the recommended amount of memory. Some of the programs require additional extended or expanded memory, so purchasing a 1Mb system will not be sufficient. Oracle, for instance, requires an AT computer with 1Mb of extended memory. When upgrading to run a specific program, check the memory, drive, and graphic requirements carefully.

Upgrading Your Bus Architecture

The computer's *bus* is the roadway through which data travels from one circuit to another. The bus connects circuit cards in the expansion slots to the microprocessor, interface ports, and other parts of your hand-me-down. In 8088 and 8086 PC systems, data moves 8 bits at a time along an 8-bit bus. The AT and other 80286 machines (as well as the 80386SX) move data along a 16-bit bus, and 80386 and 80486 computers use a 32-bit data bus.

The bus system for PC, XT, and AT machines is known as the ISA (Industry Standard Architecture). It is adequate for 8- and 16-bit computers but can not handle the data width necessary for full 32-bit operation.

To maintain compatibility with existing circuit cards, many of the first 386 systems used a 16-bit bus for all operations that didn't require a 32-bit wide path. These usually included video circuits, output ports, and the disk-drive controller. However, memory requires a 32-bit bus to work with the microprocessor, so some manufacturers installed all of their memory directly on the motherboard. Other companies developed their own proprietary buses. Their motherboards or backplanes might have several 8-bit and 16-bit expansion slots that can accept ISA cards, and one or two slots designed for their own 32-bit memory boards. If you want additional memory, you have to purchase it directly from the manufacturer because no other 32-bit memory board will work on their bus.

The PS/2 line of IBM computers is responsible for introducing the VGA standard, popularizing 3½-inch disks in the DOS world, and bringing about *Micro Channel Architecture,* or *MCA.*

MCA is IBM's approach to a 32-bit bus, and is seen by many as the 32-bit standard. A number of other vendors now sell Micro Channel compatible systems. If you purchase a 32-bit MCA board, you can use it in any MCA-compatible computer.

MCA handles data faster than ISA systems, and can address up to 4 gigabytes on an AT-style system, equalling the address capabilities of the 80386. The MCA cards also consume less power, making the system run cooler. In addition, they result in a smaller machine, taking up less of your desktop, although some add-on board manufacturers have had trouble fitting the necessary components on the smaller cards.

However, MCA expansion slots are not compatible with those in other models and will not accept PC, XT, or AT expansion cards. While the standard AT card is just over 13 inches wide and 4 inches high, the MCA card is 11½ inches wide and about 3 inches high. If you upgrade to a Micro Channel machine, you will not be able to use any expansion cards from your previous system.

In response to MCA, a group of manufacturers led by Compaq Computer Corporation joined together to promote a competing bus system, *EISA,* for *Extended Industry Standard Architecture.* EISA is an effort to establish a 32-bit bus standard in direct competition to MCA. The bus handles data faster than the ISA bus, using a special Direct Memory Access controller to take some of the burden off of the microprocessor. Perhaps the biggest benefit of EISA from the user's standpoint is its compatibility with ISA expansion cards. The extension slots are the same size and require the same power, so you can use your existing cards when moving up to an EISA system.

While the two competing products, MCA and EISA, offer two different standards, at least they are standards. If you have an MCA or EISA computer, you'll be able to purchase memory and other expansion cards from vendors other than the manufacturer.

You cannot upgrade an ISA bus to either MCA or EISA. The only way to upgrade to a different bus is to purchase a computer with the bus already installed. The move to either a MCA or EISA machine, however, should not be based on the bus alone, but on the extent to which its features will improve your efficiency and productivity. If you are considering a 32-bit machine that is not MCA or EISA, determine the availability of memory expansion. Systems that accept standard SIMM's on the motherboard can be upgraded less expensively than those requiring cards using a proprietary bus. If the company goes out of business or stops supporting the proprietary model in favor of MCA or EISA machines, you won't be able to expand memory.

Exploring New Operating Systems

Almost everything in the PC world has expanded—32-bit processing, multi-megabyte memory, high-resolution graphics—everything but DOS.

While DOS has evolved over the years, most versions are still limited to 640K of conventional memory and 32Mb hard-disk partitions, and can only run one program at a time without special multitasking software. It was only logical that a new operating system should develop to accommodate the technological advances in hardware.

Near the end of 1987, the first versions of the OS/2 operating system became available. While it has roots in DOS—many of its commands are the same and it can read and write to DOS disks—OS/2 clearly initiates a new era in computing.

Designed for 286 and 386 systems, OS/2 can address extended memory above 1Mb. The extra memory allows for built-in multitasking in the protected mode. In *protected mode,* OS/2 performs memory management tasks to ensure that there are no conflicts between existing programs—that no two programs, for example, would try to use the same memory addresses. Protected mode also allows you to run more applications than will fit in memory. When the system runs out of actual memory, it simulates additional memory by using space on your disk drive. It temporarily stores your running programs on the disk, swapping data between the disk drive and actual memory as required. While your system may only have megabytes of actual memory, it appears to have up to 4 gigabytes of *virtual,* or simulated, memory in the hard disk.

Only programs designed for OS/2 can take advantage of the operating system's protected mode. To maintain compatibility with DOS applications, OS/2 provides a second mode of operation, real mode. In *real mode,* OS/2 acts as if it were DOS, so DOS programs run normally, although still restricted to the 640K limitations.

Just as real mode eased the transition from DOS to OS/2, so does *dual boot.* You can configure your system to boot as either OS/2 or MS-DOS. One operating system is set up as the default used when you start your system. To boot the other operating system, just hold down the Alt key as the computer starts.

OS/2 was updated to version 1.1 in 1988 to include Presentation Manager (PM) and a graphic user interface much like Microsoft Windows. In 1989, OS/2 was updated to version 1.2, which includes File Manager, a DOS shell-type program for displaying and working with the directory structure. It also includes the Desktop Manager, which groups files by type and lists applications for easy execution.

With version 1.2, you can select the High Performance File System (HPFS) in place of the traditional FAT. HPFS incorporates its own disk-caching routines and allows file names of up to 255 characters. For example, instead of naming a report

BUDGET93

you can name it

OPERATING BUDGET FOR 1993

Unfortunately, HPFS is incompatible with DOS. While DOS can read and write files stored in an OS/2 partition using FAT, it cannot access files under HPFS. In addition, utility programs for undeleting DOS files won't work with HPFS.

Version 2.0 of OS/2 is being planned for use solely on 386 and 486 computers, and will allow greater compatibility with DOS applications, even allowing the transfer of text and graphics. An extended edition of OS/2 is being developed that will include its own database server and communications manager.

Now how does OS/2 affect your upgrade decisions?

Presentation Manager version 1.1 or 1.2 will boot in a machine with 1Mb of memory and it requires an 80286 or above computer, and at least a 10Mb hard-disk drive. For all practical purposes, you need extended memory (at least 4Mb to perform any useful multitasking) and a 20Mb hard disk.

Whether or not you need OS/2 is another question. You can accomplish much of what OS/2 has to offer using version 3 of Microsoft Windows or another multitasking program that provides a graphic user interface and memory management. If you have limited memory, you can multitask without the graphic environment using a number of software programs. There are even utilities that let you use longer file names and address hard-disk partitions larger than 32Mb.

While OS/2 is a powerful operating system, you need quite a bit of hardware and compatible applications to take advantage of its most important features, although you can still run DOS programs in real mode. If you don't need all of that power, investigate multitasking DOS alternatives and take a look at version 3 of Microsoft Windows.

Considering the UNIX Alternative

UNIX is an operating system first developed by Bell Telephone Laboratories in the late 1960s. Originally designed for systems larger than microcomputers, it can be used in PC's having at least the 286 processor. Like OS/2, it is a multitasking operating system. In addition, it is a *multiuser* system—it supports the simultaneous use of the microprocessor by more than one person. This makes it ideal for use in offices where several people need to share the same data.

While UNIX doesn't have the same origins as DOS and OS/2, many of its concepts are similar. It uses a *kernel* that controls system hardware, much like DOS's hidden files IO.SYS and IBMDOS.SYS. User interaction is performed through a *shell*, a command interpreter analogous to COMMAND.COM, and UNIX includes *utility programs* just as DOS includes external commands. File information is stored in directories, and the disk can be divided into directories and subdirectories.

These similarities aside, however, UNIX is a unique operating environment meant for high-performance computing. Installing UNIX on a microcomputer can be expensive and should be considered only in a multiuser environment or when you need to share programs and data with minicomputers running UNIX or one of its derivatives.

Determining Your Needs

Before you upgrade your system, carefully determine exactly what you need by developing a list of specifications. This is best accomplished by looking at the requirements of your software, or the requirements of programs you plan to purchase.

Gather together your programs and make a list of the memory, disk drives, processor, video, and other requirements. Look at the program documentation to answer these questions:

▶ Do you need to upgrade or add a hard-disk drive? What size drive will store your programs and data?

▶ Do you need to upgrade or add a floppy drive? What size and capacity do you need to run your applications?

▶ Do you need additional memory? Must it be expanded or extended?

▶ Do you need to upgrade your video system? Do you need color graphics? CGA, EGA, or VGA? Will this require a new monitor?

Make certain your upgrades are fully compatible with your hardware:

▶ Are your expansion slots 8-bit or 16-bit?

▶ Are your expansion slots proprietary 32-bit, standard MCA, or EISA?

▶ What size card can your vacant slots handle? Full-size or half-size? Can the upgrade fit in a single slot?

▶ What size bay does a new drive require? Full-height or half-height?

▶ Can your power supply accommodate an additional hard- or floppy-disk drive?

Next, consider the interface ports you need to accommodate your hardware and software:

- ▶ Do you need additional serial ports?
- ▶ Do you have a serial mouse, printer, or modem?
- ▶ Do you need additional parallel ports?
- ▶ Will you need special cables or adapters?

Also consider the physical requirements:

- ▶ How much desk space do you have available?
- ▶ Do you need external disk drives?

Then, consider convenience issues:

- ▶ Do you want to install a second floppy-disk drive for making backups?
- ▶ Do you want to install a different size disk drive to be compatible with both 5¼-inch and 3½-inch disks?
- ▶ Do you want to install a different capacity disk drive?
- ▶ Do you want to install a disk drive to be compatible with a computer at home or at the office?

Next, think of the future and give some thought to expandability. Adding a memory card that can accept only 1Mb of memory, for example, may be wasteful if you will need additional memory later.

- ▶ Should you leave an expansion slot open for later additions?
- ▶ Do you anticipate making software purchases that will change your needs?

Finally, consider the cost:

- ▶ How much to you want to spend?
- ▶ What compromises, if any, are you willing to make?

▶ Would you settle for a smaller disk drive if it were faster? A one wait state computer if it had a memory cache? A monochrome VGA system instead of color?

When you have a list of your minimum and mandatory requirements, you're ready to upgrade your hand-me-down.

Determining Your Hand-Me-Down's Future

Depending on how much you want to upgrade your hand-me-down, you may discover that the total cost of upgrading is more than the price of an entirely new system. You may also discover that even with additional upgrades, your hand-me-down will still fall short of serving your needs. When it is not practical to upgrade your hand-me-down, you should consider moving on to another system— purchasing a more powerful hand-me-down or a new computer.

As you look at possible systems, compare each with your list of specifications. Don't even consider a system that doesn't meet the minimum requirements or that costs more than the limit you've established.

Don't be misled by literature showing a basic system price but listing additional resources you need as "optional." Look for small print such as "monitor and video card not included" or "price shown without a hard disk." Insist on a price that includes the basic system, a copy of DOS, and all of the optional items that make it fit your specifications.

Ask if your company, school, or organization has special purchasing arrangements with a specific retailer. Some dealers will give educational or charitable discounts even without formal arrangements.

Software compatibility is the ultimate test. This was quite a problem years ago, when there were various levels of PC-compatibility. Some systems would run generic MS-DOS programs but not those specifically designed for the IBM-PC. A number of computers would run most DOS programs but have trouble with a few applications. The standard test was to try Lotus 1-2-3 and Microsoft Flight Simulator—if the computer ran those, it was considered IBM compatible.

While software compatibility is not as much of a problem as it was in the past, some systems may not be able to run certain programs, even if the computer is advertised as 100% IBM compatible. Whether this problem is because of the system speed, the type of video adapter, or the proprietary BIOS, a computer that cannot run your application is useless.

No matter what guarantee is given by the salesperson, it is your responsibility to make sure you can run your programs before you buy the computer. Take your application program to the computer store; install and test it if you have to. If the program doesn't work, don't accept any vague explanations or promises.

Remember the importance of an expandable system. You're upgrading now—you might have to upgrade again in the future.

What to Do with the Old System

Don't forget the investment you already have in your hand-me-down. You can try to sell it, trade it in, keep it, or hand it down to someone else.

To sell your system, spread the word to friends, run an ad in the local paper, or post a notice on the company or campus bulletin board. Look at other ads to see the market price or the price of a comparable new system. With PC prices falling, used computers are not selling for very much. After all, you can find some new hard-drive PC systems with a color monitor for about $1000, so how much could you expect for a used floppy-drive PC?

You might be able to trade in your system for a new one. A few manufacturers and dealers have trade-in programs, although they usually offer less than you can get on the open market. Trading in does save you the trouble of running ads and dealing with buyers, but if money is critical, you usually do better selling your hand-me-down yourself.

Then again, you can always keep the machine as a spare, for another family member, especially if the resale or trade-in price seems low. The computer will be available if your new system breaks down, and you might even be able to raid it for its disk drives or memory chips. If you don't have room for both computers, consider donating it to a local school or other institution. You'll get a tax deduction for the market price and the reward of helping others.

No matter how you dispose of the computer, keep in mind the legal and ethical issues involved in selling or giving away copies of software. You can legally give away a program if you do not retain any copies. Leaving programs on the hard disk while retaining floppy-disk copies is the same as giving them away on floppies—it is illegal.

Purchasing the New System

With your decision made, purchase or lease the new system—leasing reduces your initial outlay but may increase the final price. Select the dealer with the best combination of price and service, and who is willing to guide you through any rough spots. A supportive dealer is an invaluable resource, but unfortunately some dealers will talk about service and support, and then fall short when you actually need it. Spend some time listening to other customers and try to get a sense of their satisfaction. Find out who you call for service. Is there a direct line to the service or support department? If you have to go through the salesperson, who do you contact in an emergency or when the salesperson is not on duty?

Some time ago, my school received a bid on 20 systems for a computer lab. The bid was submitted by the service manager in a local branch of a nationwide chain known for support and service. The price was excellent but was for a system not normally carried by the dealer or the chain. Each time we called for details on the bid, we were referred to the service manager or put off until he could call back.

Just before signing the contract, we had a final question and insisted on speaking with the store manager, who told us that the bid was personally submitted by the service manager and was not affiliated with the store itself. Any questions, support, or warranty service were the service manager's individual responsibility. We quickly went elsewhere.

Mail-order companies are another source for systems. Some are manufacturers that deal directly with the public. Others are third-party shops that put together systems from components. Many are retailers that specialize in mail-order merchandising. As long as the system meets all of your specifications, the decision to purchase through the mail should be based on your need for service and support after the sale.

Many mail-order systems include warranty contracts honored by nationwide service firms. If you have a problem, you can call locally for service or take the system to an authorized service center. Systems that must be shipped back to the manufacturer may not be as desirable. Always select vendors that guarantee their products and preferably have toll-free support lines.

When your new system arrives, connect it as explained in Chapters 1 and 2. Personalize the system following instructions in Chapters 4 and 5, and, if necessary, configure the hard-disk drive as detailed in Chapter 14. If the need ever arises, you're now prepared to upgrade or expand your new system with additional memory, drives, and other resources.

Command Summaries for Some Common Application Programs

*M*any application programs use the function keys on your keyboard to streamline complicated tasks. If you do not have the documentation for software that you received with your hand-me-down, contact the manufacturer or purchase a book that explains how the software operates.

In the meantime, this appendix includes the key combinations used by four popular application programs. The key combinations can be of two types. You might have to press one or more keys at the same time, or you might have to press several keys in sequence. In this appendix, keys that should be pressed together are separated with a hyphen. For example, if a key combination is shown as *Ctrl-F1,* you should press and hold down the Ctrl key and then press the F1 key.

Other key combinations are pressed in sequence. These key combinations are written with a space between each key. For example, the combination *Home* ← means to press and release the Home key, and then press ←.

Finally, some commands require a combination of methods. The instruction *Shift-F8 2 1,* for example, means to press Shift and F8 at the same time, release both keys, press and release 2, and then press and release 1.

WordPerfect 5.1

WordPerfect 5.1 is a popular word processing program that requires a hard disk or two high-capacity floppy disks. To see if WordPerfect 5.1 is on your hard disk, look for a directory called WP51. You'll see several files that start with *WP.* You can work with WordPerfect by using either key combinations or a mouse.

Key Combinations Used in WordPerfect 5.1

Table 1 shows the key combinations using the ten function keys on your keyboard. If you have a distribution copy of WordPerfect, you should also have two plastic templates that explain how the function keys are used. A square template with a cutout in the middle is designed for keyboards with ten function keys on the left. Place it over the function keys and refer to it as you type. A longer template is supplied for keyboards with the function keys along the top row—place it above the keyboard (resting on the top row of keys) when you work with WordPerfect.

Table 1: *Function Key Combinations for WordPerfect 5.1*

Key Combination	Function	Key Combination	Function
F1	Cancel	F2	Search Forward
Ctrl-F1	Shell (DOS-OS/2)	Ctrl-F2	Spell
Shift-F1	Setup	Shift-F2	Search Backward
Alt-F1	Thesaurus	Alt-F2	Replace
F3	Help	F4	Indent Left Margin
Ctrl-F3	Screen	Ctrl-F4	Move and Copy
Shift-F3	Switch	Shift-F4	Indent Both Margins
Alt-F3	Reveal Codes	Alt-F4	Block
F5	List Files (DIR)	F6	Boldface
Ctrl-F5	Text In/Out	Ctrl-F6	Tab Align
Shift-F5	Date/Outline	Shift-F6	Center
Alt-F5	Mark Text	Alt-F6	Flush Right
F7	Exit (Save/Quit)	F8	Underline
Ctrl-F7	Footnote	Ctrl-F8	Font
Shift-F7	Print	Shift-F8	Format
Alt-F7	Columns/Table	Alt-F8	Style

Table 1: *Function Key Combinations for WordPerfect 5.1 (continued)*

Key Combination	Function	Key Combination	Function
F9	Merge R (End Field)	F10	Save Text
Ctrl-F9	Merge/Sort	Ctrl-F10	Macro Define
Shift-F9	Merge Codes	Shift-F10	Retrieve Text
Alt-F9	Graphics	Alt-F10	Macro Start

Alphabetic Summary of Menu Commands

You can also work with WordPerfect using a series of menus. You access the menus either by clicking the right button of a mouse, or by pressing Alt-= (the Alt and = keys at the same time).

If you have a mouse, click the right button to display the menu bar at the top of the screen, and then click on the words shown. If you do not have a mouse, press Alt-= to display the menu bar, and then press the letters shown in boldface. As an alternative to using the menus, press the key combinations shown in parentheses.

For example, the command to format characters in boldface (darker printing) is shown as

Font **A**ppearance **B**old (F6)

To perform this, you can either:

▶ Click the right mouse button, and then click on the words *Font, Appearance,* and *Bold* as they appear on the screen in menus

▶ Press Alt-= , and then the letters *O, A,* and *B* in sequence

▶ Press the F6 key

In some instances, there are keys shown after a function key command, such as

Layout **C**olumns (Alt-F7) **O**n/Off

In this case, you should either:

▶ Click the right mouse button. Next, click on the words *Layout* and *Columns* as they appear in menus, and then click either on the word *On* or *Off,* depending on whether you want to turn the feature on or off.

▶ Press Alt- = . Next press the letters *L* and *C,* and then either *O* or *F.*

▶ Press Alt-F7, and then either *O* or *F.*

Table 2 is a summary of WordPerfect's commands. The function is shown on the left, and the key combinations or mouse commands on the right.

Table 2: *Commands and Their Function Key Equivalents in WordPerfect 5.1*

Command	Function Key Equivalent
Block	Edit Block (Alt-F4)
Boldface print	Font Appearance Bold (F6)
Box	Graphics (Alt-F9)
Cancel	F1
Cancel printing	File Print (Shift-F7) Control Cancel
Center page	Layout Page Center (Shift-F8 2 1) Yes
Center text	Layout Align Center (Shift-F6)
Clear screen	File Exit (F7) No No
Column definition	Layout Columns (Alt-F7) Define
Column off/on	Layout Columns (Alt-F7) On/Off
Copy text	Edit Copy (Ctrl-F4)
Cursor movement	
Bottom of document	Home Home ↓
Bottom of screen	Home ↓
Left margin	Home ←
Next screen	Home ↓
Previous screen	Home ↑
Right margin	End

Table 2: *Commands and Their Function Key Equivalents in WordPerfect 5.1 (continued)*

Command	Function Key Equivalent
Specific page	Ctrl-Home *<page number>* ←
Top of document	Home Home ↑
Top of screen	Home ↑
Date code	Tools (Shift-F5) Date Code
Date format	Tools (Shift-F5) Date Format
Date text	Tools (Shift-F5) Date Text
Decimal tab align	Layout Align Tab Align (Ctrl-F6)
Delete to end of line	Ctrl-End
Delete word	Ctrl-Backspace
Double space	Layout (Shift-F8) Line Line Spacing 2
Double underline	Font Appearance Double Underline (Ctrl-F8 A D)
Equation	Graphics (Alt-F9) Equation
Exit without saving	File Exit (F7) No Yes
Extra large print	Font (Ctrl-F8 S) Extra Large
Fine print	Font (Ctrl-F8 S) Fine
Flush right	Layout Align Flush Right (Alt-F6)
Font size	Font (Ctrl-F8 S)
Footnote	Layout Align (Ctrl-F7) Footnote
Go to page	Ctrl-Home *<page number>* ←
Hanging indentation	Layout Indent Margin Rel (F4 Shift-Tab)
Help	Help (F3)
Hyphen, optional	Ctrl--
Hyphen, required	-
Indent, both sides	Layout Align Indent (Shift-F4)
Indent, left	Layout Align Indent (F4)
Insert mode	Ins
Italics	Font Appearance (Ctrl-F8 A) Italics
Justification off	Layout (Shift-F8) Line Justification Left
Large print	Font (Ctrl-F8 S) Large

Table 2: *Commands and Their Function Key Equivalents in WordPerfect 5.1 (continued)*

Command	Function Key Equivalent
Line numbering	Layout (Shift-F8) Line Line Numbering Yes
Line spacing	Layout (Shift-F8) Line Line Spacing
Lines	Graphics (Alt-F9) Lines
Macro, define	Tools Macro Define (Ctrl-F10)
Macro, repeat	Tools Macro Execute (Alt-F10)
Margins, left and right	Layout (Shift-F8) Line Margins
Margins, top and bottom	Layout (Shift-F8) Page Margins
Move text	Edit Select or Move (Ctrl-F4)
Normal print	Font (Ctrl-F8) Normal
Outline print	Font (Ctrl-F8) Appearance Outline
Page break	Ctrl-←
Page numbering	Layout (Shift-F8) Page Page Numbering
Page size	Layout (Shift-F8) Page Page Size
Print	
Document	File Print (Shift-F7) Full
From disk	File Print (Shift-F7) Document on Disk
Multiple copies	File Print (Shift-F7) Number of Copies
Multiple pages	File Print (Shift-F7) Multiple Page
Page	File Print (Shift-F7) Page
Quit	File Exit (F7)
Recall document	File Retrieve (Shift-F10)
Redline printing	Font (Ctrl-F8) Appearance Redline
Repeat	Esc
Replace	Search Replace (Alt-F2)
Reveal codes	Edit Reveal Codes (Alt-F3)
Save and continue	File Save (F10)
Save and quit	File Exit (F7) Yes Yes
Search backward	Search Backward (Shift-F2)
Search forward	Search Forward (F2)

Table 2: *Commands and Their Function Key Equivalents in WordPerfect 5.1 (continued)*

Command	Function Key Equivalent
Select printer	File Print (Shift-F7) Select Printer
Shadow printing	Font (Ctrl-F8) Appearance Shadow
Small capital printing	Font (Ctrl-F8) Appearance Small Cap
Small print	Font (Ctrl-F8 S) Small
Spell	Tools Spell (Ctrl-F2)
Strikeout printing	Font (Ctrl-F8) Appearance Strikeout
Subscript	Font (Ctrl-F8 S) Subscript
Superscript	Font (Ctrl-F8 S) Superscript
Switch documents	Edit Switch Documents (Shift-F3)
Tab set	Layout (Shift-F8) Line Tab Set
Tables	Layout Tables (Alt-F7 T)
Thesaurus	Tools Thesaurus (Alt-F1)
Typeover mode	Ins
Underline	Font Appearance Underline (F8)
Very large print	Font (Ctrl-F8 S) Very Large
View document	File Print (Shift-F7) View Document
Window Size	Edit Window (Ctrl-F3)

Microsoft Word 5.0

This popular word processing program from Microsoft Corporation provides a WYSIWYG environment displaying character formats such as boldface, underline, and italic on the screen. You can run it from either a hard disk or from floppy disks, although using floppy disks can be difficult if you're creating a complex document.

To see if Word is on your hard disk, look for a directory called WORD or WORD5. You can work with Word by using either key combinations or a mouse.

Key Combinations Used in Microsoft Word 5.0

Table 3 shows the key combinations using the ten function keys on your keyboard. If you have a distribution copy of Word, you should also have two plastic templates that explain how the function keys are used. A square template with a cutout in the middle is designed for keyboards with ten function keys on the left. Place it over the function keys and refer to it as you type. A longer template is supplied for keyboards with the function keys along the top row—place it above the keyboard when you work with Word.

Table 3: *Function Key Combinations for Word 5.0*

Key Combination	Function	Key Combination	Function
F1	Next Window	F2	Calculate
Ctrl-F1	Zoom Window	Ctrl-F2	Header
Shift-F1	Undo	Shift-F2	Outline View
Alt-F1	Set Tab	Alt-F2	Footer
F3	Glossary	F4	Repeat Edit
Ctrl-F3	Step Macro	Ctrl-F4	Toggle Case
Shift-F3	Record Macro	Shift-F4	Repeat Search
Alt-F3	Copy to Scrap	Alt-F4	Show Layout
F5	Overtype	F6	Extend
Ctrl-F5	Line Draw	Ctrl-F6	Thesaurus
Shift-F5	Outline Organize	Shift-F6	Column Select
Alt-F5	Go To Page	Alt-F6	Spell
F7	Previous Word	F8	Next Word
Ctrl-F7	Load	Ctrl-F8	Print
Shift-F7	Previous Sentence	Shift-F8	Next Sentence
Alt-F7	Show Line Breaks	Alt-F8	Font Name

Table 3: *Function Key Combinations for Word 5.0 (continued)*

Key Combination	Function	Key Combination	Function
F9	Previous Paragraph	F10	Next Paragraph
Ctrl-F9	Print Preview	Ctrl-F10	Save
Shift-F9	Current Line	Shift-F10	Whole Document
Alt-F9	Text/Graphics	Alt-F10	Record Style

Formatting Keystroke Commands

Table 4 shows the key combinations you use to format characters, lines, and paragraphs. Press Alt and the key shown to create the format.

Table 4: *Formatting Commands in Microsoft Word 5.0*

Key Combination	Function
Alt-+	Superscript letters and numbers
Alt-− (minus)	Subscript letters and numbers
Alt-B	Bold
Alt-C	Center text
Alt-D	Double underline
Alt-E	Hidden text
Alt-F	Indent first line
Alt-J	Justify text
Alt-I	Italic letters
Alt-K	Small capital letters
Alt-L	Left justify
Alt-M	Decrease indentation
Alt-N	Increase indentation
Alt-O	Add extra line between paragraphs
Alt-P	Return paragraph to normal
Alt-Q	Indent both margins

Table 4: *Formatting Commands in Microsoft Word 5.0 (continued)*

Key Combination	Function
Alt-R	Right justify
Alt-S	Strikethrough
Alt-spacebar	Return characters to normal
Alt-T	Hanging indentation
Alt-U	Underline
Alt-1	Single space
Alt-2	Double space

Alphabetic Summary of Menu Commands

You can also work with Word using the command menu at the bottom of the Word screen. Press Esc to enter the command area, and then select the command you want to execute. If you have a mouse, click on the command with the left button. Table 5 is a complete summary of Word commands using the command area.

Table 5: *Alphabetic Summary of Menu Commands in Word 5.0*

Function	Key Combination
Annotation	Esc F A
Automatic Numbering	Esc L N
AutoSave	Esc O
Bold print	Alt-B
Bookmark	Esc F K
Boxes	Esc F B B
Calculate	F2
Case Toggle	Ctrl-F4
Center text	Alt-C
Change disk drives	Esc T O
Character format	Esc F C
Clear document	Esc T C

Table 5: *Alphabetic Summary of Menu Commands in Word 5.0 (continued)*

Function	Key Combination
Color (boxes and lines)	Esc F B
Color (display)	Esc O
Color (printing)	Esc F C
Columns	Esc F D L
Copy text	Alt-F3
Cursor movement	
Bottom of document	Ctrl-PgDn
Bottom of screen	Ctrl-End
Left margin	Home
Next screen	PgDn
Next window	F1
Previous screen	PgUp
Right margin	End
To footnote	Esc J F
To page	Esc J P
Top of document	Ctrl-PgUp
Top of screen	Ctrl-Home
Delete	
Document on screen	Shift-F10 Del
File	Esc T D
Line	Shift-F9 Del
Not to scrap	Backspace *or* Shift-Del
Paragraph	F10 Del
Sentence	Shift-F8 Del
Text to scrap	Del *or* Esc D
Word	F8 Del
Division break	Ctrl ↵
Document retrieval	Esc L D
Double space	Alt-2

Table 5: *Alphabetic Summary of Menu Commands in Word 5.0 (continued)*

Function	Key Combination
Double underline	Alt-D
Draft print	Esc P O
Font size	Esc F C
Font type	Alt-F8
Footer	Alt-F2
Footnote position	Esc F D L
Footnotes	Esc F F
Foreign Characters	Alt-<*code number*> (use keypad)
Format	Esc F
Frame Position/Size	Esc F O
Glossary	
Clear glossary	Esc T G C
Delete to	Esc D
Expand entry	F3
Insert from	Esc I
Load glossary	Esc T G L
Merge glossary	Esc T G M
Print glossary	Esc P G
Save glossary	Esc T G S
Go to page	Alt-F5
Graphic link	Esc L L G
Graphic mode	Alt-F9
Hanging indentation	Alt-T
Header	Ctrl-F2
Help	Esc H *or* Alt-H
Hidden text	Alt-E
Hyphen	
Optional	Ctrl-- (hyphen)
Required	Ctrl- – (minus on keypad)

Table 5: *Alphabetic Summary of Menu Commands in Word 5.0 (continued)*

Function	Key Combination
Hyphenate	Esc L H
Indent first lines	Alt-F
Indent	
Decrease	Alt-M
Increase	Alt-N
Index	Esc L I
Insert mode	F5 (toggle)
Italic	Alt-I
Justify	Alt-J
Left flush	Alt-L
Line number	Esc F D L
Line spacing	Esc F P
Lines	Esc F B L
Link	
Document	Esc L L D
Graphic	Esc L L G
Spreadsheet	Esc L L S
Macros	Shift-F3
Margins	Esc F D
Merge text	Esc T M
Merge codes	Ctrl-{ and Ctrl-}
Move text	Esc D ⏎ Ins *or* Del Ins
New line	Shift-⏎
New page	Shift-Ctrl-⏎
Open paragraph spacing	Alt-O
Outline	
Collapse	– (minus on keypad)
Collapse body text	Shift-– (minus on keypad)

Table 5: *Alphabetic Summary of Menu Commands in Word 5.0 (continued)*

Function	Key Combination
Expand all headings	*
Expand body text	Shift-+ (plus on keypad)
Expand heading	+ (plus on keypad)
Lower heading level	Alt-O
Organize	Shift-F5
Raise heading level	Alt-9
View	Shift-F2
Overtype mode	F5 (toggle)
Page break	Shift-Ctrl-←
Page numbering	Esc F D P
Page size	Esc F D M
Paginate	Esc P R
Pagination toggle	Esc O
Paragraph numbering	Esc L N
Pitch	Esc F C
Printer display	Alt-F7
Printing	Esc P
Paper feed	Esc P O
Print direct	Esc P D
Print document	Ctrl-F8
Print glossary	Esc P G
Print merge	Esc P M
Print pages	Esc P O
Print preview	Esc P V
Print to file	Esc P F
Printer model	Esc P O
Printer type	Esc P O
Resolution	Esc P O

Table 5: *Alphabetic Summary of Menu Commands in Word 5.0 (continued)*

Function	Key Combination
Queue files	Esc P Q
Quit	Esc Q
Recall text	Ctrl-F7
Record style	Alt-F10
Rename file	Esc T R
Repeat	
Edit	F4
Search	Shift-F4
Replace	Esc R
Required space	Ctrl-spacebar
Revision marks	Esc F R
Right flush	Alt-R
Ruler	Esc O
Running heads	Esc F R
Running-head position	Esc F D M
Save text	Ctrl-F10
Scrolling	
Bottom of document	Ctrl-PgDn
Screen down	PgDn
Screen up	PgUp
Top of document	Ctrl-PgUp
Search	
Formats	Esc F E
Text	Esc S
Select text	
Column	Shift-F6
Document	Shift-F10
Extend	F6
Line	Shift-F9

Table 5: *Alphabetic Summary of Menu Commands in Word 5.0 (continued)*

Function	Key Combination
Paragraph	F10
Sentence	F9
Sentence left	Shift-F7
Sentence right	Shift-F8
Word left	F7
Word right	F8
Show Layout	Alt-F4
Small capitals	Alt-K
Sort	Esc L A
Spelling	Alt-F6
Standard paragraph	Alt-P
Strikethrough	Alt-S
Style bar	Esc O
Style sheets (Gallery)	
Attach style sheet	Esc F S A
Clear gallery	Esc G T C
Copy style	Esc G C
Delete style	Esc G D
Display	Esc G
Exit gallery	E
Format style	Esc G F
Insert style	Esc G I
Load style sheet	Esc G T L
Merge style sheet	Esc G T M
Name style	Esc G N
Print style sheet	Esc G P
Rename style sheet	Esc G T R
Save style sheet	Esc G T S
Subscript	Alt- – (minus)

Table 5: *Alphabetic Summary of Menu Commands in Word 5.0 (continued)*

Function	Key Combination
Superscript	Alt- + *or* Alt- =
Table of contents	Esc L T
Tabs	Esc F T
Clear tab stop	Esc F T C
Default tabs	Esc F T R
Set tab stop	Alt-F1
Text mode	Alt-F9
Thesaurus	Ctrl-F6
Underline	Alt-U
Undo	Shift-F1
Windows	Esc W
Close window	Esc W C
Move window	Esc W M
Options	Esc O
Split window	Esc W S
Zoom window	Ctrl-F1

Lotus 1-2-3

Lotus 1-2-3 is the worldwide standard in electronic spreadsheets. If you have a spreadsheet program on your hard disk or on floppy disks, it is probably either Lotus 1-2-3 or another Lotus-compatible spreadsheet. This section includes a basic set of commands for use with either version 2.2 or 3.0 of Lotus 1-2-3.

Function Key Commands in Lotus 1-2-3

Table 6 lists the commands Lotus 1-2-3 assigns to the ten function keys. If you need help with any command, press F1 to access the Help function.

Table 6: *Function Key Equivalents in Lotus 1-2-3*

Function Key	Equivalent
F1	Help
F2	Edit
F3	Name
F4	ABS (absolute cell reference)
F5	Goto
F6	Window
F7	Query
F8	Table
F9	Calculate spreadsheet
F10	Graph display

Worksheet Commands

Most spreadsheet functions are performed using the menus shown on the top of the Lotus 1-2-3 screen. You access the menus by pressing the / key. Then press the first letters of the commands you want to perform. Table 7 summarizes the most frequently used worksheet commands in Lotus 1-2-3.

Table 7: *Worksheet Commands in Lotus 1-2-3*

Command	Function
/C	Copy—copy individual or groups of cells from one location to another
/D	Data—commands to perform database functions on worksheet data
/DD	Data Distribution
/DF	Data Fill
/DQ	Data Query
/DS	Data Sort
/DT	Data Table

Table 7: *Worksheet Commands in Lotus 1-2-3 (continued)*

Command	Function
/F	File—commands to save and recall worksheets, combine worksheets, exchange data, and manage files on the disk
/FC	File Combine
/FD	File Directory
/FE	File Erase
/FI	File Import
/FL	File List
/FR	File Retrieve
/FS	File Save
/FX	File Xtract
/G	Graph—commands to design, preview, and manage charts and graphs based on worksheet data. Print graphics using the PrintGraph option on the opening command line
/M	Move—move individual or groups of cells from one location to another
/P	Print—commands to print worksheets, design printouts, and control the printer
/PF	Print to a File
/PP	Print to the Printer
/Q	Quit—exit Lotus 1-2-3
/R	Range—commands that affect individual cells or groups of cells
/RE	Range Erase
/RF	Range Format
/RI	Range Input
/RJ	Range Justify
/RL	Range Label
/RN	Range Name
/RP	Range Protect
/RT	Range Transpose
/RU	Range Unprotect
/RV	Range Value

Table 7: *Worksheet Commands in Lotus 1-2-3 (continued)*

Command	Function
/S	System—temporarily return to DOS prompt
/W	Worksheet—commands that affect the entire worksheet and screen
/WC	Worksheet Column width
/WD	Worksheet Delete rows or columns
/WE	Worksheet Erase
/WG	Worksheet Global
/WI	Worksheet Insert rows or columns
/WP	Worksheet Page
/WS	Worksheet Status
/WT	Worksheet Titles
/WW	Worksheet Window

Commonly Used Functions

You can perform complex calculations in your worksheet by using Lotus's built-in functions. Start each function by entering the @ symbol, the abbreviated function name, and then the numbers or spreadsheet cells you want to use in the calculation. For more detailed information on using Lotus 1-2-3, use the Lotus help menus or read *The ABC's of 1-2-3 Release 2.2* by Chris Gilbert and Laurie Williams ©1989 from SYBEX Computer Books. Table 8 shows the most commonly used functions.

Table 8: *Lotus 1-2-3 Functions*

Function	Command
@ABS	Absolute value
@AVG	Average of a range of cells
@COUNT	Counts the items in a range of cells
@DATE	Current system date
@EXP	Power
@IF	Logical IF function

Table 8: *Lotus 1-2-3 Functions (continued)*

Function	Command
@INT	Integer
@MAX	Largest number in a range of cells
@MIN	Smallest number in a range of cells
@MOD	Remainder of division
@PMT	Periodic payment based on principle, interest, and length of loan
@PV	Present value
@RAND	Random number
@ROUND	Round
@SQRT	Square root
@SUM	Sum (total) of a range of cells

dBASE IV

A database program allows you to collect, manipulate, and report data of all types. dBASE IV is a popular database program manufactured by Ashton-Tate, a leader in the database software field. It is the culmination of several earlier releases that quickly became the standard against which all other database programs are compared.

dBASE IV requires a hard disk. If you have the program on your hand-me-down, it will probably be in a directory called DBASE. Look for several files with the name DBASE, and other files with the extension .DBF. This is the extension dBASE assigns to database files.

Function Key Commands in dBASE IV

While dBASE IV has a complete system of menus for creating and using databases, some tasks have also been assigned to specific function keys. Table 9 shows the dBASE function key commands.

Table 9: *dBASE IV Function Key Commands*

Key Combination	Function
F1	Help
Shift-F1	Pick
F2	Data
Shift-F2	Design
F3	Previous file skeleton or topic
F4	Next file skeleton or topic
Shift-F4	Find next occurrence of search string
Shift-F5	Find first occurrence of search string
Shift-F9	Quick Report
F10	Menus

Working with dBASE Screens

There are many times when you'll be performing word processing functions while working with dBASE. You might be adding or editing a database record, or creating a database program to print a report. dBASE provides a set of commands for moving the cursor, and editing and saving your work.

While you can use the arrow and other cursor keys on the numeric keypad for moving the cursor, Ctrl-*key* combinations have also been provided for cursor movement as well as other functions.

Table 10 summarizes the cursor movement and Ctrl-*key* combinations in dBASE IV. Most of these combinations will work with earlier versions of dBASE as well.

Table 10: *Key Combinations for dBASE IV*

Key Combination	Function
Ctrl-⏎	Save work and remain in function
Ctrl-←	Beginning of previous word/field
Ctrl-→	Beginning of next word/field

Table 10: *Key Combinations for dBASE IV (continued)*

Key Combination	Function
Ctrl-Backspace	Delete previous word
Ctrl-C *or* PgDn	Next screen
Ctrl-D *or* →	Right
Ctrl-E *or* ↑	Up
Ctrl-End	Save work and exit function
Ctrl-G *or* Del	Delete item
Ctrl-Home	Move to memo field
Ctrl-KR	Recall file into current function
Ctrl-KW	Write file to the disk
Ctrl-N	Insert
Ctrl-PgDn	End of text
Ctrl-PgUp	Beginning of text
Ctrl-Q *or* Esc	Abandon changes
Ctrl-R *or* PgUp	Previous screen
Ctrl-S *or* ←	Left
Ctrl-T	Delete text to beginning of next word
Ctrl-U	Delete
Ctrl-V *or* Ins	Insert/overtype mode
Ctrl-X *or* ↓	Down
Ctrl-Y	Delete text to end of line
End	End of field
Home	Beginning of field
Shift-Tab	Previous field
Tab	Next field

TO JOIN THE SYBEX MAILING LIST OR ORDER BOOKS
PLEASE COMPLETE THIS FORM

NAME _____ COMPANY _____

STREET _____ CITY _____

STATE _____ ZIP _____

☐ PLEASE MAIL ME MORE INFORMATION ABOUT **SYBEX** TITLES

ORDER FORM (There is no obligation to order)

PLEASE SEND ME THE FOLLOWING:

TITLE	QTY	PRICE
_____	____	____
_____	____	____
_____	____	____
_____	____	____

TOTAL BOOK ORDER   ____ $____

SHIPPING AND HANDLING PLEASE ADD $2.00 PER BOOK VIA UPS   _____

FOR OVERSEAS SURFACE ADD $5.25 PER BOOK PLUS $4.40 REGISTRATION FEE   _____

FOR OVERSEAS AIRMAIL ADD $18.25 PER BOOK PLUS $4.40 REGISTRATION FEE   _____

CALIFORNIA RESIDENTS PLEASE ADD APPLICABLE SALES TAX   _____

TOTAL AMOUNT PAYABLE   _____

☐ CHECK ENCLOSED   ☐ VISA
☐ MASTERCARD   ☐ AMERICAN EXPRESS

ACCOUNT NUMBER _____

EXPIR. DATE _____ DAYTIME PHONE _____

CUSTOMER SIGNATURE _____

CHECK AREA OF COMPUTER INTEREST:

☐ BUSINESS SOFTWARE

☐ TECHNICAL PROGRAMMING

☐ OTHER: _____

OTHER COMPUTER TITLES YOU WOULD LIKE TO SEE IN PRINT:

_____

_____

THE FACTOR THAT WAS MOST IMPORTANT IN YOUR SELECTION:

☐ THE SYBEX NAME

☐ QUALITY

☐ PRICE

☐ EXTRA FEATURES

☐ COMPREHENSIVENESS

☐ CLEAR WRITING

☐ OTHER _____

OCCUPATION

☐ PROGRAMMER   ☐ TEACHER

☐ SENIOR EXECUTIVE   ☐ HOMEMAKER

☐ COMPUTER CONSULTANT   ☐ RETIRED

☐ SUPERVISOR   ☐ STUDENT

☐ MIDDLE MANAGEMENT   ☐ OTHER:

☐ ENGINEER/TECHNICAL   _____

☐ CLERICAL/SERVICE

☐ BUSINESS OWNER/SELF EMPLOYED

CHECK YOUR LEVEL OF COMPUTER USE

☐ NEW TO COMPUTERS
☐ INFREQUENT COMPUTER USER
☐ FREQUENT USER OF ONE SOFTWARE
   PACKAGE:
   NAME _____
☐ FREQUENT USER OF MANY SOFTWARE
   PACKAGES
☐ PROFESSIONAL PROGRAMMER

OTHER COMMENTS:

_____
_____
_____
_____
_____
_____
_____

PLEASE FOLD, SEAL, AND MAIL TO SYBEX

– – – – – – – – – – – – – – – – – – – –

SYBEX, INC.
2021 CHALLENGER DR. #100
ALAMEDA, CALIFORNIA USA
          94501

SEAL

SYBEX Computer Books
are different.

Here is why . . .

At SYBEX, each book is designed with you in mind. Every manuscript is carefully selected and supervised by our editors, who are themselves computer experts. We publish the best authors, whose technical expertise is matched by an ability to write clearly and to communicate effectively. Programs are thoroughly tested for accuracy by our technical staff. Our computerized production department goes to great lengths to make sure that each book is well-designed.

In the pursuit of timeliness, SYBEX has achieved many publishing firsts. SYBEX was among the first to integrate personal computers used by authors and staff into the publishing process. SYBEX was the first to publish books on the CP/M operating system, microprocessor interfacing techniques, word processing, and many more topics.

Expertise in computers and dedication to the highest quality product have made SYBEX a world leader in computer book publishing. Translated into fourteen languages, SYBEX books have helped millions of people around the world to get the most from their computers. We hope we have helped you, too.

For a complete catalog of our publications:

SYBEX, Inc. 2021 Challenger Drive, #100, Alameda, CA 94501
Tel: (415) 523-8233/(800) 227-2346   Telex: 336311
Fax: (415) 523-2373

Term	Definition
Modem	Modulator-demodulator—a device used to send and receive computer signals over the telephone network.
Monochrome monitor	A monitor that displays black and one other color.
Monochrome VGA	A monochrome monitor using the VGA standard.
Motherboard	The main circuit board that contains most of the computer circuits.
Mouse	A small hand-held pointing device that you roll along the desk top next to your computer to move the cursor on the screen and select menu options.
Multimode	Display cards that can emulate MDA, HGC, CGA, and EGA images as analog signals on VGA monitors.
Multitasking	The capability to run more than one program at a time.
Networking	The interconnection of two or more computers for the purpose of sharing files and resources.
Numeric coprocessor	A coprocessor dedicated to math functions.
Parity	A system of checking the accuracy of data and transmission; parity may be odd, even, or none.
Park	Positioning the read/write head over an unused portion of the disk to avoid damage from mechanical shock or electrical surges.
Partition	Subdivision of a hard disk.
Path	The directions to the location of a file on the disk.
PCL	Printer Control Language—used in Hewlett-Packard and compatible laser printers.
Pixel	An area on the screen corresponding to one dot on the display or one bit of computer data; short for *picture element*.
Ports	Computer connectors to attach to input and output devices.
Print spooler	A program that intercepts data being sent to the printer and stores it in high-speed RAM until your printer can accept it.
Program switching	The technique of loading several applications into memory, and then switching between them.
Protocol	The rules that must be followed in order for two devices to communicate.
RAM	Random access memory that can be written to and read from. Also called read/write and user memory.
Read/write head	The mechanism that reads data from and records data on the disk surface.